In Fond Memory
Of Piper Hauk

MONTEREY
Public Library

THE NEW COMPLETE CAIRN TERRIER

From the dim shieling on the misty isle,
Mountains divide us and a world of seas;
    Yet still our hearts are true, our hearts are Highland,
And we in dreams behold the Hebrides.

Waiting or sometimes called *Highland Dogs*, circa 1839, by Webb after Landseer. The terrier in the foreground of this interesting painting is probably typical of the prototype Scotch terrier from which the Cairn developed.

THE NEW COMPLETE

Cairn Terrier

by JOHN T. MARVIN

ILLUSTRATED

Second Edition

HOWELL
BOOK HOUSE
New York

Howell Book House
Macmillan Publishing Company
866 Third Avenue, New York, NY 10022

Collier Macmillan Canada, Inc.
1200 Eglinton Avenue East, Suite 200
Don Mills, Ontario M3C 3N1

Library of Congress Cataloging-in-Publication Data

Marvin, John T.
    The new complete Cairn terrier.

    Bibiography: p. 267
    1. Cairn terrier.   I. Title.
SF429.C3M37   1986   636.7'55   86-282
ISBN 0-87605-097-6

Macmillan books are available at special discounts for bulk purchases for sales promotions, premiums, fund-raising, or educational use. For details, contact:

        Special Sales Director
        Macmillan Publishing Company
        866 Third Avenue
        New York, NY 10022

10 9 8 7 6 5

Printed in the United States of America

To the

Terriers from Scotland, those
Gash an' faithful tykes who gat
Them friends in ilka place.

The Breakfast Party, circa 1831, by Sir Edwin Landseer. This painting **was also exhibited** under the title *Too Hot.* It shows early highland terriers of various types with a hound.

Contents

The Author

JOHN MARVIN'S active participation in dogs began more than 50 years ago. Together with Mrs. Marvin he has bred and exhibited Wire Fox Terriers and West Highland Whites with most gratifying results. There have been over 20 homebred champions from "Cranbourne," and three of the Westies were owner-handled to Best in Show awards. Since 1947 he has been licensed by the American Kennel Club to judge all the terrier breeds, and since 1967 many of the sporting breeds as well.

Mr. Marvin has judged at virtually every important show in the United States, and has officiated in the Cairn ring at the national

Specialty, Chicago International and Westminster. His profound knowledge of all terriers and his insistence on the highest quality have made him one of America's most sought-after and respected judges.

Over the years, Mr. Marvin has gained many honors while making noteworthy contributions for the betterment of purebred dogs. Long affiliations with such Clubs as the Dayton Kennel Club, The Associated Terrier Clubs and the Montgomery County Kennel Club, of which he was show chairman from 1972-1977, have been of great benefit to these organizations. In addition, he is a member and past president of the American Fox Terrier Club; past secretary and president of the West Highland White Terrier Club of America, serving as its current delegate to the American Kennel Club, a post held since 1966. He is a member of the Eastern Trial Board of the American Kennel Club while serving on various committees of that organization. He was the weekly dog columnist for the *Dayton Daily News* for some 20 years and a contributor to most dog journals including writing more than 70 articles for the *American Kennel Gazette* since 1947. In 1978, he was the recipient of the Gaines Medal for Good Sportsmanship while gaining national awards for Dog Writer of the Year in 1973 and Outstanding (Dog) Journalist of the Year in 1975 in addition to a dozen other awards for his books and articles in national competitions; he was president of the Dog Writers' Association of America from 1973-1979 and is currently a trustee of the Dog Writers' Educational Trust.

This second edition, *The New Complete Cairn Terrier,* first published in 1975, brings information on the Cairn Terrier up-to-date while maintaining all of the important historical aspects of the original effort.

Preface

THIS book was prompted by my great interest in the Terriers from Scotland. My previous efforts on the West Highland White Terrier and the Scottish Terrier uncovered a vast fund of early information concerning the Cairn Terrier that has previously been unrecorded. In the absence of any complete treatise on the breed in this country, it seemed useful to set down the facts and fancies that have been assembled which are interesting and instructive and which may be helpful in understanding the breed more completely. Further, this book is illustrated with many early prints that offer a pictorial history of the development of the old Scotch Terrier and its later offspring, the Scottish, West Highland White and Cairn Terrier.

In preparing this treatise, I have been aided by many persons whose generous help has made my task easier. Chief among these is Miss Frances Porter, who has been the breed's historian for many years past. Miss Porter has given generously of her knowledge and background and has supplied me most of the pedigree material so important to the preparation of the book. I am also indebted to the host of fanciers who have furnished information and illustrations. Of this group I wish to thank particularly, Mrs. G. W. Hyslop, Mrs. C. Groverman Ellis, Miss Helen Hunt, the late Mr. W. N. Bradshaw, Mr. M. K. McLeod, Mrs. Carl Brewer and Miss Ferlieth Hamilton, editor of *Dog World* (England), and the owner of Oudenarde Kennels, who helped tremendously in the accumulation of materials concerning English personalities, kennels and dogs.

Because of the extensive and available pedigree studies in Great Britain by Dr. T. W. L. Caspersz and Alex Fisher, and in America by Elizabeth H. Anderson, Frances R. Porter and Clara M. LeVene, no extensive effort has been made to delve deeply into ancestral backgrounds. However, brief notice of successful sires and dams is offered where appropriate, as is other significant, related material.

I have endeavored to authenticate the information herein and have included a full bibliography of sources. If any errors are noted, they are regretted and it will be deeply appreciated being advised of them so that future printings and editions may be completely accurate.

JOHN T. MARVIN

1

The Genesis of the Dog

WHILE this book is directed to the origin and history of the Cairn Terrier, it will commence with a brief general exposition of the dog, followed by the evolution of the Terrier—as a distinct strain that was bred for a specific purpose and temperament.

Theories of Genealogy

The basic genealogy of the dog is completely obscured in the dimness of the past. There is little doubt that all breeds descended from common ancestors and historian geneticists have determined that the dog and the wolf came from the same progenitors. Buffon, the celebrated French naturalist, in his genealogical chart suggests that all races of dog came from the early Shepherd's dog, but this theory was discredited over a century ago. One point upon which all historians agree, however, is that the dog, unlike the wolf, was always easily domesticated and that the strong bond of friendship between man and dog was forged originally many centuries ago.

> *Of the dog in ancient story*
> *Many a pleasant tale is told*
> —Howitt

Cave Canem. Beware of the Dog. From a mosaic found in Pompeii.

Proof of this statement may be found in the Bible where dogs are referred to some forty times. Figures of dogs and doglike deities have been found carved in stone dating back thousands of years before Christ. The early Egyptians appreciated the fidelity of the dog to such an extent that they named Sirius the "Dog Star," because of its faithful appearance as a forerunner to the great floods of the Nile, a periodic signal to move their flocks to higher ground. In ancient Roman dwellings the words *Cave Canem* (Beware of the Dog) together with the figure of a dog were often depicted in mosaic on thresholds as a warning to trespassers. The early Europeans used the dog as a symbol of fidelity and loyalty while Ecclesiastical representations of the holy patrons often include a dog as the protector and companion of the subject. In fact, the dog has been with man and his possessions in every age and in all parts of the globe, an important part of the labors and sports of men, sharing danger and pleasure with equal zeal and fidelity.

> *The poor dog in life, the firmest friend,*
> *The first to welcome, foremost to defend:*
> *Whose honest heart is still his master's own,*
> *Who labours, fights, lives, breathes for him alone.*
> —Byron

Throughout the history of civilization canines have shown unqualified love and respect for persons of all creeds, races and stations of life, asking only a little praise and affection in payment for their unfailing devotion. Truly, the steadfast fidelity of the dog is unmatched by any other member of the animal world.

> *With eye upraised, his master's looks to scan,*
> *The joy of solace, and the aid of man;*
> *The rich man's guardian, and the poor man's friend,*
> *The only creature, faithful to the end.*
> —Crabbe

Other domesticated animals submit to human control but rarely do they recognize their master except for the supply of their wants. The dog is different, he will starve with his master and suffer any hardship or indignity in order to be close to the object of his affection. Dogs have been known to grieve over the loss of their master to the extent of refusing food and drink and finally dying from a broken heart— where can one find greater love?

Glen Fishiel, a vignette by Sir Edwin Landseer, 1824. An old type terrier dog is shown sitting at the left of the group.

Uses of Dogs

Through the ages, dogs have been used for many purposes in addition to being the most popular of pets. Dogs have been trained as dray animals, hunters, vermin destroyers and companions. Today, their use differs little; we probably stress their companionship to a greater degree but our canine friends still have the same inbred abilities to which they will exert their every effort when called upon to do so. The advent of police, guard and guide work has extended their purposeful existence and today the dog enjoys its greatest era of popularity all around the globe.

Zoological Classification

To obtain a better insight into the canine race, the zoological and biological background will be of interest. The dog belongs to that division of quadrupeds called *vertebrata,* and it ranks in the class *mammalia* because the female suckles her young. It is of the tribe *unguiculata,* since it is armed with nails or claws which are not retractile and is of the order *digitigrades* because it walks on its toes. The dog belongs to the genus *canis,* in view of its tooth arrangement and the sub-genus *familiaris* by reason of the round shape of the pupil of its eye which is a distinguishing point from the wolf, fox and jackal, all of which stem from the same genus.

All members of the genus *canis* are basically carnivorous animals; that is they eat meat as a primary diet. The dog is equipped for this diet with an excellent set of 42 teeth, including 12 incisors (the small front teeth) that are adapted for cutting and seizing; four canines (the long pointed tusk-like dentitions) which are for tearing, stabbing and "fixing" the struggling prey; and 26 premolars and molars, (the heavier and broader rear teeth having substantial flat and complex crown) that are used as grinders for crushing food. The "milk" dentition, first (puppy) teeth, are fewer in number, since certain of the molars and pre-molars have no predecessors. In general, the permanent teeth begin to replace the puppy dentition at around four months of age.

The dog tears its food and often bolts large pieces with little or no mastication. The stomach is of simple structure capable of digesting this unchewed food and the intestines are of medium length between the short ones of the true carnivora and the long ones of graminivorous animals. For these reasons, dogs can easily digest diverse

17

A group of early terriers, circa 1865, from Stonehenge's *Dogs of the British Islands*, 3rd Ed. At the left are Bounce (rough-coated terrier) and Venture (rough-coated Fox Terrier). The dogs shown at the right are Rough (Scotch terrier) and Dandy (Black and Tan Terrier).

foods, including grains and vegetables in addition to meat and, therefore, thrive on mixed diets.

Variety According to Function

From the beginning of recorded history, dogs of different kinds have been known. They have been bred selectively for centuries to best serve the purpose at hand. Sight hounds, scent hounds, bird dogs of various abilities, workers, fighters and Terriers are but a few of the very special types that have been produced through the breeding skills of man.

It has been a relatively easy task to modify or change breed characteristics and by selection and cross-breeding to obtain the type and temperament of animal desired. This statement is readily proved by the fact that in 1873 there were only about forty breeds and varieties recognized generally. Today, the American Kennel Club registers some 129 breeds and varieties, while scores of breeds that are recognized in other countries are still not on the American agenda. How many additional breeds will find their way to the roll in another century cannot be conjured.

The Purebred Family Today

From the foregoing, it is apparent that all of today's recognized breeds are hybrids, crosses of various existing strains to obtain changed and desired characteristics. When these crosses, through careful selection and several generations of breeding, reproduce their kind, the strain may be termed "set" and a new and reproducible breed is established. All of today's 129 recognized breeds have attained this status. It is true, that an occasional throwback may occur, but the majority of the progeny of registered stock will breed reasonably true to type. The art of breeding show stock is, of course, a subject unto itself.

The Terrier Group

The presently recognized 129 breeds are further sub-divided into seven basic groupings, wherein the several members of each group are related by blood, use or general activity. This classification system is used to simplify judging procedures at dog shows. Cairns fall into the category labeled, "The Terrier Group" (Group 4) which includes twenty-four (24) separate breeds defined as follows:

Airedale Terriers
American Staffordshire Terriers
Australian Terriers
Bedlington Terriers
Border Terriers
Bull Terriers
(Two varieties, white and colored)
Cairn Terriers
Dandie Dinmont Terriers
Irish Terriers
Kerry Blue Terriers
Lakeland Terriers
Manchester Terriers (Standard)

(Toy, in the Toy group)
Miniature Schnauzers
Norfolk Terriers
Norwich Terriers
Scottish Terriers
Sealyham Terriers
Skye Terriers
Smooth Fox Terriers
Soft-Coated Wheaten Terriers
Staffordshire Bull Terriers
Welsh Terriers
West Highland White Terriers
Wire Fox Terriers.

As will be explained hereinafter, The Cairn Terrier has consanguinity with other Terriers of Scotch derivation and was bred for similar purposes.

And the dog is still the faithful,
Still the loving friend of man,
Ever ready at his bidding,
Doing for him all he can.
                                        Tobit

2

The Terrier

WITH the foregoing background knowledge of dogs, we will move along to the division of dogs termed Terriers. This group came from the British Isles and includes the closely related Scottish, West Highland White and Cairn Terriers, all of true Scottish descent. The group name comes from the Latin *terra,* meaning earth, for Terriers are earth dogs—dogs that go to ground for their prey. They have special temperament, high intelligence and unquestioned courage. They will fight to the death rather than yield ground or give quarter and, above all, they respect man. Oddly enough, the very first mention of The Terrier is found in Gace de la Vigne's *poeme sur la Chasse,* circa 1359 and is as follows:

> Le va querir dedans terre
> Avec ses bons cheins terriers
> Que on met dedans les terrier.

According to scholars, this offers a play on words through the double meaning of the word "terrier" which, at the time, was also used to define a burrow of an earth animal. Thus, a rather literal translation of the passage will read:

> He goes to seek in the earth
> With good terrier dogs
> That they put into the burrow.

21

Badger digging, circa 1560.

The unearthing of a fox.

It may be assumed that the "terrier dogs" of Gace de la Vigne were small French hounds of the Basset type, but more of this later. Many works of art offer interesting conjectural background for the strain and antedate the above poem by centuries. The oldest of these is a carving that depicts a kind of a fox dog of Terrier type. The animal has small upright ears and a well carried tail and offers the alert attitude of a Terrier.

Terriers in Early Art and Literature

An even more pertinent reference is an engraving entitled, *The Unearthing of a Fox* found in an ancient manuscript in the Royal library. This dates back to the early 14th century and is possibly the first known representation of Terrier work. It shows dogs, not unlike Greyhounds in general appearance, with three men engaged in the bolting of a fox which is depicted running from the scene.

Passing to books written in the English language that mention Terriers, *The Boke of St. Albans* (1486) was the first. This priceless incunabula is credited to Dame Juliana Berners and was enlarged upon by Wynkyn de Worde in 1496. Both include an early listing of different kinds of dogs, including the Terrier, as follows:

"Firft ther is a grehownd, a Baftard, a Mongrell, a Maftyfe, a Lemore, a Spanyell. Rachys, Kenettys, Teroures. Bocheris houndes, Myddyng dogges. Tryndeltayles and Prikherid currin and fmale ladies popis that beere a Way the flces and dyueris fmale fawlis."

Of Englifhe Dogges

In the year 1570, Dr. Johannes Caius gave to the world the first book that was devoted solely to dogs. It was in Latin and bore the title, *De Canibus Britannicis.*

Six years later in 1576, Abraham Fleming translated and expanded Caius' book. This English work was entitled, *Of Englifhe Dogges* and became the first book devoted solely to dogs printed in English. In this effort, available in reprint form, all known strains of dog are broadly classified into three major groupings, as follows:

All Englife Dogges be eyther of,

(A gentle kinde, seruing the game.)

{ A homely kinde apt for sundry necessary vses. }

{ A currishe kinde, meete for many toyes. }

Fleming elaborates further upon the "gentle kinds" which, according to his classification, were dogs "seruing y' pastime of hunting beastes." It is in this grouping that the Terrier is placed.

Dogges seruing y' pastime of hunting beastes.	are diuided into	Hariers Terrars Bloudhounds Gasehounds Grehounds Louiners or Lyemmers Tumblers Stealers	In Latine called VE-NATICI

Of Englifhe Dogges was an important milestone in the literature dealing with dogs. It included most of the meat of Caius' original work together with a great deal of additional material. Furthermore, the book was printed in English which made it more easily digested and left a greater impact upon English-speaking people.

Fleming's treatise offered additional interesting information on Terriers. He classed them among the "perfect smelling group" and the smallest of the hounds. Fleming followed Caius with the statement that the Terrier is a fox or badger hound and, like Caius, he failed to give any detailed description of the appearance of the dog, but followed exactly Caius' description of the work of a Terrier with the excellent passage as follows:

Of The Dogge Called a Terrar
Another sorte there is which hunteth the Foxe and the Badger or Greye onely, whom we call Terrars, because they (after the manner and custome of ferrets in searching for Connyes) creepe into the grounde, and by that meanes make afrayde, nyppe, and byte the Foxe and the Badger in such sort, that eyther they teare them to peeces with theyr teeth beyng in the bosome of the earthe, or else hayle and pull them perforce out of their lurking angles, dark dungeons, and close caves, or at least through conceaved feare, drive them out of their hollow harbours, in so much that they are compelled to prepare speedy flight, and being desirous of the next (albeit not safest) refuge, are otherwise taken and intrapped with snares and nettes layde over holes to the same purpose. But these be the least in that kynde called 'Sagax'.

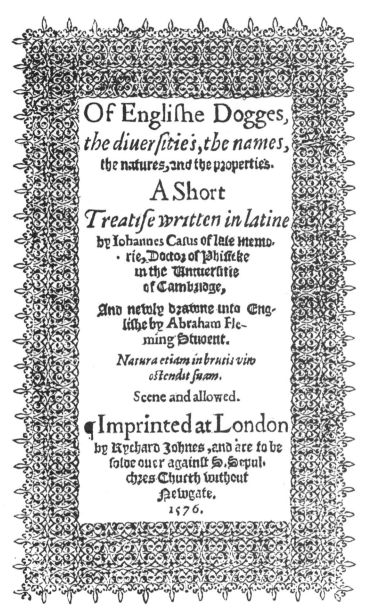

Title page of *Of Englifhe Dogges*, the first book devoted to dogs, as printed in English in 1576.

This description fits well the Terrier of today, particularly the descendents of the Scotch Terrier.

> Body and limb go cold,
>   Both foot and hand go bare;
> God send teroures, so bold, so bold,
>   Heart will harbour no care.
>   —Dr. Still, 1543

The Works of Later Writers

A number of other 16th century writers, expounding upon sporting issues offered descriptions of the Terrier in their works. George Turbeville's, *The Noble Arte of Venerie* or Hunting, circa 1575, describes "two sortes" of Terriers, a long-legged one and the "more desirable" crooked legged kind. He voiced the opinion that this latter kind came from Flanders. Jacques Fouilloux, *La Venerie,* circa 1560, includes a woodcut showing men and dogs digging out badger. The dogs are shown with collars carrying bells used at the time with dogs that had no voice to indicate audibly their progress within the earth.

Undoubtedly, these early ground-going hounds were crossed with dogs of Terrier blood, which offers an explanation for many characteristics indigenous to various Terrier strains. Croxton Smith, in his chapter on Basset Hounds found in Drury's *British Dogs,* 3rd ed., 1903, states unequivocally that "One *cannot* breed Hounds from Terriers, whereas one *can* breed Terriers from Hounds." He further brings the small Basset (*a jambes torses*) into close relationship with the Dachshund Terrier. The only explanation of the infusion of the Basset or Dachshund blood into the Terrier breeds is the invasion of the French and German strains as companions of itinerant Gypsies who went back and forth between the British Isles and their homeland. These hypotheses are supported by Stonehenge and Gray in later works of authority.

John Lesley, in his *Historie of Scotland* which bridged the era of from 1436 to 1561 offered additional interesting facts about the short-legged Terrier when he observed,

> There is also another kind of scenting dog of low height, indeed, but of bulkier body; which, creeping into subterraneous burrows, routs out foxes, badgers, martens, and wild cats from their lurking places and dens. He, if he at any time finds the passage too narrow, opens himself a way with his feet and that with so great labour that he frequently perishes through his own exertions.

26

This passage offers insight into the tenacity of the strain which by its digging abilities worked deep into the earth and in its great desire to conquer the foe sometimes died from the exertion of the effort.

In 1774, Oliver Goldsmith added the desirability of "voice" to the Terrier attributes. He wrote:

The terrier is a small kind of hound, with rough hair, made use of to force the fox and badger out of their holes; or rather to give notice *by their barking* in what part of their kennel the fox or badger resides, when the sportsmen intend to dig them out.

Goldsmith recognized that a Terrier should have "tongue". He was the first since Fleming to appreciate that Terriers do not always make a kill. Fleming mentioned that the Terrier may drive the prey out of the hole whence it can be taken in a net and Goldsmith added to this the use of "voice" to tell the sportsman in which part of the burrow the predator was holed up. Barking was here recognized as a very important adjunct to the Terrier's equipment to help guide diggers to the action.

> A small bold breed and steady to the game
> Next claims the tribute of peculiar fame'
> Train'd by the tribes on Britain's wildest shore,
> Thence they their title of Agasses bore.
> Small as a race that useless to their Lord
> Bask on hearth and beg for board,
> Crook-limbed and black-eyed, all their frame appears
> Flanked by no flesh and bristled rough with hairs
>
> But shod each foot with hardest claws is seen,
> The sole's kind armour on the beaten green;
> But fenced each jaw with closest teeth is found,
> And death sits instant on th' inflicted wound.
> Far o'er the rest he quests the secret prey,
> And see each track wind opening to his ray:
> Far o'er the rest he feels each scent that blows
> Court the live nerve and thrill along the nose.
> —JOHN WHITAKER, 1771

Vignette of early terriers from Sydenham Edwards' *Cynographia Britannica*, circa 1801.

3

The Emergence of Separate Terrier Breeds

As THE nineteenth century opened, Sydenham Edwards began publication of his excellent, *Cynographia Britannicis* (1800 et seq.) It was planned originally for quarterly issue but failed to maintain the schedule and eventually ceased publication after the issuance of eleven chapters. In the chapter titled, "The Terrier", which is not dated but which was published in 1801, the author offers a somewhat similar description to those previously set forth but adds: "In Scotland the use of the Terrier is to kill; and here they breed a fierce race; so great is their courage they will attack and destroy the largest foxes with which the country abounds, following them into chasms of rocks, where they often perish together." Edwards' most important contribution was, however, a colored plate that depicts five different Terriers including one that is unquestionably of the Scotch type. This dog has relatively short, crooked legs, is of a wheaten color and has one prick and one tulip ear. The illustration shows a bell carried around the neck of the dog, indicating that in spite of Goldsmith's earlier admonitions, some Terriers were still mute.

First Description of the Scotch Terrier

Many other descriptions are mentioned in contemporary literature of the time but most of these were merely copied from predecessors.

29

Possibly the initial breakthrough, so far as the Cairn is concerned, is found in Thomas Brown's, *Biographical Sketches and Authentic Anecdotes of Dogs* published in Edinburgh in 1829. Here the author offers a classification between the Scotch and English types of Terrier. He says,

> There are two kinds of Terriers—the rough haired Scotch and the smooth English.
>
> The Scotch terrier is certainly the purest in point of breed and the English seems to have been produced by a cross from him. The Scotch terrier is generally low in stature, seldom more than twelve or fourteen inches in height, with a strong, muscular body, and short, stout legs; his ears small, and half-pricked; his head is rather large in proportion to the size of his body, and the muzzle considerably pointed; his scent is extremely acute, so that he can trace the footsteps of all other animals with certainty; he is generally of a sandy color or black. Dogs of these colors are certainly the most hardy, the more to be depended upon; when white or pied, it is a sure mark of the impurity of the breed. The hair of the terrier is long, matted, and hard, over almost every part of his body. His bite is extremely keen. There are three distinct varieties of the Scotch terrier. Viz: The one above described. Another, about the same size and form, but with hair much longer, and somewhat flowing, which gives his legs the appearance of being very short. This is the prevailing breed of the Western Islands of Scotland. The third variety is much larger than the other two, being generally from fifteen to eighteen inches in height with the hair very hard and wiry, and much shorter than that of the others.

The description of the Scotch Terrier offers a useful delineation with the first mentioned variety seemingly being the forerunner of what we now know as the Cairn, West Highland White, Dandie Dinmont and Scottish Terrier. The second variety unquestionably defined the Skye and the third variety, is now extinct although it certainly was a progenitor of some of the longer-legged varieties of Terrier.

Later Writers (Smith and Stonehenge)

Following Brown, most authors followed by copying (sometimes incorrectly) his efforts until Charles Hamilton Smith brought out his *The Natural History of Dogs* (1839–40) wherein a full and precise catalog of known breeds is offered for the time. This, incidentally, is the first dog book printed in Scotland to include colored plates. The Terrier is classified under the broad title of "The Cur Dogs".

30

A grouping of early terriers, circa 1890's, showing three of Scotch heritage. The two dogs at the left appear to be a Cairn and a West Highland White, while the dog in the center is of the Dandie Dinmont stamp. Also shown is a Manchester Terrier, a Fox Terrier and a Bull Terrier.

Skittles, an early Scottish Terrier, circa 1882.

Vixen (1821), by Sir Edwin Landseer, a Scotch terrier owned by the artist. She was a famous ratter in her day, as the painting indicates.

The colored illustrations furnished are interesting, however, since they identify specifically the Isle of Skye Terrier and the Scotch Terrier while depicting several other types ranging from smooth to long coated dogs. The Scotch Terrier has a wiry-textured coat, and is shown to be black with tan and white shaded markings (see illustration). The text states that the Scotch Terrier is "the more ancient and genuine breed," among the several varieties. This Terrier was bred initially on the Isle of Skye and other islands of the West Hebrides as well as in the nearby Highlands of the Scottish mainland. The broad term as originally used must perforce be considered generic to all of the Terriers of Scottish descent which includes the present day Scottish, West Highland White, Cairn, Skye, and Dandie Dinmont breeds. All came from the same base stock and were developed subsequently through selection to provide the size and kind of dog most suited for the specific purpose at hand.

Little is added by the literature for many years thereafter that had not previously been suggested. "Stonehenge" (J. W. Walsh) in his book, *The Dog in Health and Disease,* first published in 1859 with many subsequent editions, made one of his infrequent errors when he depicted a nondescript dog as a Scotch Terrier. This error was admitted by him in a later edition but indicates that the Scotch Terrier was of small moment at the time. "Stonehenge" was an important man and judged the first dog show at Newcastle-on-Tyne in 1859. He was also the long-time editor of *The Field* and his descriptions of the various breeds of dog in the aforementioned book were used as the standards by which the breeds were judged in both Great Britain and America for many years.

Early Records of The Kennel Club (England)

Possibly the most useful means for tracing the progress of the Scotch Terrier is to be found in the stud book records of The Kennel Club (England). In Volume 1 of this publication a listing of all show placements from 1859 to 1873 is carried (where available). This offers interesting reading and also helps confuse later-day researchers because of the confusion of breed names used. The initial entry, so far as the Terrier is concerned is directed to the third show held in England, Birmingham, December 3 and 4, 1860. Here Terrier classes are listed, to wit: Black and tan Terriers, White and other English Terriers and a class for Scotch Terriers. This last had two contestants, a "white Skye" and an imported Skye (?). No additional explanatory material was offered and it may be assumed that the white dog was of a type similar to a West Highland White.

The next show recorded was at Leeds, July 16, 17 and 18, 1861. Here four classes for Terriers were offered: Black and Tans, English, except black and tan, Scotch and Bull Terriers. In the Scotch Terrier classification, the placements were unusual since three dogs ended in a dead heat for first place, three shared second including one with two puppies while three were in third.

At the London show in 1862, the Scotch Terrier class was divided into dogs weighing over six pounds and under six pounds. This same event was the first to offer a more useful breakdown when it classified "Dandie Dinmonts" and Skye Terriers in different classes than Scotch Terriers.

That interest was on the rise is undeniable since at London in 1863 many additional classes were offered for Scotch-type Terriers. These included classes for Skyes and Dandie Dinmonts together with separate classification for White Scotch, Fawn Scotch and Blue Scotch Terriers. As time progressed the picture became increasingly complicated. By about 1873 the only classifications for the Scotch branch of the Terrier family were Skye Terriers and Dandie Dinmont Terriers. As will be noted hereinafter, many Scotsmen insisted that the names Scotch Terrier and Skye Terrier were synonymous.

The Dispute Over Classification

In fact, later accounts found in Thomson Gray's book *The Dogs of Scotland* (1889 and 1891) disclose that the name became a serious bone of contention between supporters of the breeds we know today as the Scottish, Cairn and West Highland White Terriers. All were entered as Skyes together with the longer-haired member of the family. The argument over a proper name for the several varieties of the breed was surely responsible for negating progress and made the establishment of workable breed clubs difficult.

The Dogs of Scotland offers the most extensive and accurate history for the period from about 1870 to 1889. It tells of the many disagreements, the problems among fanciers of the several strains and, of course, the derivation and separation of several breeds as we know them today. It is a well conceived effort written by an authority of the day. Gray quotes Mr. John D. McColl who collaborated with Captain Mackie as follows: "The Scottish Terrier is the original Highland or Cairn Terrier kept by the tod-hunters who were paid by the

ART I.   PRICE ONE SHILLING.

THE

DOGS OF SCOTLAND:

THEIR VARIETIES, HISTORY, BREEDING,

EXHIBITION, AND MANAGEMENT.

ILLUSTRATED.

By D. J. THOMSON GRAY ("Whinstone").
Editor of "The Scottish Fancier and Rural Gazette."

DUNDEE: JAMES P. MATHEW & CO., 17 and 19 COWGATE.
LONDON: L. UPCOTT GILL, "THE BAZAAR" OFFICE, STRAND, W.C.
EDINBURGH AND GLASGOW: JOHN MENZIES & CO.

1887.

Cover of the book *Dogs of Scotland,* by D. J. Thomson Gray, 1887.

several districts in the Highlands of Scotland for keeping down foxes and other vermin. The Terriers were, and still are, hunted in packs, and as the huntman's livelihood depended upon effective service with his gang, he, as a rule, bred carefully and cherished the game ones." To further confuse the issue, a dog that hunted the fox was ofttimes called a Fox Terrier and this term was used in Scotland as well as in the south.

These were the problems of the day and it is small wonder that modern authors, who do not research their subject too well, become confused by the terminology found in old stud books and catalogs. Let it be said that before about 1875 the terms Scotch Terrier, Skye Otter Terrier, Tod-hunter, Rough-haired Terrier, Skye Terrier and even Fox Terrier (in Scotland) were often all used interchangeably to the confusion of the issue.

Thereafter, the terms, Scotch and Scottish Terrier began to assume a different meaning. Generally these names were associated with the three strains we know today as the Scottish, West Highland White and Cairn Terriers. All came from the same stock and often came from the same litter. The late Walter Reeves, a widely known and respected judge, once told me that he had seen dogs from a single litter sold as representatives of the several strains and classified by color alone. Surely, this was true since pedigrees of early dogs often included names of individuals identified under different breed listings. Possibly the best proof that all came from common ancestors may be found in extended pedigrees of famous dogs of the past, but more about this later.

Another interesting piece of information, that I have in my possession, is a letter written by the son of Colonel E. D. Malcolm (who is credited generally as being the "father" of the West Highland White Terrier.) This letter states that the Colonel, upon returning from the Crimean war (circa 1860) was hunting with his Terrier pack and shot one of his favorite dogs, a reddish brindle fellow, who was scampering through the underbrush, having mistaken him for a hare. The loss of this dog so grieved the good Colonel that he vowed on the spot to propogate only "white 'uns" in the future so that a recurrence of the tragedy would never again occur. This narrative indicates beyond question that the Colonel's pack included red brindles as well as whites, all from the same breeding stock.

With the foregoing background information indicating the undeniable common blood among the various Scottish breeds, several works of art should be mentioned, as they strengthen the conclusion and offer additional interesting data concerning the presence of a Cairn type among the Scottish branch of the family. Following the Edwards tableau, discussed earlier in this chapter, we have an 1835 caricature executed by James Robertson and titled, *Scotch terriers at work in a Cairn in the West Highlands.* Surely, these dogs, while offering a wide range in size, show the unmistakable type of the early breed representatives. In 1839 Sir Edwin Landseer completed his painting *Dignity and Impudence,* which depicts a Bloodhound with a small, white Highland Terrier, both peering out of a dog house. The small white dog has prick ears and a typical short head of the Highland breed. While the color suggests a West Highlander, it should be remembered that white was permissible in the Cairn Standard, (England) until 1923.

This illustration by James Robertson, circa 1835, shows a pack of terriers hunting otter in the West Highlands of Scotland. It bears the inscription, "Scotch Terriers at work on a Cairn in the West Highlands." (The word "Cairn" defined a pile of rocks at the time.) It is highly possible that these same dogs were the ancestors of the present-day Cairn Terrier.

36

Dignity and Impudence (1839), is one of the better known animal paintings of Sir Edwin Landseer.

Dandie Dinmont by Sir William Allan, R. A. Engraved by Sly. From Waverly Novels, Abbotsford Ed., published 1842, pg. 435.

Another interesting painting is that of *Dandie Dinmont and His Terriers,* by Sir William Allan, R. A. Here the jovial Dandie Dinmont is shown surrounded by small terriers of several types. The one facing the master is a good example of the old Scotch or Highland Terrier from which the Cairn was propagated.

In view of the early works of art and the documented records and statements set forth here, it is apparent that proponents of the several Scottish breeds of Terriers must be content with the fact that "first blood" is not attributable to any one of today's strains. All came from the same base stock, all were known to exist at the same time and sometimes were interbred. It is more realistic to admit the early consanguinity of the breeds and use this fact to aid in intelligently eliminating faults that still occur, albeit rarely, that are directly traceable to the hardy dogs, wrought in the hills of the rugged Hebrides—common forebears of the Cairn, West Highland White and Scottish Terrier, as we know them today.

> No product here the barren hills afford
> But man and steel, the soldier and his sword.

Highland Terriers with Queen Victoria, Prince Albert and the infant Prince of Wales. The dogs are Cairnach, Boz and Islay with the Greyhound, Eos. Atkinson after Landseer, 1850. Cairnach will be found in other Landseer paintings. Reproduced from a photograph loaned by Gerald Massey.

Puffin Shooting. Lithograph after T. M. Baynes, circa 1830. This is a rare print of an unusual sport. The scene represents one of the islands of the Hebrides. It will be noticed that while the loader is wearing trousers, the gentleman actually shooting is in Highland dress.

4

The Road to Breed Recognition

THE EARLY history offered in previous chapters indicates that the Scotch Terrier (as differentiated from the "true" Skye) began to be accorded recognition around the middle 1870s, although much turmoil and argument still existed between the proponents of its several strains. This is shown by the multitude of identifying names that were fostered at the time, including the likes of Scotch Terrier, Short-haired Skye Terrier, Highland Terrier, Skye-Otter Terrier, Todhunter, etc. By 1881, however, some real progress was made through the formation of a club that drew and approved a Standard for Hard-Haired Scotch Terriers (1882). This description applied equally well to all three branches of the family as we know them today—Scottish, West Highland White and Cairn Terriers. While white markings were stated to be a fault, Gray's book (1889) says that "an all white color is much prized". Thus, the West Highland was certainly not excluded while the present-day Cairn was adequately covered by the inclusion of brindle, red and wheaten colors in the specification.

Separation of the Breeds

Type, however, was beginning to change. Those breeders who were oriented primarily towards the Scottish Terrier type (a dog with an exaggerated length of head and more bulky body) were surely in the majority and changes occurred that began to cleave a definite schism in the fancy. This was clearly indicated by 1899 when a group known as "The White Scottish Terrier Club," petitioned the Kennel Club for separate classes for whites. The request was denied on July 3, 1900. In 1907, however, classes for Whites were on the agenda of the Crufts show and the West Highlander entered the stud book as a separate breed, although no dogs were registered until 1908.

Breed Recognition

In spite of this activity, Cairn fanciers were still without autonomy although a substantial number were dedicated to this small Scotch Terrier. It was possibly unfortunate that many fanciers of the Cairn were also devotees of either or both of the other two related breeds, Scottish and West Highland White Terriers. This situation obviously led to some confusion and certainly lessened the force with which the drive for separate status was propelled. Initial action towards breed recognition came when classes for "Short-haired Skyes" were first offered at the 1909 Inverness show with the redoubtable Theo. Marples judging. Entries at this event were owned by Mrs. McDonald, who captured first with Fassie and Mrs. Alastair Campbell who had the remaining three entries comprising, MacLeod of MacLeod, Doran Bhan and Roy Mohr.

That the new breed was not widely known at the time is indicated by Robert Leighton's remarks concerning his judging of the Crufts show in 1909: "I happened to be the appointed judge of Skye terriers. I had got through my work, as I thought, when I discovered that there were additional classes to be judged under the unrecognized breed name of 'Short-haired Skyes'."

Leighton praised the exhibits highly and declared them to be very similar to terriers he had owned as a boy in Argyll, saying that they were the original, unspoiled working terriers of the Highlands:

Properly speaking, they were not Skye Terriers, whatever their connection with the misty island might be. But they were certainly interesting. Small, active, game and very hardy in appearance, they were strongly though slimly built; somewhat long in the back, deep in the ribs, with short, fairly straight legs and turned out feet adapted for burrowing. Their heads were small, but proportionate to the size of the body, with erect, pointed ears, and a tapering muzzle which gave them an almost foxy aspect. In colour they were varied from wheaten-red and grey-brindle to dark heather brindle. The coats

Painting of two highland terriers by P. Jones (1858). Reproduced from a photograph loaned by Gerald Massey. Note varying colors and cut ears.

Ch. Morven, one of the early, important West Highland White Terrier stud dogs, also figured in the background of some noteworthy Cairn Terriers during the early years of the 20th century. During this period a number of influential dogs of both breeds were acknowledged to be of "mixed blood."

seemed too soft and silky to afford protection from wet; but on closer inspection I found the hair hard and wiry, with a closer, woolier undercoat well calculated to resist snow and rain and to remain dry after a day's work in an otter burn. . . . And the more I handled them the more I admired them."

The dogs were from the kennels of Mrs. Alastair Campbell, who had brought them all the way from Ardrishaig, on Loch Fyne. Leighton awarded 1st, 2nd and 3rd to Doran Bhan (a light red with dark muzzle and ears), Roy Mohr (a red brindle) and Cuilean Bhan (wheaten with black points) respectively. All were subsequent winners with Roy Mohr becoming a widely-known sire.

Leighton continues that after the judging, the Skye Terrier Club held a meeting and many protests were made. There is no doubt that many fanciers did not like the name and this feeling was not limited to fanciers of the Skye alone. At the 1910 Crufts show, Mrs. Campbell and Miss Hawke drew the controversy into the open by entering their dogs (Cairns) in classes for Skye Terriers, *even though classes had been provided for Short-haired Skyes*. The judge, Miss A. K. Clifton, refused to judge the dogs as Skyes and marked her book, "Wrong class." This action brought the matter to a head and the Skye Terrier Club appointed a committee comprising Sir Claud Alexander, Robert Leighton, James Porritt and E. R. Sandwich to resolve the matter. This group went to the Kennel Club on April 6, 1910 with the problem. Concurrently, the Kennel Club had been receiving letters concerning the matter and in one from the Countess of Aberdeen was the suggestion that the breed be called "Cairn Terriers of Skye." The committee was urged by Leighton to accept the Duchess' proposal in the shortened form of "Cairn Terriers" and this name was agreed upon. The Kennel Club then decreed that all Short-haired Skyes would be transferred to the new register (Cairn Terriers) without fee until July 1, 1910. So ended the controversy, much to the benefit of the breed.

Leighton, in his enthusiasm for the Cairn, goes on to state:

This official recognition of the breed encouraged the Scottish Kennel Club to offer classes *and Challenge Certificates* for Cairn Terriers at their Edinburgh show in October, 1910, when I was again the appointed judge . . .

This statement is in obvious error, for Challenge Certificates were not available at the time. Neither does the record indicate that Cairns were shown under Leighton at Edinburgh in 1910. Actually, it was

Mrs. Alastair Campbell with three of her Cairns in 1909. The dog in her arms is MacLeod of MacLeod. The dog on her right is Roy Mhor and Doran Bhan is on her left.

Bride, Bridget and Bruin, owned by the Hon. Mary Hawke were "road markers" in the breed's early history in this century just as their owner was one of the first pioneering stalwarts of the Cairn's best interests.

not until May 29, 1912 that a separate breed register was opened indicating that the Cairn had at long last attained a recognized status and could compete for Challenge Certificates at designated events.

The First Champions

Four shows were approved for the year 1912. The first was at Richmond, on July 2nd with Mrs. Campbell judging. She awarded the coveted and long-sought certificates to Firring Fling and Firring Flora, both owned by Messrs. Ross and Markland. Doncaster was the next stop on the show trail and neither of the aforementioned dogs was successful in defending the challenge. Fling, however, captured his second ticket at Edinburgh with Tibbie of Harris gaining the bitch CC. The fourth accredited event for 1912 was held at the Crystal Palace in London with the redoubtable Hon. Mary Hawke on the podium. She awarded Tibbie her second CC and gave the dog honors to a Cairn named Gesto, but more about him later. Thus, the first year of accredited competition failed to produce a champion indicating that differences of opinion existed between judges, then as now.

In 1913, the breed burgeoned with eleven shows being designated as championship affairs. Tibbie of Harris (Reg. #525-S), owned and bred by Lady Sophie Scott, took her third ticket at Birmingham in January of that year to become the first champion of record in this newly accredited but ancient breed. Gesto (Reg. #112-R) gained his third major win at Ayr in April to make him the first male titleholder. Three others gained the title during the year, Firring Frolic, Skye Crofter and Shiela of Harris to make 1913 a "very good year" for the Cairn.

Important Early Fanciers

Before continuing with a chronological history of Cairn development, a few of the more important persons who helped guide the destinies of the breed during its emergence and subsequent recognition should be mentioned. Possibly one of the most important, although not prominent as an exhibitor, was A. R. Macdonald of Waternish, Skye. He and Mrs. Alastair Campbell, became president and secretary, respectively of The Cairn Terrier Club which was formed at a meeting following the judging at Edinburgh in 1910.

Macdonald had long been an advocate of the breed which was sometimes referred to as a "Waternish Terrier". I have in my posses-

Ch. Firring Frolic, one of the first Cairns to become a champion. *Hedges.*

Ch. Gesto completed the requirements for his English championship in 1913. In so doing, he became the first male champion in the breed. *Thomas Fall.*

sion a copy of a letter (given to me by M. K. McLeod) from Macdonald to Miss Hawke, dated October 30, 1911, setting forth an interesting and early narrative of the strain at Waternish where it had been propagated since about 1863 when Dr. Mackinnon gave his uncle a white bitch. He remarked that she was of a "Cairn type", not a West Highland White. The dogs at Waternish were of all colors, however, "with soft and hard coats and of all sizes, ranging from 18 pounds down to about eight pounds and that the medium-sized ones, with short coats, were the best for going into cairns and dens of otters".

The letter is both historical and important since it points to the fact that the early dogs of the breed varied tremendously and that courage was the major requirement. Surely, Mr. Macdonald was an early promoter and an important person in the "new breed."

The Club progressed after its formation and by the time of its 1911 meeting at Edinburgh included among others Lady Sophie Scott, Lady Charles Bentinck, the Hon. Mary Hawke, Mrs. Fleming, and Mrs. Florence M. Ross—who became the breed's historian and author of an excellent treatise on the breed. Thereafter, interest grew and more fanciers began to breed and exhibit. Among these were the Baroness Burton, Lady Kathleen Pilkington, Lady Hermione Buxton, Lady Muriel Worthington, Mrs. Charles Howard, Mrs. Basset, Mrs. L. Dennis, Mrs. Stephen, Mrs. C. H. Dixon, Miss Viccars, Miss Lucy Lockwood and many others to add to the growing fancy.

Particularly active in the fancy was, of course, Mrs. Campbell, without whom the destinies of the breed would have been delayed many years. She single-handedly fought the battle for recognition and a place at the shows. Her actions, with those of Miss Hawke, forced a change in name in 1910 and her early exhibition of Cairns at a time when the breed was neither recognized nor known widely, helped immeasurably in bringing the breed to its early position of importance. Truly, Mrs. Campbell's contribution can never be repaid fully. Further, her "Brocaire" prefix was known at the shows for many decades, showing that her interest was genuine and not a passing fancy.

Of the remaining fanciers mentioned, Mary Hawke, Mrs. Fleming, Mrs. Ross, the Baroness Burton, Miss Viccars and Miss Lockwood appear to be of greatest importance, although all of the early Club members offered strong contributions to the launching of this "new breed" into the world of recognition.

Baroness Burton with Ch. Dochfour Vuiach Vorchad and Dochfour Brigand. *Thomas Fall.*

The Affect of World War I

With the coming of the war in 1914, just two years after official recognition of the Cairn, the requirements of every day life became far more important than breeding dogs. In spite of this, some effort did continue and the Cairn made slow but steady gains both in support and popularity. Upon the conclusion of hostilities, enthusiasm heightened and the Cairn began to gain new supporters on both sides of the Atlantic.

Interbreeding and Early Type

However, it was apparent that a defined type was lacking from the beginning and this fact was of vital concern to all true supporters of the breed. The condition was probably due to the wide variance in opinion among knowledgeable fanciers who fostered different views and who practiced various means to attain their goals. These means, while not illegal, caused the problem to be even more difficult to solve. The variation in type came from several directions but the most serious was the continued interbreeding of West Highland Whites and Cairns. The two were closely allied in basic blood and many breeders still kept both breeds. Interbreeding was used to improve the Cairn which had been down in size and sometimes lacked the bone and substance desired. The practice of interbreeding the two strains was condoned by both the English and the American Kennel Clubs for some time, and in England the get were registered as "Cairn-West Highland crosses" but were exhibited in classes for Cairns when color permitted. The white ones from a litter were probably sold as West Highland Whites although no specific information is available. That no stigma was attached to the practice is proved by the fact that Ch. Gesto (whelped March 22, 1909), a pillar of the breed and the first male titleholder was sired by a West Highland White named Sgithanach Bhan (Conas ex Deochil) out of a Cairn bitch, Torvaig (Fruchan ex Corvaig). Gesto became one of the great early stud forces and his "mixed blood" surely produced some white offspring, particularly since many of the bitches put to him were themselves products of this curious practice.

The American Position on Interbreeding

The entire procedure of mixed blood was clarified in The United States in 1917 when the American Kennel Club took action and barred any Cairn from registration if it was a product of such mixed breeding practice. This action caused the English to take a "second look", and thereafter the dog press was full of editorial comments from breeders concerning the practice and some of these offer interesting, revealing and thought-provoking reading today. The Baroness Burton (Dochfour) did not support the practice but she was apparently in the minority. Miss Constance Viccars, on the other hand, was a strong advocate of interbreeding. Miss Viccars bred Cairns under the "Mercia" banner and was also a devotee of the West Highlander. The continuing controversy was carried on the pages of *Our Dogs* (England) and is worthy of limited quotation. Miss Viccars offered the following observation:

Sir,—As this very important question is now being brought before breeders of both these Terriers, I think it is important that the views of those who have had long experience in these terriers of Scotland should be given, and I hope others will help by writing their views on the subject. The burning question of the moment is: "May the cross of West Highland White and Cairn be allowed?" At present it is allowed by the English Kennel Club, but not by the American Kennel Club. By next year, or rather, at the end of this year, I understand that unless our Kennel Club finds that breeders wish the rule to remain as it is (i.e., allowing the cross), it will be altered to the ruling of the American Kennel Club, and no terrier bred from the cross can be registered.

It is up to breeders to consider the subject well and decide which is best for the breed. I personally think the rule should remain, because I know that originally these terriers were one and the same breed, white being one of the colours in Cairn litters, just as much as grey, sandy, brindle, red, etc. In fact, when I wrote to the keeper of a well-known breeder in Scotland for a White West Highland years ago, the answer was: "I will try to save you a white one out of the litter. We usually, however, keep the dark ones, being better for our work, and destroy the light colour and white ones." Old John Macdonald, of Skye, also sold me what he called "White Cairns," which won as White West Highlanders, and two of my own full-champion West Highland Whites of former days had a Cairn parent on one side. In fact, in the pedigrees of all our best of both breeds the cross is found; but most present-day breeders do not realize it, as they do not know the dogs' names of those days.

Now it is seldom done in this country: because we have so many of each variety it is unnecessary, and I, with other people, prefer to mate Cairns with Cairns and Whites with Whites. But if others find that the cross produces a perfect specimen of either breed, I fail to see what objection there can be to their doing so. It benefits the breed—which is undoubtedly getting too miniature—by giving out-cross blood.

It is still constantly done in Scotland, with the best results, and why should these people (who really know their own breed best) be forbidden to show a beautiful Cairn because it is not bred in accordance with American or some others' ideas? Nature produced the variety of colours and included white in the original colours of Cairn Terriers, and I think Scotsmen will continue to follow nature and their forbears' way of producing the best, whatever rule there may be against it. It's asking a good deal of human nature to declare the colour in a pedigree (where the parents are not show dogs and registered) if by doing so the pup is damned as an alien!

As things stand at present with our Kennel Club, a white pup from two Cairns must be registered as a "white Cairn," and may be shown as such. I am afraid few judges will give it the same chances as a darker one, but, if this remains the rule, they ought to. I do not know if the American Kennel Club will accept a "white Cairn" in their drastic refusal of a West Highland White in any pedigree for three generations back. In one way they benefit the breed in England, as by thus ruling they prevent the progeny of most of our best Cairns being imported into their country, so they remain in England—for there are very few good Cairns with no West Highland White blood for three generations discoverable.

There are other breeders far older in experience than myself (though I have had both breeds since almost the commencement of their show careers), and I do hope they will give us the benefit of knowing their opinion from long experience of what is going to be best for the breeds in the future. —Yours, etc.,"

She was taken to task concerning her terminology by *Charouin,* who said her entire argument failed because of the use of the term *crossing* when in fact the Cairn and the West Highland White were merely color varieties of the same breed (which they were originally). he suggested that the term *interbreeding* would better define the practice, a criticism to which Miss Viccars concurred readily.* In spite of the heavy and continuing editorial comment, the Kennel Club (England) did take positive action on Nov. 18, 1924 when it handed down a ruling, to wit:

> The Committee considered the question of interbreeding between Cairn Terriers and West Highland White Terriers, and decided that the application be refused.

---

* It was even suggested to have classes for *White Cairns.*

The matter was finally settled for the good of the breed. However, it is pointed out that the practice so long held legal negates to a large degree statements made by many so-called experts, that the two breeds in no way resembled one another. It is true, that through the years the West Highlander has been bred a bit up in size through standard changes that have raised the lower limit from eight to about ten inches and has been shortened in back, while the knowledgeable Cairn fancy has endeavored to maintain the smaller size and a back of moderate length, not too long *nor* too short. However, the Cairn and the Westie do have many similar characteristics and well they should since less than sixty years have elapsed since it was legal to interbreed the two. Even today, a throwback does occur, mute testimony of the early and persistent practice and this is, in no way a disgrace nor a mark against either the sire or the dam of such white offspring. The "sport" is merely the normal function of the laws of heredity wherein occasional reversions occur. This diversion into the realm of past practices has been set forth to offer background for the uninitiated so that they may have the benefit of knowledge that will explain the presence of certain isolated faults as they appear today.

This closes the early history of the founding and subsequent development of the breed as an entity in Great Britain. Chapters to follow will bring this British history up-to-date and will then offer similar material on the American metamorphosis together with a biographical history of specific dogs and their breeders in both countries.

Mrs. Alistair Campbell with Brocaire Gaol at the Cairn Terrier Club show, 1946. This photo was taken shortly before the death of the great breed pioneer.

An historic group, Lady Bentinck, Mrs. Noney Fleming and Lady Sophie Scott with their winners, c. 1913.

The MacLennan family with six of their "Carngowans."

54

5

Cairn History in Great Britain (From World War I to World War II)

At the conclusion of the first World War there remained a coterie of founding and early fanciers still active and interested. Chief among these was Mrs. N. Fleming whose "Out of the West" suffix was widely known from the beginning and who continued her interest and support of the breed for decades thereafter. Her early champion, Fisherman Out of the West and his sire Doughall Out of the West were two important sires in the '20s. The Baroness Burton was another who remained steadfast in her support. Her "Dochfour" Cairns were much in evidence in the ring and the Baroness was much in demand as an arbiter. D. McLennan of "Carngowan" fame, who held the early record for championships completed with no less than seven by 1922 continued with strong activity while Mrs. A. Campbell's contributions through the years can never be fully set forth. The mistress of "Brocaire" with her many fine Cairns will always be remembered for she was probably the greatest single influence towards breed acceptance and early growth. Miss Viccars and Lady Sophie Scott among others deserve a place in that small group who began activity before the war and who maintained their interest for many years thereafter.

One more of the old guard needs recognition even though he was virtually out of the breed by the war's end. This man was Errington Ross of Glenmhor fame. He dispersed his fine kennel during the hostilities after nearly forty years of successful activity with the forerunners of both West Highlands and Cairns. Much of his most useful stock went to a relative newcomer in Cairns, J. E. Kerr, proprietor of the Harviestoun prefix. So important were the accomplishments of Harviestoun, that a detailed history will be offered to yield further insight to the practices used and the results obtained.

An early and important dog in Kerr's extended breeding plans was Harviestoun Yorrick, a white son of Glenmhor Chief ex Glenmhor Grougach. Yorrick, when bred back to his dam produced Harviestoun Kim who, when put to Harviestoun Tibbie produced the great Harviestoun Raider on November 9, 1919. Before delineating the many accomplishments of this dog, one should investigate his background.

According to the records (supported by the breed chroniclers Beynon, Fisher and Caspersz) Yorrick's sire, Glenmhor Chief was a West Highland White sired by Ch. Glenmhor Pride, a pillar of the Westie breed. Further, Yorrick's dam, Glenmhor Grougach, was sired by Ross-shire Helvellyn, another West Highlander.

Curiously, Mr. Ross always contended that Helvellyn was a "white Cairn" but his pedigree belies the statement, as his sire was Ch. Atholl who in turn was sired by Ch. Morven, both early bastions of the West Highland White. Helvellyn's dam was another white one, Inverness Wasp, although both of her parents were dogs of color. Thus, the blood on the sire's side of Raider's pedigree was heavy with the white influence. So far as the distaff side was concerned, Harviestoun Tibbie was all Cairn until her maternal grandsire, Sgithanach Bhan, a white one long to be remembered as the sire of the one and only Ch. Gesto who was a silver grey dog. Of course, in view of the many gaps in Tibbie's pedigree, there may have been other whites but that will remain unresolved. In view of these disclosures, one cannot deny that Raider's blood carried a generous sampling of West Highland White Terrier which may have contributed to his great bone and substance.

In spite of this background, Harviestoun Raider, a red brindle, was destined to become the first "great sire" in the Cairn breed. In

Ch. Fisherman Out of the West, owned by Mrs. N. Fleming, was an important sire during the '20s and a winner of 22 Challenge Certificates.

			MacNeill
		Macdonald	Frimley Pixie
	Macdonald of Crastock		Cairn Reich
		Kitty of Frimley	Lassie of Frimley
Doughall Out of the West			Firring Fling
		Dochfour Speach	Moccasin Tibbie
	Morag		Mannie
		Dochfour Talli	Callach
CH. FISHERMAN OUT OF THE WEST			Ch. Firring Frolic
		Firring Forge	Firring Flora
	Ch. Breakwater		Ninfield Mist
		Eiley of Ninfield	Eilid Mohr
Kyley Out of the West			Conas
		Cloughton Jock	Fetach
	Cloughton Bunty		Sandy
		Zaffy of Skye	The Imp

```
                              Glenmhor Chief (W)          Ch. Glenmhor Pride (W)
              Harviestoun Yorrick (W)                     Glenmhor Wasp (W)
                              Glenmhor Grougach            Ross-shire Helvellyn (W)
      Harviestoun Kim                                      Deilie
                              Ross-shire Helvellyn (W)     Ch. Atholl (W)
              Glenmhor Grougach                            Inverness Wasp (W)
                              Deilie                       Inverness Sporran
HARVIESTOUN RAIDER                                         Wellwood Queen
                              Cluaran                      Unknown
              Cairn Reich                                  Unknown
                              Dotaig                       Unknown
      Harviestoun Tibbie                                   Unknown
                              Sgitanach Bhan (W)           Conas
              Moccasin Topsy*                              Deacheil
                              Moccasin Molly               Unknown
                                                           Unknown
```

```
                                    Harviestoun Yorrick   Glenmhor Chief
                    Harviestoun Kim                       Glenmhor Grougach
                                    Glenmhor Grougach     Ross-shire Helvellyn
            Harviestoun Raider                            Deilie
                                    Cairn Reich           Cluaran
                    Harviestoun Tibbie                    Dotaig
                                    Moccasin Topsy        Unknown
                                                          Unknown
HARVIESTOUN BRIGAND                                       Coruisk
                                    Will o'the Wisp       Callaig
                    Harviestoun Wisp                      Ross-shire Helvellyn
                                    Glenmhor Grougach     Deilie
            Harviestoun Jet                               Glenmhor Pride
                                    Glenmhor Chief        Glenmhor Wisp
                    Harviestoun Jean                      Ross-shire Helvellyn
                                    Glenmhor Grougach     Deilie
```

The lineage of Moccasin Topsy is open to question. Dr. Caspersz, in his book on the Cairn Terrier published in 1957, notes that the parents of Topsy are "unknown." In Beynon's book on the breed, as revised by Alex Fisher and published c. 1950-51, Moccasin Topsy is accorded parents, to wit: Sgitanach Bhan ex Moccasin Molly. On the other hand, the same Fisher, in his List of Names of Cairn Terriers with Names of Sires and Dams, etc., c. 1953, fails to list Moccasin Topsy, indicating the absence of information regarding her lineage.

DOUGHALL OUT OF THE WEST	Macdonald of Crastock	Macdonald	McNeill: Loch Handa, Isean
			Frimley Pixie: Ch. Skye Crofter, Niseag
		Kitty of Frimley	Cairn Reich: Cluaran, Dotaig
			Lassie of Frimley: Ch. Firring Frolic, Frimley Pixie
	Morag	Dochfour Speach	Firring Fling: Doran, Stratag
			Moccasin Tibbie: Moccasin Garry, Moccasin Effie
		Dochfour Talli	Mannie: Frasgan, Ban Bharan
			Callach: Donan, Culag

CH. DUD OF HYVER	Ch. Gillie of Hyver	Ch. Carngowan Murran	Raeburn Conas: Ch. Firring Frolic, Raeburn Morag
			Lugate Lively: Gaywulf Sands, Chevet Sionnach
		Gillassie of Ninfield	Strathpeffer Gillie Ruadh: Jack, Deantag
			Raitts Rainnach: Unknown, Unknown
	Knipton Dian (late Cloughton Beana Bharain)	Ch. Carngowan Murran	Raeburn Conas: Ch. Firring Frolic, Raeburn Morag
			Lugate Lively: Gaywulf Sands, Chevet Sionnach
		Girlie	Little Bruce: Bruce, Prickles
			Yorna: Ch. Gesto, Brigit

Ch. Gillie of Hyver.

Ch. Beechacre Bouncer

all he fathered 11 titleholders, an unprecedented record for the time. Chief among his progeny was a son, Ch. Harviestoun Brigand (red) who carried his sire's prepotency.

Harviestoun Raider was not himself a show dog; his bone and substance made him "too strong" for the Cairn competition but these same attributes were possibly the reasons for his success in the breeding pen. A list of his champion offspring, in addition to Brigand include; Chs. Harviestoun Chieftain, Diana and Rustler, together with Chs. Brocaire Donan of Gesto, Brocaire Hamish of Gesto, Brocaire Jura, Moccasin Betsy, Divil of Gunthorpe, Derelict Out of the West and Geum Woffington. A study of this list shows both Mrs. Campbell and Mrs. Fleming had Cairns sired by Raider. Both ladies had been strong opponents of mixing Cairn and West Highland blood but the abilities of Raider to produce exceptional stock overcame their reluctance to participate. Mrs. Campbell bred her three Brocaire champions out of two different bitches while Mrs. Fleming purchased Ch. Derelict Out of the West from the breeder, T. G. Cox and affixed her kennel suffix. Derelict was a litter sister to Ch. Geum Woffington.

In retrospect, Harviestoun Raider stands alone as major influence on the breed. Study of early pedigrees indicates that his blood flowed through the veins of a majority of the winning dogs of the twenties and thirties, and this concentration surely strengthened breed progress. His only possible rival was Ross' 1913 champion Firring Frolic (Red) bred by J. Macdonald and by Doran ex Stratag. Admittedly, Frolic never had the opportunities presented to Raider but he did establish his influence through MacLennan's "Carngowans" and was later supported by Mrs. Stephens' "Hyver" line.

Other Important Breeders and Dogs of the Period

Returning to the period under discussion, in addition to Kerr, there were a number of others who entered the lists or became increasingly active during the ten or twelve years following the close of the war. Chief among them were: Miss M. Irving with her homebreds, Chs. Beechacre Berry, Blaeberry and Bouncer — this last tracing back to Harviestoun Raider on both sides through successive Beechacre breedings. Bouncer was a strong sire and produced well, including such get as Chs. Beechacre Beatrice and Bruin. In all some seven titleholders carried the Beechacre prefix. Mrs. M. Johnson's, 'of Keycol

The Prince of Wales with a Cairn Terrier. This tableau, taken from an oil painting, was the cover illustration for the June 1926 *Pure-Bred Dogs—American Kennel Gazette*. It was first published in the *Illustrated London News*.

strain included the strong silver-grey stud, Ch. Sammy of Keycol in 1927, followed by Ch. Bruin of Keycol and other winners. Along with these were: Mrs. Charles H. Dixon (Gunthorpe) with such studs as Harviestoun Forgie, a Raider son and his son Dan of Gunthrope; Mrs. W. Stephens with the Hyver dogs including Chs. Gillie, (red brindle), Laddie and Dud all "of Hyver"; A. Mackenzie (Moccasin), breeder of another good Raider son by the name of Moccasin Magnet; Mrs. C. M. Bird (Placemore), long active with both Cairns and Westies and owner of Placemore Croonach by Dochfour Brigand (light brindle); Mrs. Langton Dennis (Offley); Mrs. Basset with a host of good Frimley dogs such as Ch. McRob of Frimley, a silver with black mask and Ch. Ian of Frimley (grey brindle with black mask); Mrs. Mirrlees (Shinnel) breeder of Ch. Shinnel Simon; Dr. Caspersz, breeder of Ch. Charming Eyes out of Laughing Eyes by Bouncer of Hyver, Ch. Turfield Mystic Eyes, etc., and Alex Fisher with the widely known Ch. Fimor Ben Breac (dark red brindle), etc.; (Dr. Caspersz and Alex Fisher were both tireless workers for the breed and widely known for their extensive literary efforts and pedigree studies.); Col. Whitehead (Guynach), also a tireless club worker, with the Guynach dogs including Ch. Guynach Eachunn; W. Moyer (Bogton) with Chs. Bogton Balloch, Brindle and Breda; Mrs. Prichard (Donnington), a long time club worker and breeder with Chs. Donnington Badger and Cheeky and many other winners; Miss Reoch with Ch. Valiant Pirate, a silver brindle son of Ch. Harviestoun Brigand and others; together with Mrs. Drummond (Blencathra) and Capt. Townley (Carysfort) whose activities will be delineated hereafter.

The Thirties

Passing to the decade of the thirties, Cairn fortunes boomed. The breed grew to keep step with interest and several new faces became prominent upon the scene. Such dogs as: Chs. Dud and Frolic of Hyver, Harviestoun Brigand and Aristocrat; Divor of Gunthorpe, Sammy of Keycol, Ross-shire Warrior and Tam O'Shanter Out of the West continued to be in the public eye through their issue and these were augmented by a host of new dogs whose accomplishments met or surpassed those of many of their predecessors. Among this group was Capt. Townley's great Ch. Fearnought of Carysfort, a Ch. Fang of Hyver son together with Fearnought's classic daughter, Ch. Fear Nil of Carysfort, winner of an unprecedented 24 Challenge Cer-

Lt. Col. and Mrs. Whitehead in 1921 with Eng. Ch. Guynach Eachunn.

tificates; Ch. Dochfour Ean, linebred from Ch. Harviestoun Brigand and a product of the still very active Baroness Burton's kennels; Ch. Caradoc of Crockshed, owned by Misses Allen and Turner and strong in the blood of the prepotent Gillie of Hyver and last, but by no means least, the great Ch. Splinters of Twobees, owned by Mrs. Butterworth and Miss Bengough. This one deserves special mention for his overall greatness in the ring, the breeding pen and for his longevity. The dog came along before the start of the war and sired a number of champions while winning well in the ring. During the conflict, he was virtually unused but upon its conclusion, he continued to produce top quality stock. Splinters of Twobees was sired by Mrs. T. Rudland's Ch. Trashurst Chip, a double cross of Ch. Gillie of Hyver through his sons, Donnington Gillie and Ch. Dud of Hyver. Splinter's dam was Sorag of Twobees, strongly linebred to Harviestoun Raider on both sides. Thus, Splinters combined the best producing bloodlines of his time, small wonder as to his abilities.

World War II

It is regrettable that many fine dogs of the late thirties did not reach full potential because of the interruption caused by the war. The conflict caused all activities to cease and only small "radius shows" or matches were continued. Food rationing, the bombings and other problems stifled breeding and only a very few were able to continue, and on a much reduced scale. These unhappy circumstances did little to perpetuate the names of a host of useful dogs that were in their prime during the period; many would have fared far better in both the ring and the breeding pen had it not been for this interruption. Suffice it to say, the Cairn Terrier, as with most other breeds, survived the war and emerged from the trial to become stronger than before, a tribute to the indomitable spirit of the British people.

It will be noted that the catalog of dogs offered for the period of from about 1918 to 1940 is quite short. Many fine Cairns have not been mentioned and the accomplishments of others have been offered in abbreviated form. In many instances, further detail will be found in the chapters directed to United States activity, since a host of British Cairns were exported to America where they extended their earlier careers. Some others have been omitted for the sake of brevity. For those who wish to delve deeper into the British history of the breed, a number of books on the subject have been listed in the bibliography of this book.

At this point mention must be made of the excellent and exhaustive pedigree study made by T. W. L. Casperz who, in 1932, published a compilation of pedigrees of all Cairns that had completed their English championships until that time. In the same vein, Alex Fisher compiled another listing of British Cairn Terriers together with their sires and dams with emphasis on "Lines and Families" that appeared in 1953 with an addendum through 1954. These pedigree studies together with the Casperz publication, noted above, offer breeders of Cairn Terriers valuable information that would require months of effort to assemble from the general stud records and books. Unfortunately, neither listing is readily available being quite scarce due to limited publication.

Alex Fisher's Ch. Fimor Ben Breac, from a painting by H. Crowther, circa 1926. The painting is now owned by Milton K. McLeod.

Ch. McJoe of Twobees (Joe of Twobees ex Gem of Twobees).

6

Post-War Cairn History in Great Britain

AFTER the Second World War, Cairn activity resumed in all of its branches. Breeders expanded their kennels, exhibitors were anxious to get back into the ring and all cooperated to make these desires realities. It was not long before the breed surpassed pre-war activity on all fronts. As shows were restored, entries flooded the secretary's offices and the Cairn Terrier was again an active and vital force in England's resumption of one of its favorite sporting endeavors. Study of statistics reveals that the activity in the world of dogs in general never enjoyed such interest and support.

The Fancy After the War

As would be expected, many of the pre-war Cairn breeders were no longer active. There was a substantial segment that continued but the majority of the post-war fancy were a "new breed". Among those who carried over were: Miss Allen (Crockshed); Mrs. Bird (Placemore); Mrs. Rudland (Trashurst); Miss Bunbury (Shielings); Mrs. Dixon (Gunthorpe); Mrs. Mirrlees (Shinnel); Mrs. Prichard (Donnington); A. Mackenzie (Moccasin); Miss Viccars (Mercia); Capt. Townley (Carysfort); Col. Whitehead, deeply involved in Club activities; the Baroness Burton, still interested in all phases of the breed; Miss Reoch (Valiant) with a new dog, Ch. Valiant Rob Roy of Rhosbridge, winner of nine CC's and one of the first post-war titleholders;*

* Ch. Normanhurst Penelope was the first, post-war bitch champion.

Ch. Splinters of Twobees (Ch. Trashurst Chip ex Sorag of Twobees).

		Donnington Gillie	Ch. Gillie of Hyver
	Trashurst Sandyman		Chip of Hardings
		Eaton Wendy	Sweep of Frimley
Ch. Trashurst Chip			Dochfour Flora Ruadh
		Ch. Dud of Hyver	Ch. Gillie of Hyver
	Cherry McBryan		Knipton Dian
		Haggis of Sandi-	Strathblane Chaillean
CH. SPLINTERS OF TWOBEES		acre	Stew of Sandiacre
		Offley Brimon	Ch. Harviestoun Brigand
	Ch. Quicksand Out of the West		Canna of Frimley
		She	Ch. Quicksilver Out of the West
Sorag of Twobees			Dderfel Caraid
		Glenmhor Rascal	Harviestoun Raider
	Mulaidh of Twobees		Sorag
		Glenmhor Coullie	Harviestoun Raider
			Mulaidh

An unposed grouping of four widely-known Twobees champions: (l. to r.) Ch. Bonfire of Twobees (by Ch. Splinters of Twobees), Ch. Simon of Twobees (by Ch. McJoe of Twobees), Ch. Brindie of Twobees (by Ch. Bonfire of Twobees) and Ch. McJoe of Twobees (by Joe of Twobees).

Mrs. Drummond* with Chs. Blencathra Sandpiper and Sandboy, both by Donnington Sandboy ex the top producer, Blencathra Radiance and Miss Bengough and Mrs. Butterworth with Ch. Bonfire of Twobees and, of course, his sire, Ch. Splinters of Twobees. Splinters owns the splendid record of having sired nine titleholders before and another nine after the war. What this dog might have accomplished without the war years hiatus is conjectural but the total would surely have been considerably greater. In any event, he stands among the great studs in the history of the breed. Miss Bengough had many other successes among them being Ch. McJoe of Twobees (Joe of Twobees ex the aforementioned Gem of Twobees) and Ch. Brindle of Twobees (Ch. Bonfire of Twobees ex Foundation Sylvia).

W. N. Bradshaw

Of course, there was a great influx of new faces upon the scene. Many of these had begun interest before the war but in most instances, their names became prominent subsequent to the close of hostilities. These included a relative newcomer to the breed in the person of

*Mrs. Drummond died on July 20, 1980, at the age of 93. She began her interest in the breed in 1923 and her first titleholder was Blencathra Sandpiper in 1947 while her last were Chs. Blencathra Barrett and Blencathra Buccaneer in 1971.

Ch. Redletter McJoe (Ch. Bonfire of Twobees ex Redletter My Choice), owned and bred by W. N. Bradshaw, made a great name for himself as a winner and a greater one as a producer. He sired nine champions, one of which was Ch. Redletter McMurran the first Cairn Terrier in England to win Best in Show at an all-breed Championship event.

```
                                                          Trashurst Sandyman
                                    Ch. Trashurst Chip    Cherry McBryan
                        Ch. Splinters of Twobees          Quicksand Out of the West
                                    Sorag of Twobees      Mulaidh of Twobees
            Ch. Bonfire of Twobees                        Billy Bright Eyes
                                    Silver Golden Rogue   Gina of Thaxted
                        Mitzie of Zeliah                  Carmichael of Crockshed
                                    Chelmor Beauty        Erica's Caroline
CH. REDLETTER McJOE                                       Thistleclose Twinkle
                                    Bravado of Bann       Wee Jean
                        Sir Launchalot                    True Shot
                                    Beauty Queen of Bann  Colwell's Choice
            Redletter My Choice                           Braweeyin Fearnil
                                    Happy                 Braweeyin Garbo
                        Pride of Cronshaw                 Brentleigh Wheaten Ensign
                                    Sporty of Cranbery    Sporty of Brentleigh
```

W. N. Bradshaw (Redletter). Mr. Bradshaw was no stranger to dogs, having been active in several breeds including Flat-Coated Retrievers since sometime in the '20s. Just before the war, he took notice of the Cairn and exhibited briefly with moderate success. So important is the post-war effort of the Redletter Kennels, both in England and the United States, that a rather detailed history of its major accomplishments will be offered here.

Shortly after the close of the war, Mr. Bradshaw purchased two bitch puppies that were named Redletter My Choice and Redletter Mayflower. The first was bred to Ch. Bonfire of Twobees and the resulting litter brought forth a dog puppy, Redletter McJoe, whelped on August 22, 1948.

The youngster showed early promise and at eight months of age captured best puppy at the Club Show. Within a year he was made up, claiming his third CC at the following Club event. McJoe was not the first titleholder for Bradshaw, however. That honor goes to Ch. Redletter Magnet (Standholme Dusty Prince ex Carnochan Lass). In any event, McJoe was campaigned for a period of three years and did very well. His chief claim to fame, however, was his ability in the breeding pen where he sired some nine champions and many more Certificate winners.

Of all of McJoe's get, Ch. Redletter McMurran stands alone. McMurran won a total of 26 CC's and was the first Cairn Terrier in England to capture Best in Show at a Championship event. This he did at Paington in 1955. One of McJoe's daughters, Ch. Redletter Elford Mhorag, out of Foundation Sylvia and a litter sister to Ch. Brindle of Twobees, won 18 CC's during her show career. McMur-

```
                                                                  Ch. Trashurst Chip
                                        Ch. Splinters of Two-      Sorag of Twobees
                    Ch. Bonfire of Twobees          bees          Silver Golden Rogue
                                        Mitzie of Zellah           Chelmor Beauty
        Ch. Redletter McJoe                                        Bravado of Bann
                                        Sir Launchalot             Beauty Queen of Bann
                    Redletter My Choice                            Happy
                                        Pride of Cronshaw          Sporty of Cranbery
CH. REDLETTER McMURRAN                                             Killearn Mr. Chips
                                        Rascal of Rhu              Morag of Rhu
                    Free Lance of Carysfort                        Tigger of Carnwell
                                        Foula of Carysfort         Foxglove of Carysfort
        Cairncragg Binkie                                          Braw Dusty
                                        Grey Monarch               Betsy of Marchmont
                    May Moon of Mercrogia                          Kim of Smallthorne
                                        Trixie of Poplars          Glenryan Gaiety Girl
```

ran and Mhorag, half-brother and -sister, broke a long standing record by winning both the dog and bitch Certificate at five different championship affairs. Both were strong in Splinters of Twobees blood —both being sired by McJoe, a Splinters grandson, while tracing back to Splinters on their dam's side through Killearn Mr. Chips in the case of McMurran and through Foundation Twig and Titania of Hearn for Mhorag.

McMurran, mated to Ch. Redletter Miss Splinters, produced a pair of champions in Redletter McBryan and Redletter McBrigand and, when put to Redletter Miss Muffet, sired Ch. Redletter Miss Madam. McBryan was a strong winner in this post-war period. He captured 17 CC's while siring 13 champion offspring, the best known being Ch. Redletter Master Mac. Another McBryan son, Ch. Redletter Maestro was bred twice to Felshott Araminta and produced three titleholders, Ch. Redletter Twinlaw Sea Spirit, Ch. Twinlaw Blithe Spirit and Ch. Redletter Twinlaw Melissa. Seaspirit was later purchased by Mrs. Betty Hyslop and has done some good winning in the U.S. and Canada, but more importantly he became the second Cairn in history to win Best in Show at a championship event in England, while still owned by Bradshaw. This time the triumph was at Manchester in 1968. Thus, Redletter dogs have the singular honor of being the only Cairns in British history to gain the pinnacle at Championship affairs. Of course, other Cairns have captured the supreme award at Open affairs, but none other at the prestigious Championship level.

Bradshaw never made a choice between his several top dogs. He agreed, however, that three in particular merit special mention when anyone begins to catalog the great Cairns in the history of the breed. These include: McMurran, a great showman and a fine producer; McBryan, another excellent producer and—in Bradshaw's own words— "a true gentleman"; and last but not least the bitch, Ch. Redletter Marcel (by Ch. Redletter Michael), who captured 16 CC's in a single year. Marcel was dam of the excellent show bitch, Ch. Redletter Moonraker, who died in her prime in 1973.

Chs. Redletter Elford Mhorag (winner of 18 CC's), Redletter McRuffie (winner of 3 CC's in England and later an American and Canadian champion for Mrs. Hyslop) and Ch. Redletter McMurran (26 CC's and the first Cairn to go Best in Show at an English championship event).

W. N. Bradshaw with three generations of great Cairn breeding; (r. to l.) Ch. Bonfire of Twobees, Bonfire's son Ch. Redletter McJoe and McJoe's son Ch. Redletter McMurran.

73

Regrettably, Mr. Bradshaw died on July 2, 1982, at the age of 86 to end an era of great success. Whether the prefix will be carried on is not known. His last champion was Redletter Martini. During his long interest in the breed, Bradshaw held the record for titleholders with a total of 42. So closes an era of great success that has been evidenced throughout the world by Redletter exports that have done well wherever they have been exhibited.

Other Prominent Fanciers

Continuing the roll of selected post-war breeders and owners, we find that Mrs. E. F. Leverton had good success with Ch. Merrymeet Medea (Broadwater ex Merrymeet Novera Diana); Medea's son, Ch. Merrymeet Jason (by Merrymeet Jenmar Silver); and Ch. Merrymeet Tathwell Therese (by Jason out of Toptwig Sorag). Mrs. E. M. Yeend has done some fine winning with homebreds such as, Ch. Yeendsdale Masterpiece, a Redletter McJoe son out of Ch. Joyous of Yeendsdale; Ch. Yeendsdale Merry Fiddler, by Masterpiece out of Gay Girl of Yeendsdale and Ch. Yeendsdale Inspiration by Merry Fiddler out of Yeendsdale Never Say Die among others. Another kennel that has both background and a presently high rating is the Oudenarde establishment of Miss Ferlieth Hamilton*. It has enjoyed substantial success for many years and is among the present leaders in the breed. Represented in the past by the likes of Chs. O. Souvenir, O. Fellamelad, O. Caroline, O. Fancy Light and her sire and dam, O. Special Edition and Light Melody, the kennel has prospered in spite of the death of Mrs. Hamilton as will be seen from the survey to follow which lists new Cairn champions by year for the period of from 1975-1984 inclusive. Mrs. B. Shea (Redstacks) with homebreds such as Ch. Redstacks Kerry Dancer and Ch. Redstacks Demoiselle; Misses J. Marshall and H. Longmore and the Unique Cottage dogs** including, Ch. Unique Cottage Sir Frolic, sire of Mrs. B. M. Dixon's, Ch.

---

*Previously listed under the ownership of Mrs. D. Hamilton and Miss F. Hamilton with Miss Temple and now noted under the name of Miss Ferlieth Hamilton. Mrs. Diana Hamilton died, October 10, 1979; her obituary will be found in the Christmas issue of (Eng.) *Dog World* (1979).

**Unique Cottage Cairns are now owned by Mrs. Parker-Tucker who was Miss Marshall before her marriage. Mrs. Small (nee Longmore) is now the owner of the well-known Avenelhouse prefix.

A grouping of the Oudenarde Cairns; (l. to r.) Ch. Oudenarde Midnight Chimes, Oudenarde Streamlight, Oudenarde Carefree Pete and Oudenarde All-A-Light. *Thomas Fall.*

Am., Eng. Ch. Toptwig Fly by Night of Oudenarde, bred by Gay Marsh and owned in England by Mrs. D. and Miss H. Hamilton.
Dog World (England).

Ch. Oudenarde Sea Venture, owned by Mrs. D. and Miss H. Hamilton. *Fall.*

Am., Can., Eng. Ch. Oudenarde Sea Hawk, owned by Betty Hyslop and bred by Mrs. D. and Miss H. Hamilton, showing an example of an especially good headstudy. *Fall.*

Ch. Felshott Silly Season of Oudenarde was the last champion bitch finished by Mrs. D. and Miss H. Hamilton. She was bred by the Misses Hall and Wilson and was by Ch. Oudenarde Raiding Light. *Fall.*

Rossarden Mighty Star. *Fall.*

Ch. Rossarden Drambuie. *Fall.*

77

Whinyeon of Rossarden, the same lady's Ch. Rossarden Macdougall of Whimpas bred by Mrs. Heery. Both these noted Cairns were owned by the Rossarden Kennels of Miss Charlie Dixon and the late Miss B. M. Dixon (d. 1969), an establishment that has been in operation many years. Begun in the thirties, the kennel has been kept relatively small while carefully planned, selective breeding within established bloodlines has maintained a high level of quality. This type of effort has permitted Rossarden to produce Cairns that are both competitive and reproduce their kind. To date, some 10 Cairns have made their titles with many more gaining challenge certificates. One of the best-known dogs of the kennels was the aforementioned, Ch. Whinyeon of Rossarden who, with Ch. Rogue of Rossarden had highly successful careers in the ring. Miss Dixon is known in the United States through her judging, the latest assignment having been in 1982. Miss M. D. W. Gibson with Ch. Geroff of Mistyfell (Ch. Blencathra Redstart ex Sadie of Mistyfell); Mrs. H. L. Manley (Lofthouse) with Ch. Lofthouse Geryon of Mistyfell, a litter brother to the aforementioned Geroff, together with Ch. Lofthouse Victoria (Ch. Lofthouse Geryon of Mistyfell ex Ch. Lofthouse Golden) and Ch. Lofthouse Davey (Geryon ex Dorseydale Justeena) who came to the United States and captured the National Specialty show in 1966 under Mrs. Drummond; Mrs. D. Seymour with Ch. Dorseydale Tammy, a litter brother to Ch. Lofthouse Davey and both bred by Mrs. Seymour; Misses M. and D. Hall with the Felshott dogs including Ch. Felshott Taste of Honey by Ch. Redletter Master Mac ex Ch. Felshott Bryany; Mrs. M. Mawson with Chs. Glenmacdhui Mohra by Ch. Blencathra Redstart and Ch. Glenmacdhui Doonrae Memsie by Ch. Lofthouse Davey; the Toptwig dogs of Mrs. G. Marsh and Mr. J. H. Danks including Chs. Toptwig Tilden, Toptwig Mr. Defoe and Toptwig Miss Defoe, and the Cairns from Mrs. M. Jaggers Vinovium Kennels including Chs. Vinovium Pledwick, Vinvovium Graham and Vinvovium Errol Flynn who was exported to Mrs. Hyslop's Cairndania Kennels. Throughout the entire period, Mrs. Drummond continued her efforts with very good success with the likes of Ch. Blencathra Milord (Ch. Blencathra Chieftain ex Blencathra Milady), Ch. Blencathra Brochter and his son, Ch. Blencathra Elford Badger, and more lately with Ch. Blencathra Brat. Many more excellent breeders have come upon the scene since the war and it would be impossible to catalog all who deserve notice. Those mentioned have been representative of the fancy, a blend of old and

Ch. Unique Cottage Sir Frolic. *Cooke.*

Ch. Yeendsdale Inspiration. *Thomas Fall.*

Ch. Blencathra Brat, sire of Mrs. Hyslop's Fox-grove Susanella who was Best of Breed at the Cairn Terrier Club of America's 1974 Specialty show.

Ch. Blencathra Milord (Ch. Blencathra Chiefton ex Blencathra Milady). *B. Thurse.*

new tempered with great enthusiasm towards furthering the best interests of the breed.

Col. H. F. Whitehead

In retrospect, Col. Whitehead was still actively judging and attending shows until his untimely and tragic death in an accident in the late sixties. I had met him at Chicago when he judged the Specialty show of the Cairn Terrier Club of America in 1961 and drew the largest entry on record to its time, 122 dogs. He placed Mrs. G. W. Hyslop's Ch. Rossmar's Clanruf O'Cairndania Best of Breed. Thereafter, I had the pleasure of visiting the Colonel at his home in Armadel

Col. H. F. Whitehead was one of the foremost stalwarts of the Cairn Terrier breed. He is shown here making a Best of Breed award to Mrs. Hyslop and her Ch. Rossmar's Clanruf of Cairndania at the Cairn Terrier Club of America Specialty in 1961. *William Brown.*

near Edinburgh on three separate occasions over a period of years and always found him to be a warm and intelligent person, dedicated to the breed and overflowing with sound knowledge. Col. Whitehead, although never one of the outstanding breeders or exhibitors in Great Britain, had the background to help the newcomer and oldtimer alike and many persons on both sides of the Atlantic have benefited from his sound advice.

Alex Fisher

Another lifetime enthusiast, Alex Fisher, died in 1972. It was a great loss to the fancy as this man contributed tremendously to the breed's historical background. His early stud force, Ch. Ben Breac (Whelped in 1924) won consistently and produced equally well. He was by Ch. Cheek ex Guynach Nan, a bitch bearing Col. Whitehead's prefix. Fisher's constancy of effort is best demonstrated by viewing the record which shows Ch. Fimor Katrine and her winning sister, Fimor Kyle (1952) to be direct descendants of Ben Breac. In all, twenty Cairns are in the direct line of descent, all owner bred.

The Baroness Burton

Study of show results since the war brings to light the interesting fact that the Baroness Burton was still exhibiting as late as the 1958 Crufts show. The Baroness' name was the last of the founding group to come to notice. Her interest in dogs was no passing matter. She began in the early 1890s with a French Bulldog, then owned Westies, Pekingese and finally Cairns, all the while keeping Keeshonden, Labradors and Gordon Setters. All of her sporting dogs were worked by the Baroness herself and she did not give up shooting until she was 75—a remarkable person.

Prospects for the Future

Today, none of the early fanciers who were so very important in the founding years and in then bringing the breed into the public's eye, are with us. The success of the Cairn Terrier in the future depends upon the current group of whom there are many. It is hoped that their interest will have the longevity and devotion that was evident among the likes of Mrs. Alistair Campbell, the Baroness Burton, Mrs. Fleming and Miss Viccars in particular, aided by a host of others who were responsible for the prominence the breed now enjoys.

81

Since there are many new supporters of the breed in addition to a host of enthusiastic "holdovers," it appears that a useful manner for introducing them is to offer a survey of show activities by year from 1975. This is best accomplished by listing new champions by year which, through kennel name presence, will indicate those establishments that are breeding winners, a useful manner of recognizing breeding skills. For example, in 1975 there were ten new titleholders. They were, Chs. Avenelhouse Golden Oriole, Whimpas Mark, Tablin Rollo, Brucairn Quality Street, Heshe Miss Emm Dee, Sine of Clandranald, Redletter Millie, Redletter Miss World, Felshot Hillarity and Felshot Russell. In 1976 the total was eleven, to wit, Redletter Midsummer, Unique Cottage Grey Wagtail, Rossarden Minerva, Twinlaw Barnstormer, Detchmont Catrona, Unique Cottage Pippit, Bankfoot Devoran, Toptwig Fly By Night of Oudenarde, Toptwig Dawnlight of Oudenarde, Redletter Miss Marcella and Scottishe of Selkirk. 1977 new titleholders numbered twelve and included Robinson Crusoe of Courtrai, Brucairn Jonnie, Brucairn Chimes Beay Belle, Oudenarde Sea Venture, Ugadale Leadall, McBean Procyon, Craiglyn Caledonian, Pinetop Simply Super, Camcairn Cordelia, Lynwil Sarah Jane, Oudenarde Fair Thrill and Redletter Moon Marcel. The 1978 roll embraced 13 new names including Redletter Midsummer, Unique Cottage Grey Swift, Courtrai Sally Ann, Unique Cottage Whinchat, Velora Dancing Light, Thimswarra Roulette, Rustlebury Taragon of Ramslow, Avenelhouse King's Frolic, Oudenarde What Next, Felshott Silly Season of Oudenarde, Pinetop Victoria, Stanedykes Pete, and Courtrai Triella Trudy. The 1979 titleholders numbered ten including, Heshe Rough Cut, Ljekarna Jolly, Heshe Charmer, Camcairn Claudette, Cairntop Master Simon, Rossarden Royal Star, Straniver Red Regent, Unique Cottage Fly Catcher, Kinkim Lohna Lady Can and Penticharm Golddigger. The 1980 champions included Stanedykes Thourso, Roseview Lancelot, Glencarra Bright Spark, Oudenarde Night Watch, Hamish Selkirk, Cruzo Carousel, Sandaig Sula Rhu, Monary Roda, Heshe Happy Talk, Clanranald Laetare, Thimswarra Estelle and Harlight Honeysuckle (ten in all). Finally, the 1981 recipients that numbered ten, to wit, Chs. Pinetop Montanam Strathinver Red Rufus, Unique Cottage Tree Creeper, Redletter Martini, Camcairn Beaulah, Avenelhouse Acrobat, Penticharm Catherine, Penticharm Charlie Girl and Saucy Miss Monary. This listing includes names of kennels that have done well in the past while also embracing a host of new prefixes that are rapidly becoming better known, many of which will be the foundation of the future fortunes of the breed.

While many are aware of the procedures used in England for gaining the championship title, many newcomers are not and for them an explanation is furnished. At English championship events, of which there are a limited number in each breed, all champions must be entered in the open classes. This means that these same dogs are in direct competition for the coveted challenge certificate (akin to the winners ribbon in the United States and Canada) with all non-champions. This is the reason why relatively few new titleholders are crowned each year as compared to United States statistics. It also suggests that these same new champions are fully worthy of the title as they must meet and defeat the best in order to prevail.

The Lindsley Tappins with Chs. Roddy and Knipton Dean O'Tapscot. Dean was an outstanding sire and consistent winner during the early '30's.

Ch. Prometheus (1914–1928).

7

The History of the Cairn Terrier in America— 1913-1930

THE VERY early development of the Cairn in America lagged British action by a few years and is quite obscure today. Undoubtedly, many American fanciers had "Cairns" at the same time that the British were developing the breed under its early name of the "Short-Haired Skye." Further, the West Highlander was established and recognized in America by 1908, and this fact points to probable "Cairn type" offspring that must have been present in many litters.

The First Cairns in America

However, documentation of the Cairn has eluded this author prior to statements giving credit to Mrs. Henry F. Price of Riverside, Connecticut, as having imported "the first known Cairns." In September of 1913 she brought over Sandy Peter Out of the West and Loch Scolter's Podge, both bred by Mrs. Fleming. Contrary to general information stating that she entered both in the Miscellaneous Class at Danbury in October of 1913, American Kennel Club records indicate that Sandy Peter was the lone entry in the class and obviously placed first. This dog had the more impressive honor of being the first Cairn to gain AKC registration, also in 1913, being assigned number 173555 in the stud record. Curiously, he was the only registrant for the year.

The following year, 1914, five Cairns were recorded in the stud registry and Sandy Peter Out of the West gained additional acclaim by placing third in a big Miscellaneous Class at Westminster. The same year, Mrs. H. W. Warden of Philadelphia had the distinction of registering the first American-bred Cairn, Lorne Spirag, #185653, the product of a mating between Lorne Padraig ex Lorne Feorag and whelped May 7, 1914. In 1915, no Cairns were registered but eight were shown. These were owned by Mrs. Price and included Sandy Peter Out of the West, and his get, Peter Piper, Prometheus, (a champion in 1921) and Miss Prim. The others were owned by Mrs. H. W. Warden, bearing the names of Lorne Feorag, Lorne Padraig II, Lorne Spirag and Lorne Stratay. The following year (1916) was not any better as the total exhibits again numbered eight including dogs owned by Mrs. Warden, Mrs. E. Lehman, Mrs. Edward Schmidt, Miss McAllister, Nelson Warwick and Mrs. William Nichols. The registration figures for the year matched exactly the number shown.

The Breed Takes Hold

In 1917 began a strong upsurge in registrations with 32 being added to the stud book and it became apparent that the new breed had come "of age" in America. On December 18 of this same year (1917), The Cairn Terrier Club of America gained membership in the American Kennel Club, its first officers being: Mrs. Payne Whitney, president; William R. Wanamaker, vice president; Mrs. Byron Rogers, secretary, and Mrs. H. F. Price, treasurer. This was, of course, most important to the breed since the national club gave backing and added prestige to this relatively new breed. The Cairn Terrier Club of America was the ninth Terrier breed club to become an American Kennel Club member and has been a strong and stabilizing factor in the growth and direction of the breed in this country.

As noted, in the very early days of the breed's official existence, Cairns had been shown in the Miscellaneous classes. This was normal procedure for little-known breeds. At the time, each show-giving club could limit its agenda to specific breeds and those not included in the classification were relegated to, and had to be exhibited in, the Miscellaneous Class. The classification differed from show to show and in 1915, for example, the Cairn was exhibited variously in Miscellaneous classes and in separate breed classes. The first club to offer separate classification was the Ladies Kennel Association of Mineola, New York, on June 3 and 4, 1915. Here separate classes were on the agenda and the redoubtable Holland Buckley was the judge. The same year both Gwynedd Valley and Devon kept the breed in the Miscellaneous Class while Danbury, held in October, offered separate classification. To make the issue more confusing, 1916 found a mixture of classes for the breed, with Boston held in November of that year relegating Cairns to the Miscellaneous grouping.

The First Champions

As the breed expanded numerically, an increasing number of shows began to enjoy entries in the breed and the Cairn soon became a known entity among the several recognized breeds of dog. This metamorphosis occurred during the war period (1914–1918) when American activity actually increased while British support was declining. In 1918, Mrs. Payne Whitney's imported, Greentree Ardsheal Gillie Cam qualified for the title of champion, the first American champion of record. Two years later (1920), Mrs. Winans Burnett's, Goldthread of Quinnatisset made the grade and became the initial American-bred titleholder. At this time, Mrs. Burnett was surely the most successful and active exhibitor, as she owned all four champions for the year 1919 (all imported) and four of the eight that qualified in 1920, an excellent and enviable record.

The Important Contributions of Early Fanciers

Of the several early fanciers mentioned heretofore, Mrs. Price (Robinscroft), Mrs. Whitney (Greentree), Mrs. Burnett (Quinnatisset) and Mrs. Rogers (Misty Isles) were the most active and important up to about 1920. Further, they all maintained their interest in the breed and helped strengthen it further through their background knowledge.

Special mention must go, however, to two of these because of their very special contributions towards breed growth and interest. Mrs. Price will be remembered as the importer of the very first Cairn to officially come to this country. For this she is acknowledged to be the founder of the American fancy. However, Mrs. Price did not rest upon her laurels; she bred and exhibited faithfully for many years and may be found as an exhibitor at shows in the early forties, surely a fancier with a life-time interest.

Mrs. Rogers entered the breed a bit later but shared the enthusiasm of Mrs. Price. English by birth, she was interested originally in Sealyham Terriers and used the kennel name Llandoyley. As her interest in dogs grew, she included Cairns in the effort which, of necessity, matured from a hobby into a business. Mrs. Rogers began to exhibit in 1917 and wrote the first book on the breed, *Cairn and Sealyham Terriers* in 1922.

As her importing business expanded, she moved to Bedford, Massachusetts and in 1924 changed the name of the kennels to Misty Isles. Concurrently, she began to expend increasingly greater time and effort to Poodles which became eventually her major interest. Indeed, the 'of Misty Isles suffix became so important that dogs bearing it are to be found in the backgrounds of most of the present day representitives of that breed. So far as Cairns are concerned, while Mrs. Rogers name does not appear often as a breeder of Cairns, the 'of Misty Isles appendage is found quite often in the names of early imports. (An excellent biography of Mrs. Rogers, written by Mrs. Erlanger, will be found in the book, *Poodles In Particular,* by Alice Lang Rogers.)

After the conclusion of the war, activity in both England and America heightened. By 1920, the Cairn Terrier was becoming a reasonably well-known breed and with this recognition came a host of new supporters to add to the several holdovers mentioned previously. In the new group were such stalwarts as Mr. and Mrs. W. Brydon Tennant (Glenconnor) who owned Ch. Joker of Harris, imported by Mrs. Rogers. The Tennants were active for about two decades and added much to the early stature of the Cairn. Additionally, Mr. and Mrs. Norman W. Ward (Cornor) promoted the breed for many years and owned a host of fine dogs including, Chs. Cornor Ross-shire Trefoil and Cornor Rosshire Trefusis; Miss Edith McCausland (Kedron) whose early imports Dochfour Callum and Ch. Barlae Jackie were well used at stud; Mrs. Edward Loomis (Knocwood) with Ch. Offley Misty Morn and his daughters, Chs. Knocwood Jean and Biddy of Misty Isles: the Henry Slacks (Rosscamac) who exhibited many top dogs including Ch. Offley Gilladdie of Rosscamac and Mr. and Mrs. Kenneth Harlan of the California-based Marken Kennels who had the good fortune of owning the first Cairn to go Best in Show in the United States. This dog, an American-bred, was named Jinx Ballantrae.

Ch. Greentree Ardsheal Gillie Cam, owned by Mrs. Payne Whitney, was the first Cairn to become an American champion.

Jinx Ballantrae, with owner Marie Prevost (Mrs. Kenneth Harlan), was the first Cairn Terrier to win a Best in Show in the United States. This occurred 1927 in Portland, Oregon. *Lester Rounds.*

In March of 1927 he was exhibited at Portland, Oregon and was selected best dog in show by J. W. Burton. The event had an official entry of 481 dogs and the win completed championship requirements for the dog. Mr. Harlan was a widely-known movie star and Jinx was handled to the triumph by his equally famous actress wife, Marie Prevost.

Another top win was consummated the following year by Mr. and Mrs. Richard Stix' imported, Ch. Gillad of Cairmore. This triumph was over an entry of 497 dogs at the April 1928 show in St. Louis and the judge was the redoubtable Frank Addyman. This act followed closely the dog's Best of Breed win at Westminster where he came up from the classes over a host of toppers. Mr. and Mrs. Stix' (Cairmore Kennels) activities were doubly interesting in that it was they that took the breed out of its Eastern stronghold to Cincinnati where a substantial kennel was established. In addition to the aforementioned Gillad (sire of Ch. Fiddown Thistle), there were such dogs as Chs. Dalle of Gunthorpe Cairmore, Brocaire Nigean Hamish (dam of Ch. Cairmore Gesto), Harvest Out of the West (sire of Ch. Cairmore Dark Harvest), Ch. Fascinating Eyes of Dew Hollow and many more. Unfortunately, the establishment was not of great longevity but it certainly helped the breed during its term of effort and it introduced interest in the Cairn to the Midwest. All of the foregoing fanciers must be remembered and recognized for their strong contributions during an important era in breed growth.

Special mention must be accorded two additional fanciers who began their interest during the 1920s and who contributed immeasurably to the stature of the breed. They were, Mrs. Amy Bacon (Cairnvreckan) and Mr. and Mrs. Lindsley Tappin (Tapscot).

Cairnvreckan

Mrs. Bacon was a fancier of life-long interest. Her efforts were intense and she bred well and exhibited consistenty, beginning in the early twenties and continuing until her death in the mid-fifties. She was quite successful in the ring with more than two dozen titleholders being bred by Cairnvreckan. I had the honor of knowing the lady through our mutual interest in West Highland Whites. This indicates that Mrs. Bacon was not one who expended her sole efforts on Cairns but who was interested generally in dogs. Mrs. Bacon was indeed

This beautiful painting is of interest for a variety of reasons. Executed by the renowned animal artist, Enno Meyer, it depicts Chs. Gillad of Cairmore and Dallee of Gunthorpe Cairmore, owned by Mr. and Mrs. Richard Stix. The painting was reproduced in color for the December 1, 1928 issue of *Pure-Bred Dogs—American Kennel Gazette*. It is now the property of Mrs. Carl Brewer.

a credit to the dog game. It is also of some importance that she was a breeder, first, last and always. She was not a buyer of either English or American stock. She generally exhibited what she bred—no greater tribute can be offered. A few of the better known dogs bred by her include: Chs. Knocwood Daintyness, Cairnvreckan Merlin, Cairn-vreckan Darach, Cairnvreckan Dewar, Cairnvreckan Kinchin, Cairn-vreckan Stelvio and Cairnvreckan Unique one of her last.

Tapscot

The Lindsley Tappins with their extensive Tapscot kennels actually re-made the Cairn fancy at the time. Tapscot was a large and success-ful effort that endured for many years and which, during its term of activity, dominated the shows. More than 45 titleholders were on its roll, a record for the time. Because the story is so un-usual, a rather detailed account of the effort will be offered. The inter-est began with a single, rather poor specimen of the breed. His tempera-ment "sold" his owners and they began to look about for another and better dog. Their quest led them to the import, Dollis Dawn, who was registered with the suffix 'of Tapscot attached in 1927. Dawn gained the points for her title the same year and became the first in a long line of titleholders that would carry the 'of Tap-scot legend. At the time, the Tappins were living in an apartment on Park Avenue in New York City. Not wishing to change their abode and not dreaming the extent of future expansion, they housed the dogs in pens and wicker crates that took over several bedrooms in their spacious quarters. The kennel set-up posed no deterrent to breed-ing and in 1928 the Tappins made five more champions. All of the dogs in this "city kennel" were exercised three at a time on leads by either Mr. or Mrs. Tappin, aided by others as the kennel population expanded. All dogs were housebroken at an early age and the more adult ones had the run of the apartment. The Tappins credited their unique kennel set-up for the fine dispositions of its inmates.

As time passed the dogs multiplied, the Tappins finally had to move their base of operations to Wilton, Connecticut where they pro-vided spacious new quarters for the steadily growing kennel popula-tion. Through nearly two decades of strong activity, a steady outpour-ing of top Cairns were housed at Tapscot including the likes of; Chs. Patience of Otford of Tapscot, Duke of T.; Dean Again of T., sire of Diana; Duke, Best Boy, Jere and Peppermint, all of Tapscot. Ch. Jere O'Tapscot was one of the big winners to his time and captured the breed at Westminster twice while winning the National Specialty in both 1941 and '42 before he was four years old. In addition, he became a strong sire, his most notable son being Ch. Jayson O'Tapscot who was acquired by Mrs. Allen's Craigdhu establishment, where he was responsible for over twenty titleholders, an all-time record to its time. Add to this list, four outstanding stud dogs: Ch. George of Hyver O'Tapscot who sired Chs. Major, Pippin, Una's Cheery Boy, Persistence, Pirate, Troona, Thrill, Gallant Boy, Gallant Man and Gay Boy, all O'Tapscot, together with Ch. Cornor George; Ch. Knipton Dean of Tapscot whose get included Chs. Darkie, Brownie, Mist, Deacon, Dean Again and Greta, all O'Tapscot together with Chs. Hollow Tree Margaret and Heather; Ch. Tinker of Tapscot, a homebred who sired Chs. Dalrigh and Dunbar of Cairndania and Ch. Blinkbonny Thrums among others; and finally, Ch. Tommy Tucker O'Tapscot, a dog out of Persistence, who sired the likes of Chs. Petticoat, Whizz II, Gillyflower and Best Boy, all O'Tapscot. Surely, this partial listing of Tapscot inmates togther with some of their accomplishments stamps the kennel as the leading effort until its time. The desire to excel, the ability to import, breed and exhibit, all helped the Cairn Terrier attain stature within the Terrier group and among all breeds of dogs. Tapscot closed its doors in about 1943 and Riot O'Tapscot was the last Champion to carry the name.

Summary

So ends the saga of the Cairn Terrier through the 1920s. This was a critical period, for without steady growth and strong, intelligent breeder support, the breed could have been obscured for many years to come. Luckily for the Cairn, the period was one of controlled growth, one where fanciers were impressed with quality and when many had the funds to import the best and to exhibit so that the Cairn Terrier became known widely by the public.

Because of the relative importance of these founding years, a chronological list of all Cairn Terrier champions from the beginning of the breed through 1930 is appended hereto. It is interesting to note that in spite of the breed's growth that imports exceeded American-breds about three to one during the period. The total number of champions listed is 91, of which only 30 are American-breds. Oddly enough the last few years showed an even greater percentage of disparity.

Cairn Terrier Champions through 1930
(An asterisk before a dog's name indicates American-bred)
1913 through 1917

None

Name   Owner

1918

Greentree Ardsheal
  Gillie Cam   Mrs. Payne Whitney

1919

Castlehill Ooa   Mrs. Winans Burnett
Fraoch Gael Out of the West   Mrs. Winans Burnett
Lugate Lucid   Mrs. Winans Burnett

1920

*Goldthread of Quinnatisset   Mrs. Winans Burnett
Greentree Broc   Mrs. Payne Whitney
Greentree Folly's Sister   Mrs. Payne Whitney
Ian of Mercia   Mrs. Winans Burnett
Offley Misty Morn   Mrs. Edward N. Loomis
Spangle Out of the West   Mrs. Winans Burnett
*Tempest's Kiltie of Misty
  Isles   Mr. A. U. Whitson
Tempest Out of the West   Mrs. Winans Burnett

1921

*Grosse Point Cheeky Girl   Mrs. H. Stephens
Mairlan Mirk   Mrs. J. Marwick
Sorag of Misty Isles   Mr. Joseph Friedlander
*Winsome Bairn of Misty
  Isles   Mrs. Winans Burnett
*Prometheus   Mrs. Henry F. Price

1922

Eskside Jock   Mrs. Edward N. Loomis
Fluff Out of the West   Mrs. Henry F. Price
*Grosse Point Rags   Mrs. H. Stephens
Merivale Rahab   Mrs. Alfred C. Kluepfel
Shona of Misty Isles   Miss Elsie G. Hydon
*Sprite of Quinnatisset   Mrs. C. A. Orcutt
Westbourne Shoran   Mrs. Alfred C. Kleupfel

Name	Owner

1923

*Fore of Quinnatisset	Mrs. Winans Burnett
Greentree Southboro Sonata	Mrs. Payne Whitney
Greentree Southboro Signum	Mrs. Payne Whitney
*Greentree Squirrel	Mrs. Payne Whitney
Quinnatisset Rags of Bonshaw	Mrs. Winans Burnett
*Ragbag of Quinnatisset	Mrs. Winans Burnett
*Sydward Ruddy Girl of Misty Isles	Mrs. Edward M-P. Murphy
Wee John of Quinnatisset	Mrs. Winans Burnett

1924

*Biddy of Misty Isles	Mrs. Charles F. Aldrich
Dochfour Oliver	Mr. Francis L. Robbins, Jr.
Flare of Keycol	Mr. Francis L. Robbins, Jr.
*Greentree Ailsa Craig	Mrs. Payne Whitney

1925

Brian of Trefusis	Mr. Frank C. Wymond
Cornor Jemima of Trefusis	Mr. and Mrs. Norman W. Ward
Cornor Ross-shire Trefoil	Mr. and Mrs. Norman W. Ward
Darach Out of the West of Misty Isles	Mr. Frank C. Wymond
Joker of Harris	Mr. W. Brydon Tennant
*Kinlock Lass of Misty Isles	Mr. W. Brydon Tennant
*Knocwood Daintiness	Mrs. Edward M. Loomis
*Moorland Lassie of Quinnatisset	Miss Gertrude S. Thomas
*Rincon Bell Bonus	Mr. Frank C. Wymond
*Stand Pat Bobs	Stand Pat Kennels
*Thorn of Quinnatisset	Miss Gertrude S. Thomas

1926

*Cairnvreckan Merlin	Mrs. Amy L. Bacon
Darling of Gunthorpe	Mrs. De Lancey K. Jay
*Knocwood Jean	Mrs. Henry Slack and Miss Rosalie Slack
Robinscroft Robach of Fair City	Mrs. Henry F. Price
*Rose-Bay's Wee Jean	Mrs. William C. Hill

95

Name	Owner
1927	
Barlae Jackie	Miss Edith McCausland
Cornor Inverness Froach	Dr. M. McCabe
Dallee of Gunthorpe of Cairmore	Mr. and Mrs. Richard Stix
Dollis Dawn of Tapscot	Mr. and Mrs. Lindsley Tappin
*Harlan's Sheila	Mr. Kenneth Harlan
*Jinx Ballantrae	Mr. Kenneth Harlan
Kayenne Not so Dusty	Mrs. F. Younghusband
*Kedron Gesto	Mrs. Grace Hayward
Offley Gilladdie of Rosscamac	Mrs. Henry Slack and Miss Rosalie Slack
Offley Skirl of Sydward	Mrs. Edward M-P. Murphy
Ross-shire Groggie of Cornor	Mr. Frank C. Wymond
1928	
Bhen Troona of Tapscot	Mr. and Mrs. Lindsley Tappin
Dochfour Cluin	Miss Edith McCausland
Dream of Hyver	Mr. and Mrs. Lindsley Tappin
Flower of Kayenne	Mrs. F. Younghusband
Gillad of Cairmore	Mr. and Mrs. Richard Stix
Knipton Dean of Tapscot	Mr. and Mrs. Lindsley Tappin
Pamela of Trefusis	Major and Mrs. Louis P. Baker
Brocaire Nigean Hamish	Mr. and Mrs. Richard Stix
Snelston Simon of Tapscot	Mr. and Mrs. Lindsley Tappin
*Wee Drappie of Tapscot	Mr. and Mrs. Lindsley Tappin
1929	
Reverly Darkie of Cairmore	Mr. and Mrs. Richard Stix
*Craker of Tapscot	Mr. and Mrs. Lindsley Tappin
Patience of Otford of Tapscot	Mr. and Mrs. Lindsley Tappin
Roddy of Tapscot	Mr. and Mrs. Lindsley Tappin

Name	Owner
Southboro Sanoper of Tapscot	Mr. and Mrs. Lindsley Tappin
Una of Keycol of Tapscot	Mr. and Mrs. Lindsley Tappin
Harvest Out of the West	Mr. and Mrs. Richard Stix
Knipton Cannach of Cair-more	Mr. and Mrs. Richard Stix

1930

*Nordhoff Rincon of Brickietosh	Frank W. Simmons
Prudence of Otford of Tapscot	Mr. and Mrs. Lindsley Tappin
Shinnel Silver Doctor	Miss Joan and Miss Diane Newton
George of Hyver of Tapscot	Mr. and Mrs. Lindsley Tappin
Knipton Dahlia of Cairmore	Mr. and Mrs. Richard Stix
*Brownie of Tapscot	Mr. and Mrs. Lindsley Tappin
*Deacon of Tapscot	Mr. and Mrs. Lindsley Tappin
Dunwich Brymay	Miss Joan and Miss Diane Newton
Hoax of Hyver of Tapscot	Mr. and Mrs. Lindsley Tappin

Ch. Cornor Ross-Shire Trefoil and Ch. Cornor Jemima of Trefusis.

Ch. Fear Nil of Carysfort, owned by Major H. A. Townley.

8

The Cairn Terrier in America—1930-1946

THE CAIRN Terrier progressed as rapidly in America as it did in Great Britain during the decade of the thirties. Fanciers were drawn to this appealing breed. It required little trimming and displayed all of the virtues of other strains while being contained in a small package, ideal for city or country living. In contrast to Britain, breed prosperity did not suffer too much during the war years, probably because restrictions were not as severe in America as across the sea.

American Cairns in the Thirties

In spite of the great depression experienced during the early 1930s, the period found dogs in general and Cairns in particular well supported both in the ring and the kennel. Many holdovers from the decade of the twenties, who have been discussed in the previous chapter, were still quite active and among these are included: Mrs. H. F. Price (Robinscroft), the doyen of the breed and still exhibiting her dogs, as were the F. C. Browns (Pinegrade), the Wards (Cornor), the Paul Renshaws (Hollow Tree) with the likes of Ch. Hollow Tree Margaret, Ch. Swashbuckler of Crockshed O'Hollow Tree and many others were actually increasing their activity while Mrs. Amy Bacon's Cairnvreckan dogs were more in evidence than ever before. The

Tapscot Kennels continued to be strong but the Cairmore compound of the Richard Stix's began to fade during the early portion of the period. Mrs. Loomis's Knocwood dogs with Chs. Offley Misty Morn and his daughter Ch. Knocwood Jean, Miss McCausland's Kedron prefix with an import, Dochfour Callum and Mr. and Mrs. Henry Slack's Rosscamac Cairns were also in evidence.

In addition to this strong nucleus of established fanciers, there was added a host of persons who began to bolster the breed's position. These included Mrs. G. W. Hyslop (Cairndania), Mrs. Groverman Ellis (Killybraken), Miss Helen Hunt (Shagbark), Mrs. Lillian Wood (Melita) and Mrs. R. T. Allen (Craigdhu) all of whom will be discussed in detail in the next chapter. In addition to these, Miss Elizabeth Braun of Pittsburgh was an important breeder whose Bethcairn prefix dated back to the middle 1920s but which did not become prominent nationally until the early '30s when Ch. Hazel of Fosseway (Fearless of Hyver ex Witch of Fosseway) came upon the scene. This good winner was followed by a host of fine specimens including the wheaten Ch. Nicolette of Crockshed (Carmichael of Crockshed ex Willow of Crockshed), the outstanding Ch. Fiery Rob of Carysfort, a red wheaten, whelped in 1934 by Eng. Ch. Fidelity of Carysfort ex Fair Suzanne of Carysfort, who became a multiple Group winner and a dominant sire with the likes of Chs. Bethcairn Fiery Jester, Bethcairn Fiery Lass, Bethcairn Judith, Bethcairn Robinhood and Gildor's Bairn O'Rob who was out of Ch. Petticoat O'Tapscot, all to his credit.

The Forties

The establishment continued to enjoy great success through the 1940s and into the '50s with such representatives as Chs. Bethcairn Diana (Brindle) by Ch. Fear Nix of Carysfort ex Bethcairn Robinette, Bethcairn Radia (Ch. Bethcairn Highland Fling ex Bethcairn Jolly), Bethcairn Dauntless by Bethcairn Cheftain ex Bethcairn Electra, and Ch. Bethcairn Soutar Johnny by Ch. Bethcairn Robinhood ex Jester's Chatterbox, etc. In more recent years dogs from this establishment have become progressively less in evidence at the shows although Miss Braun, now Mrs. Paul Ernst and her husband, Dr. Ernst, still maintain a strong interest in the breed.

Continuing with other fanciers of the period, Mrs. H. Terrell Van Ingen (Pinefair) was both a successful and enthusiastic exhibitor with such dogs as: Chs. Stelvio of Happy Hobby, an imported red brindle

Ch. Nicolette of Crockshed, owned by Mrs. Paul Ernst. This bitch was a champion in England and America and was Best of Breed at Westminster in 1938. *William Brown.*

Ch. Fiery Rob of Carysfort, owned by Mrs. Paul Ernst.

Ch. Bethcairn David, bred by Mrs. Paul Ernst and owned by Mrs. Taylor Coleman. *Rudolph Tauskey.*

Ch. Sally of Sporle of Pinefair, owned by Mrs. H. Terrell
Van Ingen.

Ch. Letter Perfect of Dowsfort, owned by Mr. and
Mrs. Charles Forrest Dowe. *William Brown.*

dog by Achilti Bobbie ex Bronzeray of Kennelride; Sally of Sporle of Pinefair, a gray brindle (Deft of Gunthorpe ex Dilidem of Gunthorpe); Flornell Simoon by Fearnaught of Carysfort ex Blencathra Mignon; Maruna of Hyver of Pinefair by Kruso of Hyver ex Barleyhill Ace, a daughter of the great Gillie of Hyver; Ribbledene Ripper a black brindle by Ch. Merry Max ex Zoe of Mandrake who was sired by McRob of Frimley and a host of other winners. The dogs were often handled by the redoubtable Percy Roberts. The Charles Scribners' Dew Hollow dogs including Chs. Hausell's Betty Bouncer, bred by Mrs. Caspersz by Phantom of Crockshed ex Turfield Smiling Eyes; Buccaneer of Ullathorpe a red cream son of Seadog Out of the West ex Sunshine Sally; Fascinating Eyes of Dew Hollow, a cream bitch sired by Ch. Harvest Out of the West ex Fascinating Fanny; Kindly Eyes of Ryma, a wheaten bitch bred by the Rev. Casperzs by Crack of the Wyns ex Tugrah Trustful Eyes whose dam was named Friendly Eyes of Crockshed. The Sherwood Hall Cairns, including Chs. Cragwood Mister Glencannon by Rincon Gillie ex Cragwood Pixie; Whiskerette of Beresford, a red brindle by Jimmy of Keycol ex Cairnvreckan Lady Stormont and Cairnvreckan Dewar a gray son of Cairnvrec-

Ch. Gildor's Bairn O'Rob, owned by Mrs. Gilbert C. Bird.

103

Ch. Sylvia of Dowsfort, owned by Mr. and Mrs. Charles Forrest Dowe. *William Brown.*

Ch. Green Light of Dowsfort, owned by Mr. and Mrs. Charles Forrest Dowe. *Rudolph Tauskey.*

kan Gairlock ex Down East Busybody; Mrs. Howard L. Platt's East-cote dogs with Chs. Hilary of Eastcote, a wheaten by Prince of Hyver of Eastcote ex Heiress of Eastcote; Dividend of Eastcote by Ch. Divor of Gunthorpe and his son, Ch. First Preferred of Eastcote. Mrs. Ballinger Mills' large Bayou Haven Kennels housed Ch. Brigand O'Bayou Haven, a red cream (Bally O'Bayou Haven ex Tilly O'Tap-scot), together with Ch. Til O'Bayou Haven and her daughter, Ch. Wendy O'Bayou Haven; Mrs. Eugene Untermyer with Ch. Dunbar of Cairndania, a gray son of Ch. Tinker O'Tapscot ex Bunty of Cairn-dania; Ch. Fairey of Carysfort, a full sister to Ch. Fiery Rob of Carys-fort, and the dark grey homebred, Ch. Wee Devil by Ch. Chunk of Crockshed ex Ch. Brechin who was out of Fairey by Dunbar and owned jointly with Miss Hunt; Mrs. N. B. Smith breeder of Chs. Crag-wood Gallant Fox, Cragwood Gillie and Cragwood the Witch; Mrs. Ray Crump with Ch. Kirth of Cairndania; Mrs. G. C. Bird (Gildor) who will be discussed in more detail in the following chapter and Mr. and Mrs. Charles Forest Dowe and their strong Dowesfort estab-lishment. This kennel was of considerable importance for an extended period. Many of its early dogs came from England and Bob Craighead was used extensively as a handler. Among the more prominent pre-war Cairns were the likes of the Group-winning Ch. Fear Nix of Carysfort (Silver Hawk Out of the West ex Fear Nil of Carysfort), Ch. Fast Step of Carysfort and the Fear Nix daughter, Ch. Sylvia of Dowesfort.

Ch. Fear Nix of Carysfort, owned by Mr. and Mrs. Charles Forrest Dowe. *William Brown.*

Ch. Chrystobel of Crockshed, owned by Mrs. G. W. Hyslop.
Rudolph Tauskey.

Ch. Pimpernel of Mercia, imported prior to World War
II and owned by Mrs. G. W. Hyslop. *Rudolph Tauskey.*

Ch. Knipton Dean of Tapscot, owned by Mr. and Mrs. Lindsley Tappin, made a name for himself as an outstanding winner and sire in the early thirties and was Best of Breed at the 1931 Westminster show. *Rudolph Tauskey.*

			Harviestoun Kim
		Harviestoun Raider	Harviestoun Tibbie
	Ch. Divil of Gunthorpe		Ninfield Mist
		Peggy of Gunthorpe	Offley Cuag
Boldre Dagger			Doughall Out of the West
		Warrenhurst Dirk	Warrenhurst Ruadh
	Boldre Zephyr		Crofter of Frimley
		Boldre Oofles	Clio of the Creek
CH. KNIPTON DEAN OF TAPSCOT			Ch. Firring Frolic
		Raeburn Conas	Raeburn Morag
	Ch. Carngowan Murran		Gaywulf Sands
		Lugate Lively	Chevet Sionnach
Knipton Dian			Bruce
		Little Bruce	Prickles
	Girlie		Ch. Gesto
		Yorna	Brigit

Ch. Red Pride of Tapscot, owned by Mr. and Mrs. Charles Bates Dana, was a consistent winner and a noted producer during the early thirties.

Ch. Jayson O'Tapscot, owned by Mrs. R. T. Allen and bred by Tapscot Kennels. He was one of the champions of 1944.

		Ch. Pirate O'Tapscot	Ch. George of Hyver O'Tapscot
	Ch. Jerry O'Tapscot		Ch. Patience of Otford O'Tapscot
		Music of Tapscot	Ch. Knipton Dean of Tapscot
Ch. Jere O'Tapscot			Marchfield Maureen O'Tapscot
		Statestreet	Southboro Squib
	Ch. Bad Girl of Idle Creek		Ch. Knipton Dahlia
		Dinah of Idle Creek	Ch. Knipton Dean of Tapscot
CH JAYSON O'TAPSCOT			Betsy of Idle Creek
		Ch. Offley Skirl of	Harviestoun Chieftain
	Ch. Cracker O'Tapscot	Sydward	Harviestoun Mola
		Vixen of Invercairn	Teilum
Jolly Girl O'Tapscot			Sandie of Invercairn
		Ch. Gallant Boy	Ch. George of Hyver O'Tapscot
	Jill of Tapscot II	O'Tapscot	Goldie O'Tapscot
		Joy O'Tapscot	Ch. Knipton Dean of Tapscot
			Gyp of Hyver O'Tapscot

American and Canadian Ch. Chunk of Crockshed was an important prewar import of Mrs. G. W. Hyslop. He was sired by the renowned Ch. Splinters of Twobees and was himself the sire of American and Canadian Ch. Kilmet of Cairndania. *Rudolph Tauskey.*

```
                                                    Donnington Gillie
                                 Trashurst Sandyman  Eaton Wendy
                  Trashurst Chip                     Ch. Dud of Hyver
                                 Cherry McBryan       Haggis of Sandiacre
     Ch. Splinters of Twobees                        Offley Brimon
                                 Quicksand Out of the She
                  Sorag of Twobees           West    Glenmhor Rascal
                                 Mulaidh of Twobees   Glenmhor Coullie
CH. CHUNK OF CROCKSHED *                              Doughall Out of the West
                                 Dusk of Cleasby      Shinnel Storm Cloud
                  Salutation Ian                     Raitts Roisgeach
                                 Placemore Grey Lady  Placemore Lassie
     Puffin of Crockshed                             Pibroch of Glenfang
                                 Red Pride of Otford  Darwin Daffodil
                  Salutation Irma                    Dochfour Meanach
                                 Bean of Otford       Belinda of Otford
```

This brief outline offers some small insight into the activities of a few of the many persons who were active in the breed during the period under consideration. Some of these have extended their activitives into the next era of Cairn progress as will be delineated in the chapter to follow. It is interesting to note that the war, while it did cause a reduction in size and number of shows in America, did not have the very drastic effect on the breed that was apparent in Britain. Many established kennels continued to breed, albeit on a reduced scale, and made some of the shows whereby interest was maintained and the desire to progress was whetted as was proved by the post-war activity.

Before passing to contemporary times, suitable credit must be accorded to Elizabeth H. Anderson (Down East Kennels), Frances R. Porter and Clara M. LeVene (Tana) who were solely responsible for the extensive breed records that are so vital today. These ladies expended great effort and many hours of laborious work to research and record the pedigrees of all American Cairn champions from 1920 through 1952. This group did for American Cairns what Caspersz and Fisher had done for their British counterparts. Miss Anderson pursued the original effort covering all pedigrees from 1920 through

Mrs. G. W. Hyslop with two of her standard-bearers during the late 30's, Ch. Tinker of Tapscot (right) and Ch. Dalrigh of Cairndania. *Millar Studios.*

Ch. Tam's Grey Girl of Cairndania, owned by Mrs. G. W. Hyslop. *Rudolph Tauskey.*

Ch. Cairnvreckan Kasida, owned by Amy L. Bacon. *Rudolph Tauskey.*

Ch. Dypsee of Gunthorpe, owned by Amy L. Bacon. *Rudolph Tauskey.*

Ch. Cairnvreckan Marquis, owned by Amy L. Bacon. *Rudolph Tauskey.*

Ch. Cairnvreckan Fyord, owned by Amy L. Bacon. *Rudolph Tauskey.*

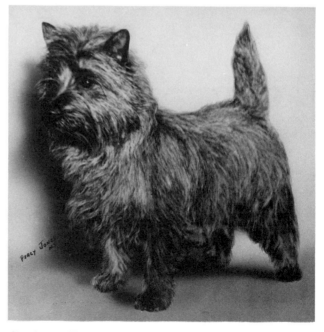

Ch, Jere O'Tapscot, owned by Mrs. Lindsley Tappin, was best Cairn at the 1942 Westminster show. *Percy Jones.*

1933, a work that was published in 1934. Porter and LeVene carried on through 1952. This was accomplished in two steps with the initial volume covering the years from 1932 through 1942 and the second volume completing the period through 1952. Thus, Cairn fanciers in America have a counterpart of the British index that has meant so much to breeders and researchers alike. In each instance, the compilers have delineated producing lines, and families to aid later-day breeders in their efforts.

These exhaustive studies make the tracing of pedigrees relatively simple as they offer a complete record which would require untold research if the same information concerning even a single dog or family were to be obtained through the more conventional and bulky kennel club records. Today, we are living in an era when activity in dogs has been accelerated ten-fold over the last few years. Who will shoulder and continue the laborious work of these three dedicated persons to maintain the record up-to-date from 1952? It poses a question that is difficult to answer.

The ladies, as was the case with their British counterparts, were all breeders and exhibitors while Miss Porter carried the added burden of being the breed's historian for many years with her excellent articles in the various dog journals.

Ch. Foxgrove Susanella, Mrs. Hyslop's celebrated Blencathra Brat daughter, won the 1974 CTCA Specialty soon after her North American debut. She followed this up with a long string of important wins at shows in the United States and Canada.

Ch. Redletter McRuffie, owned by Mrs. G. W. Hyslop, was one of the breed's most memorable winners and producers. Best of Breed at Westminster three times and at the CTCA Specialty twice, he was also a multiple group winner when such wins by Cairns were few and far between. *Evelyn M. Shafer.*

9

The Cairn Terrier in America Since World War II

U PON the conclusion of hostilities and when general conditions nationally had again settled into a more normal pattern, shows blossomed and dogs gained their greatest popularity in history. This was probably caused by the relief enjoyed by all and the desire to again compete in normal sports and activities.

Increased Popularity

Cairn fortunes improved dramatically as compared to those of many other breeds of dog. This was evidenced by registration figures for the breed as compared with those for all breeds of dog. The following chart offers the American Kennel Club statistics in five year increments for a 35 year span since the conflict:

Year	Cairn Registrations only	Registrations for all breeds
1946	426	204,957
1951	501	264,415
1956	752	430,900
1961	1,076	493,300
1966	2,883	809,400
1971	7,738	1,129,200
1976	6,432	1,048,648
1981	6,346	1,033,849

Thus, during the period of the past 25 years, registrations for Cairns have increased some eighteen times while the same figure for all breeds of dog has only grown slightly more than five times. This comparison is frightening to dedicated fanciers since it brings the Cairn ever closer to the "popular breed" status, something that has never improved the overall quality of any breed that has gained this position.

The best bulwark against regression is a strong group of dedicated fanciers whose efforts are directed towards breed improvement. The Cairn was fortunate in having a large number that fall into this category as many of the fanciers from the pre-war period were still active.

The Fancy in the Post-War Period

Among this group was Mrs. Amy Bacon who is mentioned frequently throughout this book. After the war, her Cairnvreckan dogs were just as active as before and until her untimely death in the middle fifties, she bred or owned an additional dozen or so champions including such dogs as Chs. Cairnvreckan Robert, Raleigh, Sirius, Stelvio and Portia, to name a few. Mrs. Bacon was always an avid breeder and, while she owned a number of imports, was a champion of the American-bred Cairn. Her death was a great loss to the fancy as it is doubtful that any other person helped so many fanciers become successful in the breed.

In addition to Mrs. Bacon there was a host of others including; Miss Elizabeth Braun (Mrs. Paul Ernst) with Chs. Bethcairn Highland Fling, Bethcairn Souter-Johnny, Blencathra Bonny Lad, etc.; the Paul Renshaws with Ch. Hollow Tree Forbes; Mr. and Mrs. Charles Obenauer with Ch. Shagbark Kilty and others; Mr. and Mrs. Dowe with Chs. Full Glory, Glittering Light, Fortune Hunter, etc., all 'of Dowesfort; Mrs. Untermyer with Ch. Shagbark Canny Mac; Mrs. H. L. Platt and a host of Eastcote dogs; Vera Tim and Clara LaVenc with the likes of Chs. Tana's Ross-shire King, Tana's Wolscot Mercury and Tana's Stardust, the sire of many champions; the Sherwood Cairns of Lydia Hopkins and Mrs. Linda Avenali; Mrs. Ray Crump (Kencairn), breeder of Bethcairn Highland Fling and Bethcairn Radia and the previously mentioned Gildor Kennels of Mrs. G. C. Bird of Ohio. Mrs. Bird was one of the many that gained pre-war support from Tapscot when she purchased the bitches, Petticoat O'Tapscot (Ch. Tommy Tucker O'Tapscot ex Persimmon O'Tapscot) and Bella Donna O'Tapscot (Ch. Duke O'Tapscot ex

A view of Cairndania. From this Canadian-based operation have come a steady succession of consistent winners in the keenest of competition. Imports and home-breds both have had a share in writing permanent records in the breed. *Rudolph Tauskey.*

Ch. Rogerlyn Sea Hawk's Salty Sam, owned by Betty Hyslop, a multiple Specialty and BIS winner in the United States and Canada, he proved also to be a notable sire.

American and Canadian Ch. Kilmet of Cairndania. *Rudolph Tauskey.*

Belle O'Tapscot) that were made up in 1938 and '40 respectively. Petticoat, when bred to Miss Braun's great stud, Ch. Fiery Rob of Carysfort produced Ch. Gildor's Bairn O'Rob who sired a half a dozen titleholders. Mrs. Bird had excellent success in the breed and it suffered as her interest waned in the early post-war period.

In addition to the abbreviated listing noted above, there are five other kennels that stand apart because of their longevity and accomplishments. None has been discussed at length heretofore because their influence on the breed reached its height during the post-war era. Four of the five are still quite active. They include the Cairndania establishment of Mrs. G. W. Hyslop; Mrs. C. Groverman Ellis and Miss Mary Jane Ellis's Killybracken effort; Miss Helen Hunt and the Shagbark Cairns; the late Mrs. L. M. Wood's Melita Kennels and Mrs. R. T. Allen's strong Craigdhu establishment. Each will be discussed separately and in some detail.

Cairndania

The first to be discussed is the very strong Cairndania Kennels of Mrs. George W. Hyslop, based at Brockville, Ontario, Canada. It has been in continuous operation for more than 50 years. Throughout this entire period, Mrs. Hyslop has, more often than not, handled her own dogs although the services of Alf Loveridge and more recently, Roberta Campbell have been used.

The name "Cairndania" suggests that both Cairns and Great Danes are of interest and this is the case although the former has been increasingly important over the past twenty years and today makes up most of the kennel's population. Mrs. Hyslop has always been a heavy importer. Generally, when she has seen or heard of a top dog in England, she has tried to add that dog to her kennel population. This practice has kept quality high and has given great latitude to her breeding operations. It has also had a salutary affect upon the American fancy since this imported blood is made available to all breeders and has thus widened their choice of stud dogs.

It should be understood that her efforts have not been limited to importation only since she has been very active as a breeder, using her fine stock to the fullest advantage to keep her puppy pens full of promising youngsters and exhibiting her homebreds with the same zeal and success that has marked her efforts with imports. The consistency of the operation is best told by its score which shows

Ch. Redletter Miss Splinters, owned by Mrs. G. W. Hyslop, was a standout winner in the breed. Shown a total of sixty times, she was defeated in the breed on only one occasion. *Rudolph Tauskey.*

				Ch. Bonfire of Twobees
			Ch. Redletter McJoe	Redletter My Choice
		Ch. Redletter McMurran		Freelance of Carysfort
			Cairncragg Binky	May Moon of Mercrogia
	Crowtree Splinters			Person of Carysfort
			Peter Pan of Crowmere	Salopian Silver Wings
		Redletter Diana		Altbeck Athlete
			Sparklet of Bourton	Rags of Bomton
CH. REDLETTER MISS SPLINTERS				Killearn Mr. Chips
			Ch. Rufus of Rhu	Morag of Rhu
		Blencathra Ruffian		Brackendene Brig of Conrlynn
			Ch. Fincairn Gillian	Fen Cairn Jennifer
	Foxearle Goldfinch			Donnington Sandboy
			Ch. Blencathra Sand-	Blencathra Radiance
		Foxearle Goldilocks	piper	Kelpie of Foxearle
			Glenn of Foxearle	Pixie of Foxearle

that 93 homebred and imported Cairns have made their American titles through 1972 with the majority completing their Canadian Championships as well. These figures will be increasing constantly since Mrs. Hyslop is one of the strongest of current exhibitors.

When her interest started in 1928 she purchased her first Cairn, Placemore Peekaboo, from Mrs. Bird's kennels in England. This one was followed by Eng. Ch. Seaworthy Out of the West and Moccasin Mercy. Cairndania began exhibiting in the United States in 1931 when Mrs. Hyslop took her first homebreds to Westminster. Since that time she has captured top wins in the breed at this event many times. Much of her early success may be attributed to the grand import, Eng., Can. & Am. Ch. Divor of Gunthorpe (1931) by Ivor of the Mist ex Deggie of Gunthorpe who sired many of the kennels early winners. He was followed by Am. and Can. Ch. Tinker O'Tapscot (1934) who also became a top producer. In 1938 she imported Pimpernel of Mercia (1939) who quickly established herself as a topper by winning at Morris and Essex and continuing to her title with Best of Breed at Westminster in 1939. Thereafter, a steady outpouring of imported and homebred greats have come into the ring under the Cairndania banner. A complete list would be impossible but a few that come readily to mind and listed in chronological order include; Ch. Chunk of Crockshed (1941) a Splinters of Twobees son and a great stud force; Ch. Kilmet of Cairndania (1943) by Chunk and winner of the U.S. Specialty four consecutive times; Ch. Tam's Grey Girl (1944); Ch. Kindon Saucy Sue (1948), an unforgettable bitch that lived up to her name in showmanship; Ch. Kiltie's Foxglove of Cairndania (1951); the immortal Ch. Redletter McRuffie (1954), a Group winner who also captured three national specialties and became one of the all-time top sires with 26 champions (American) to his credit; Ch. Redletter Miss Splinters (1957), widely known winner and dam of Chs. Redletter McBrigand (1959), a Best in Show winner and Cairndania McRuffie's Splinter (1962) one of three from Miss Splinters by McRuffie; Ch. Cairndania McBrigand's Holbrig (1963) a Best in Show winner; Ch. Unique Cottage Mr. Bradshaw (1962), a Best in Show winner in 1963; Ch. Cairndania McBrigand's Brigrey (1964), a son of McBrigand out of Ch. Cairndania Clansman's Grey Girl (1960), a Best in Show winner in 1965; and sire of at least 16 U.S. titleholders; Ch. Lofthouse Davey (1966) by Eng. Ch. Geryon of Mistyfell ex Dorseydale Justeena; the great Ch. Cairndania Brigrey's Berry-Red (1968), a consistent winner; Ch. Redletter Twinlaw Seaspirit (1968), top sire for 1971 with six champion get

Ch. Redletter McBrigand, owned by Mrs. G. W. Hyslop.
Rudolph Tauskey.

Ch. Cairndania Clansman's Grey Girl, owned by Mrs.
G. W. Hyslop. *Rudolph Tauskey.*

Ch. Cairndania's McBrigand's Brigrey, a Best in Show
winner, owned by Mrs. G. W. Hyslop. *Rudolph Tauskey.*

together with Chs. Vinvovium Errol Flynn (1969), Tammy of Mistfell (1969), and the more recent standard bearers including Chs. Foxgrove Susanella, Rogerlyn Sea Hawk's Salty Sam, Foxgrove Jester and Ch. Foxgrove Jeronimo among a host of others. All of the dogs mentioned have impressive records in both Canada and the United States where they have scored many Specialty and Best in Show triumphs.

In July 1984, Roberta Campbell, long-associated with Cairndania as the presence at the other end of the lead, retired from professional handling. She is currently working in the Education Department of the American Kennel Club. Mrs. Hyslop still continues showing herself but now uses Elliot Weiss when the services of a professional handler are required. Mrs. Hyslop and her new handler have both continued the winning tradition of the Cairndanias with such recent winners as Ch. Cairndania's Sam's Sundew who was Best of Breed under Mildred Bryant at the AKC Centennial event and Ch. Gaelic Haggis MacBasher among others.

Ch. Foxgrove Jester, another of Mrs. Hyslop's celebrated winners, is shown here being awarded BIS at the 1977 Rhode Island KC event under Mrs. J. H. Daniell-Jenkins. Roberta Campbell handled Jester to the win, as she has so many of the Cairndanias. *John Ashbey.*

Am., Can. Ch. Gaelic Haggis McBasher is one of Mrs. Hyslop's mid-1980s BIS dogs. His record also includes BB at the 1985 Westminster KC show. *Alex Smith.*

Am., Can. Ch. Wee Gaelic Todd Cairndania, one of Mrs. Hyslop's mid-1980s winners and one of the last shown by Roberta Campbell. He is shown winning under Dr. Masley enroute to his American title. *Alverson.*

Since the middle 1930s, Mrs. Hyslop has been most successful at U.S. fixtures, winning the national specialty innumerable times and capturing the breed at Westminster, Morris and Essex and the International with great consistency. The steady success of Cairndania indicates sound judgment and knowledge in purchasing top English dogs and in the breeding plans to produce offspring that can hold their own against the best of "both worlds". One important fact, Cairndania is not a commercial kennel and never has been. It is conducted for the pleasure of its owner and for the sport that it affords her. Stud dogs are available to all and this has made it easy for small breeders to avail themselves of the best of English and American bloodlines. Truly, Cairndania is one of the great kennels of the age as proved by its continued record of excellence and accomplishment.

Killybracken

The Killybracken Kennels, of Mrs. C. Groverman Ellis and her daughters, became interested in Cairns in the early thirties. The breed was added to an already expanding population of Irish Wolfhounds that gained favor in about 1928. Since that time, Killybracken has housed many champion Cairns, including 36 that were homebreds. In addition to bench activity there has been a steady interest in Obedience and many Cairns have gained their C.D. and C.D.X. degrees including Ch. Tam Glen of Killybracken who is believed to be the only Cairn ever to gain the difficult and coveted Tracking degree.

In 1933, the dog Fiddown Firecracker (Cairnvreckan Dewar ex Fiddown Firefly) came to the Ellis' from Mrs. Catherine Irwin of Atlanta and started it all. Firecracker was bred to Brocaire Crisp-Jura, one of three bitches imported from Mrs. Alistair Campbell, and among the progeny was a dog, Scott of Killybracken who ultimately sired Ch. MacScott of Killybracken. Another early acquisition was Red Magnet of Mercryd (Yorick of Mercryd ex Ross-shire Tatcho) purchased while the Ellis' were at the Crystal Palace show in 1937. This one was strong in Harviestoun Raider blood through a double cross of Moccasin Magnet. When bred to the aforementioned Fiddown Firecracker, she produced Bang of Killybracken who was the grandsire of Ch. Tibbie of Killybracken. Thus, Fiddown Firecracker, together with the bitches Brocaire Crisp-Jura and Red Magnet of Mercryd, became important foundation stock for the endeavor and

Ch. Alex of Killybracken, owned by the Killybracken Kennels of Mrs. C. Groverman Ellis (handling) and Mary Jane Ellis. Alex, a Best in Show winner, represents a long line of winners and producers spanning a period of several decades. *Frasie.*

Ch. Spray of Killybracken won the Cairn Terrier Club of America Sweepstakes in 1954 under the late Alva Rosenberg. *Evelyn Shafer.*

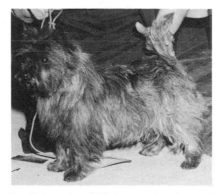

Ch. Catescairn Chitchat, a daughter of Ch. Spray of Killybracken, duplicated her mother's 1954 Sweepstakes win in 1960 under Mrs. Sherman Hoyt. *William Brown.*

their names will be found in the pedigrees of many present-day Killy-bracken Cairns, albeit some ten to twelve generations back.

Additional purchases to offer latitude in breeding included, Kencairn Jeffrey, Ch. Cairnvreckan Trian, Cragwood Merrie-Go-Round and Ch. Scarlet of Killybracken. Other inmates through the years include, Ch. Bheg of K. (Blaise of K. ex Belpie of Kencairn); Chs. Trig, Trim and Trigo of K., all by Kencairn Jeffrey ex Jingle of K., a daughter of Cragwood Merrie-Go-Round; Chs. Laurie of K., Tam Glen of K., C.D., Alex of K., a dog by Trim out of Ha'Pence of K., etc., and more lately, Chs. The Dragoon of K. (Ch. Lofthouse Davey ex Ch. Blyman Bit of Killybracken) and Ch. Dhu's Ditto of Killybracken (Kelso of K. ex Ch. Bunty Dhu of K.) etc. It is interesting to recall that Mrs. Ellis transferred her good bitch Ch. Spray of Killybracken to the Stewarts', Catescairn Kennels and subsequently obtained her daughter, Catescairn Chitchat by Ch. Catescairn Crackerjack in return. Spray was the winner of the national club's Sweepstakes in 1954 while Chitchat duplicated the feat in 1960. Of course, both bitches made their titles for the respective owners.

Of all the Cairns at Killybracken, Mrs. Ellis believes that Chs. Trig, Spray and Alex were probably tops. Alex was one of the few that was campaigned and he did extremely well winning two Groups, placing in a host of others and climaxing his career by going Best in Show at Kalamazoo in 1957. As will be indicated from this short history, Killybracken is and always has been a breeding kennel, relying upon its homebreds to perpetuate the stock. Few outside dogs have been purchased and then only to establish new blood that will niche well with the old. Further, the Ellis' have usually exhibited their own Cairns, seldom using outside help. In the very few instances that a professional has been used, Virginia Hardin has taken over.

The kennels were originally located in Illinois where Mrs. Ellis gained great prominence in the dog world through her long-time efforts as president or show secretary of the International Kennel Club of Chicago. In later years, Mrs. Ellis resided in Francestown, New Hampshire. Her daughter, Mary Jane, a well-known judge, now makes her home in Woodbine, Maryland.

Ch. Simon of Twobees, an import owned by Miss Helen Hunt and the sire of four champions. *William Brown.*

Ch. Berry of Buttermere, an import, owned by Miss Helen Hunt. *William Brown.*

127

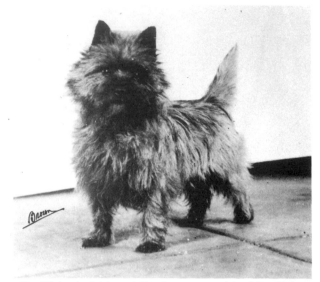

Ch. Whimsical Mac of Twobees, owned by Miss Helen Hunt. *William Brown.*

Ch. Cairngorm Catriona, dam of three champions, owned by Miss Helen Hunt. *Wiliam Brown.*

Shagbark

Shagbark is the kennel name applied to dogs from Miss Helen Hunt's kennel that is located in Washington, Conn. It began operations in the thirties when she brought Drungewick Julia home from England. Following closely were such Cairns as Cairnvreckan Elin, Dunmore Taffy, Ch. Best Girl of Tapscot, Ch. Twobees Knurl of Crantock, (a Splinters son), Wistful Eyes of Crockshed (by Ch. Chunk of Crockshed) and Lockyers Evening Glow. The last three imports formed the nucleus for a program based upon linebreeding to the great Ch. Splinters of Twobees.

With the advent of the war, activity ceased and was not resumed until the close of hostilities. At this time, her first homebred champion, Shagbark Sparkle (a holdover from pre-war activities by Ch. Twobees Knurl of Crantock ex Wistful Eyes of Crockshed) and his daughter, Ch. Shagbark Miss Muffet formed the foundation for the post-war program. Miss Muffet produced three champion daughters in Shagbark Misty, Misky and Marigold while Sparkle sired the likes of Chs. Sparklet of Ros, the aforementioned Miss Muffet and Windswest Eve among others.

An important post-war addition was the dog, Ch. Whimsical Mac

Ch. Shagbark Sparkle, owned by Miss Helen Hunt, was Winners Dog at the Westminister Kennel Club at only six months of age. *William Brown.*

of Twobees, chosen by Miss Bengough as a suitable outcross to compliment the Splinters line. This dog was not only a stud force but an outstanding show animal who topped the breed in strong Eastern competition some fifty times. Another import, Ch. Simon of Twobees was also highly useful in building the Shagbark line. He produced, among others, Chs. Shagbark Katrine, Bengo, Sovereign and Simon Eyes, Cairndania Muldoon and Crofter's Sally. Many other champions have been inmates of this small but select kennel including the likes of Chs. Berry of Buttermere, Cairngorm Catriona (dam of Chs. Shagbark Katrine, Whimsical Kate and Canny Mac), Shagbark Tuppence, Whimsical Gael and Bluebell, etc.

In all, more than thirty Cairns bred or housed at Shagbark have made their American titles, and by 1956 Miss Hunt had a full five generations of her own breeding housed in the kennels. Representatives of this line were: Ch. Shagbark Sparkle, his daughter, Ch. Shagbark Miss Muffet, her daughter, Ch. Shagbark Marigold, her daughter Ch. Shagbark Kilspindle and finally, her daughter, Ch. Shagbark Kilty, an enviable accomplishment. Miss Hunt has been prominent in Club affairs for many years and has raised several other breeds, including Welsh Terriers (with a homebred champion), Border Collies and Jack Russell Terriers to demonstrate her wide range of interest in dogs.

Melita

Melita is another Canadian kennel of long standing. Owned by the late Mrs. L. M. Wood, of Victoria, B.C., it began operations in the early 1930s. As with so many establishments, Melita became increasingly prominent after the close of hostilities and has since shown its stock with much greater frequency on both sides of the border. Among the Cairns that require mention is the dog, Ch. Woody Woodpecker of Melita who was sired by a Melita stud, John of Blarneystone ex Ch. Keithcairns Trinket and was purchased as a youngster. He made his titles in both the United States and Canada before his second birthday and as a champion captured many breeds, two Groups and a host of other placements before being sold to the States at four years of age, where he became a Group winner for his new owners, Fred and Ethel Stott. Woody's Flicka of Melita was acquired by Eleanor Finkler of Crete, Illinois, and became a part of the foundation for her successful

130

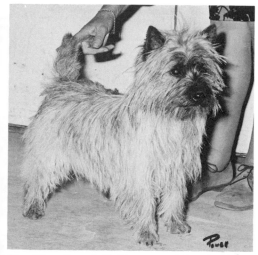

Ch. Warspite of Melita, owned by the late Mrs. L. M. Wood. *G. Wynne Powell.*

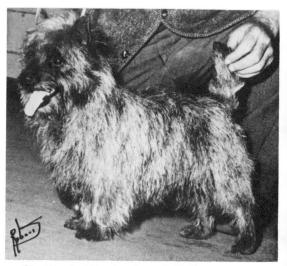

Ch. Woody Woodpecker of Melita was one of Mrs. Woods' well-known sucessful campaigners. *Lewis Roberts.*

An interesting study in Cairn development. These are four Melita Cairns at ages of one year, nine months, six months and four months (left to right). All are now champions. Note particularly, differences in size and coat.

kennel. Ch. Balgrochan Scotch Whiskey was another who bears mention, together with Chs. Hobgoblin of Melita a winner at Westminster, his son Ch. Posh of Melita who came to the States and Ch. Santa Claus of Melita owned by Mr. and Mrs. John D. Orman of Memphis when he captured Best in Show at Biloxi in 1967. Additional Melita products include, Chs. Jolly Roger, Duncannon, Hawk, Woody's Warbler, etc., all of Melita; together with two imports, Ch. Felshott Dempster, Ch. Felshott Whisper, a Best in Show winner in Canada; and the 1973 winner, Ch. Buckshot of Melita, owned by Doris L. Harris and shown expertly by Daisy Austad at West Coast events.

Mrs. Wood was highly successful throughout her extended activity by using a blend of domestic and imported bloodlines always keeping temperament in mind as a necessity. She did not care for overly agressive animals since her dogs ran together and fighting could not be tolerated. A survey of the nearly 40-year history of this establishment will show that it had been consistently successful in the ring on both sides of the border.

Ch. Bucksnot of Melita (Ch. Felshott Dempster ex Ch. Craiglyn Corrina), owned by Doris L. Harris, was a well-known winner during the early 1970s. Shown here with his handler, Daisy Austad, his record includes a group 2nd at Westminster 1974. *Bill Francis.*

132

Ch. Craigdhu Sir Echo, owned by Mrs. R. T. Allen. *Evelyn Shafer.*

Craigdhu

Mrs. R. T. Allen's Craigdhu Kennels at Rockford, Illinois, is the final venture to be discussed in depth. It has done well for over 45 years and is again, an establishment that obtained early stock from Mrs. Bacon (Ch. Cairnvreckan Krags is an example). Mrs. Allen later bred Ch. Tommy Tucker of Craigdhu (Ch. Cairnvreckan Gwynn ex Crudal) who became a useful stud, while Ch. Cairnvreckan Kinchin and Ch. Dargent of Gunthorpe were others that helped the early success of the kennels. Probably the most significant sequence of events, so far as Craigdhu is concerned, began in 1943 when Mrs. Bacon obtained a young dog, Jason O'Tapscot (Ch. Jere O'Tapscot ex Jolly Girl O'Tapscot) from Mrs. Tappin. She campaigned him for a while and then transferred title to Mrs. Bird (Gildor) who quickly completed his title in 1944. Shortly thereafter, Jason came to Mrs. Allen, and a fortunate acquisition it turned out to be. The dog, who had been under four different ownerships in about two years, came into his own and sired more than twenty titleholders during his life, a record to its time.

He had phenomenal success when bred to his kennelmate and half-sister, Ch. Craigdhu Opal (Ch. Jere O'Tapscot ex Hey Diddle-Diddle O'Tapscot) who had previously been acquired from Mrs. Tappin, through Mrs. Bacon. This niche produced eight champions with C. Butterscotch, C. Bittersweet and C. Sir Echo (a Group winner) in a single litter. These were followed by Chs. C. Nutmeg, C. Gallant, C. Sugar N'Spice, C. Calico and C. Cinnamon, Jason did well with another Craigdhu inmate, Ch. Graff's Lassie (Peter Flashaway ex Happy Find of Clairmar), who whelped Chs. Craigdhu Just Bill, Just Velvet and Just Sue by him.

The aforementioned Ch. Craigdhu Sir Echo was another strong sire and maintained the family bloodlines with the likes of Chs. Craigdhu Polly Prim, C. Topper, C. Velveteen, C. Speculation, C. Spoofer, C. Joker, C. Piper, C. Robin and Craigdhu Wilwyn to his credit. This last one was a Group winner and a useful sire. He was backed by Ch. Theodore Mack Ruckus, a big winner in the '60s. Surely, Craigdhu has been most successful in both the breeding pen and the ring and while operations have slowed over the past few years, Mrs. Allen still has strong interest in the breed and in club activities while judging assignments take up much of her time.

Ch. Theodore Mack Ruckus, owned and handled by Mrs. R. T. Allen. He is shown winning a Group under judge Forest N. Hall. *Page of New York.*

Ch. Topcairn Tomasine, owned and handled by Girard A. Jacobi, was WB at the Cairn Terrier Club of America's 1970 Specialty under Mrs. R. T. Allen. *Evelyn Shafer.*

Ch. Craigdhu Wilwyn, owned by Mrs. R. T. Allen.
Rudolph Tauskey.

Ch. Catescarin Caper, owned by
Mrs. H. Bartlett Stewart. *Rudolph
Tauskey.*

Ch. Catescairn Camelot, owned
by Mrs. H. Bartlett Stewart.
Rudolph Tauskey.

This reservoir of activity and knowledge has been aided immeasurably by a host of newer faces, persons who, for the most part, are later additions to the group that fancies this small, attractive Terrier.

Catescairn

In this expanding company we find Mr. and Mrs. H. B. Stewart Jr., from Ohio. Their Catescairn dogs had a substantial impact and provided basic breeding stock for several other important establishments. Here again were fanciers that acquired Cairns from Mrs. Bacon in the persons of Ch. Cairnvreckan Rogue and Cairnvreckan Rilla, who in union produced Ch. Catescairn Conquest. Rilla, when bred to Ch. Chunk of Cairndania was responsible for Chs. Catescairn Crickett and Caper. All of these dogs were important as were Chs. Catescairn Checkers (Ch. Heathcairn Cuthbert ex Catescairn Crackerjill), Catescairn Cocoa and her son Ch. Catescairn Camelot by Ch. Redletter McRuffie, Catescairn Charm, Catescairn Chitchat and many more. Chitchat went to Mrs. Ellis as noted earlier, while Conquest was sold to Mr. and Mrs. Carl Brewer and became an important cog in the extended breeding plans of their select establishment. Several other excellent specimens were acquired by the Crestcairn establishment of Mr. and Mrs. Buell E. Herrick. Indeed, Catescairn was an important and successful operation for many years.

Heathcairn

Before leaving this area, the efforts of the Brewers will be expanded. Mr. and Mrs. Carl Brewer began their very strong but select Heathcairn establishment around 1950. Mrs. Bacon was asked to recommend a good stud and she suggested Mrs. Stewart's youngster, Catescairn Conquest (Ch. Cairnvreckan Rogue ex Cairnvreckan Rilla). The Brewers were fortunate to acquire the dog for he had just taken the points at Westminster. In any event, they did buy him and he was soon a champion. They next enlisted the aid of Col. Whitehead in quest of a good English bitch to be bred to Ch. Bonfire of Twobees before shipment to America. The Colonel suggested Sorrel of Glen (Woodthorpe Glendenning ex Sorag of Glen), who was purchased and bred to Bonfire according to plan. Heathcairn Splinters, Hector and Bonfire, the resulting litter of three, all made their titles. Sorrel was later bred to Conquest and produced Ch. Heathcairn Cuthbert who,

Ch. Heathcairn Charlie (Hearn Thunder Thighs ex Holemill Candlestick), owned and bred by Mrs. Carl E. Brewer.

Ch. Heathcairn Grayson, a full brother to Charlie, is also owned by Mrs. Brewer and was successfully campaigned by her. *Booth.*

Ch. Heathcairn Cuthbert, owned by Mr. and Mrs. Carl Brewer. *Frasie.*

Ch. Heathcairn Burleigh (Ch. Heathcairn Cuthbert ex Ch. Heathcairn Bonfire), owned by Mrs. Carl E. Brewer. *Frasie.*

the Brewers believe to be, the best that they bred. He was not only an excellent specimen of the breed, having captured the 1959 Club Specialty and the International Group, but he was a top stud and his efforts surely brought success, not only to the Brewers' efforts but to the Norris's Bairdsain establishment as well, as will be discussed later in connection with the vignette directed to that kennel.

Among the many other Cairns housed at Heathcairn one must also remember Ch. Heathcairn Burleigh (Cuthbert ex Ch. Heathcairn Bonfire), a Group winner, Ch. Heathcairn Rosebud, bred by Mrs. Bacon, Ch. Heathcairn Typhoon, and Ch. Heathcairn Roland.

Regrettably, Mr. Brewer died in 1975 and kennel activity was reduced for a time, but Mrs. Brewer has continued the effort with good success. Two of her more recent titleholders are Ch. Heathcairn Charlie, who finished at 10 months of age, and Ch. Heathcairn Grayson.

Bairdsain

Since Ch. Heathcairn Cuthbert had a strong role in the success story of the Bairds' Kennels, later registered as Bairdsain, a short resume of its activities is in order here. It was begun by Charles and Audrey Norris in Gates Mills, Ohio, around 1955, later moving operations to Indian Hill, Cincinnati. Possibly their most fortunate move was to purchase the bitch Shaldar of Rossarden who was bred subsequently to the Brewers' Ch. Heathcairn Cuthbert resulting in a litter of four. It included two males, Baird's Bramble and Shaldar's Boy and two females, Baird's Thorn and Thicket. The entire quartet gained their titles, but Bramble and Thorn were surely the most outstanding. While still puppies, they won top Terrier Brace at the International in 1962 after Bramble had taken the dog points in the breed. Ch. Baird's Thorn was Best of Breed at the 1963 National Specialty with Ch. Baird's Bramble taking the breed the following day at Westminster. Both were consistent thereafter, winning and placing in innumerable Terrier Groups, while Bramble captured a Best in Show at Erie in 1964. Ch. Baird's Shaldar's Boy, a much less publicized member of the litter did well at many other events but was overshadowed by the accomplishments of his brother and sister. A repeat breeding of Shaldar of Rossarden to Cuthbert brought another big winner for the kennel in Ch. Baird's Euclid, together with a litter

Ch. Baird's Bramble, owned by Mr. and Mrs. Charles B. Norris.
Rudolph Tauskey.

Ch. Baird's Thorn, owned by Mr. and Mrs. Charles B. Norris.
Rudolph Tauskey.

sister, Ch. Heathcairn Tow. Bairdsain Kennels have bred many fine Cairns but the accomplishments of the littermates Thorn and Bramble, and the productivity of Shaldar of Rossarden in union with Cuthbert, overshadows all.

Other Successful Kennels

Continuing the inventory of other successful kennels in the post-war era we find the late Celeste Hutton and her Greysarge dogs with Ch. Kilmet's Chunk of Braemuir, C.D., C.D.X., his daughter Greysarge Pixie, C.D., Ch. Greysarge Flare and Ch. Greysarge Naughty Marietta, etc.; Mrs. Doris Ticehurst with a host of titleholders including that oustanding litter by Eng. Ch. Redletter McMurran ex Redletter Melody comprising, Ticehurst's Black Douglas, Gay Spirit, Melody and Murran Ruadh, all of whom made their American titles along with their dam; the successful Canadian-based Balkaren Kennels of Mrs. J. T. Shirkie with the likes of Chs. Balkaren Perky Fox, Balkaren Ruffian of Cairndania, Kyleakin Perky of Balkaren and Balkaren Stuart, etc., together with Mr. and Mrs. James MacFarlane's relatively small but select Badenoch Kennels.

Badenoch

MacFarlane began his interest in the breed as a young man in Scotland. In 1920 he had a kennel of some 15 dogs but had to disperse it shortly because of business pressures. Years later, when the MacFarlanes were relocated in Canada, the desire to reenter the fancy was revived and a bitch, Badenoch Cubbie of Kenten (Balkaren Leetle Bateese ex Kenten of Kilmarnock) was purchased. MacFarlane wrote to his uncle, the redoubtable Col. H. F. Whitehead for advice and was delighted when he discovered that the Colonel had traced "Cubbie's" pedigree all the way back to Ch. Guynach Eachunn (1921), an early favorite of Whitehead's and his first champion. Armed with this lineage, Cubbie was bred to Can. Ch. Kindon Jaycenth and her initial litter produced two useful offspring, Badenoch Bonny Heather and Badenoch Foxy Sue. The latter developed into a fine producer. Bred to Ch. Redletter McRuffie she welped Ch. Badenoch Hamish Ruadh who was a good show dog and a strong stud force.

Ch. Unique Cottage Goldspur, owned by Mr. and Mrs. James G. MacFarlane, at 13 years.

In 1956, Ch. Cairndania Redstart's Redspurn was purchased, bred to Hamish and produced Ch. Badenoch Redham's Chieftain who developed into a prolific sire. Ch. Uniquecottage Goldspur (Eng. Ch. U.C. Maningay ex Eng. Ch. U.C. Blackgold) was next bought through Col. Whitehead in 1964 and became a Group winner but more importantly, an excellent outcross for the kennel's bitches. Possibly the most successful show dog to date was Ch. Cannycairns Fergus (Wendanny Fionn ex Can. Ch. Polly of High Hedges) who held a high rank among all Cairns in the ring during the years 1969, '70 and '71.

Two later inmates that have done well were Chs. Avenelhouse Bright Tweed and High Hedges Skipper of Badenoch. Incidentally, the kennel prefix was derived from the name of the district in Inverness-shire where McFarlane was born. The kennels enjoyed an excellent record for a small establishment and has owned and produced a host of champion Cairns during its tenure.

Regrettably, James MacFarlane died in 1981 and kennel activity was discontinued.

Braemuir

The Braemuir Kennels of Mr. and Mrs. Philip Thompson (Amsterdam, New York), was another operation that benefited from breeding stock bearing the Cairnvreckan prefix. Several dogs were obtained in the middle 1950s to augment the likes of Chs. Braemuir Greyling, Braemuir Caradoc, and others already in residence. As time progressed, Ch. Hillston Jeremy of Braemuir came upon the scene together with Barney of Tonderghie an import that was campaigned quickly to his title. He in turn, when bred to Cairnvreckan Zsa Zsa and Ch. Cairnvreckan Wisteria, sired Chs. Braemuir Noel and Braemuir Breacan respectively. The kennel was quite successful during its span of activity which began to diminish during the decade of the '60s.

Bellacairn

The Thompsons were good breeders and their efforts were responsible for the foundation stock of the very active Bellacairn establishment of Mrs. Isabel Eckfeld of California. This began when Mrs. Eckfeld lived in the East and purchased her first Cairn from Braemuir. Upon

Ch. Badenoch Fersue's Tarra, owned by Mr. and Mrs. James G. MacFarlane.

Ch. Cannycairn's Fergus, owned by Mr. and Mrs. James G. MacFarlane.

moving to California she endeavored to obtain additional stock only to discover that some of the Braemuir dogs had been acquired by Mrs. Amy Katz's California-based Kandykate Kennels. Her first purchase from Mrs. Katz was a bitch, Kandykate's Kadence (Ch. Thax Personality of Braemuir ex Braemuir Gwynneth.) She finished her championship handily and when bred to Toffee of Cairn Den produced the littermates, Chs. Bellacairn's Bit O'Scotch and Bellacairn's Blend of Cairn Den. A repeat breeding brought forth, Ch. Bellacairn's Kandy's Kid. Bit O'Scotch has done some exceptional winning under the expert guidance of Daisy Austad including a number of Terrier groups topped by a prestigious Best in Show at Beverly Hills Kennel Club in 1968.

Ch. Kandykate Kadence proved to be a very worthwhile acquisition as she has produced eight titleholders from three different studs, including Ch. Bellacairn's Black Bottom, a red sired by Ch. Caithness Rufus and a current winner, and Ch. Bellacairn's Fanciepants, a silver bitch that is doing well in the ring. Ch. Kandykate's Kilpatrick, by Ch. Greetvale Mickey Boy (a Group winner owned by Mrs. Katz), ex Ch. Ticehurst's Kandy Kim, has proved to be another useful stud with Ch. Bellacairn's Karen to his credit, among others. Thus, while the kennel is relatively small, it has housed some top Cairns during the years. Mrs. Eckfield continues to exhibit at a number of West Coast and some important Eastern fixtures. One of her more recent entries was Ch. Gairlock's Rascal O'Ragtime.

Milbryan

Another kennel that has some early roots tracing back to both Catescairn and Braemuir is Mrs. David W. Bryant's Texas-based Milbryan establishment. Early titleholders included Chs. Tana's Sunny Eilean and Braemuir Raffan II (Shagbark Simon Berry ex Ch. Braemuir Wistful) who had the distinction of placing Best in Show at Fort Sill in 1961, together with the very important Ch. Catescairn Chance For Me (Ch. Redletter McRuffie ex Ch. Catescairn Cocoa). This one did well in the ring, sired five titleholders, and will be found in the backgrounds of scores of contemporary Milbryan Cairns. Other inmates that have distinguished themselves include; Ch. Milbryan McGillicuddy (Betcha Boots of Braecroft ex Ch. Miss Sue

Ch. Kandykate Kadence (Ch. Thax Personality of Braemuir ex Braemuir Gwynneth), owned by Isabel Eckfeld and bred by Kandykate Kennels. This bitch became a champion at 16 months and went on to be a producer of quality stock. *Joan Ludwig.*

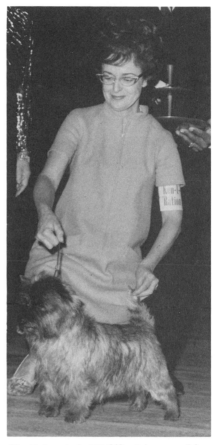

Ch. Bellacairn's Fancie Pants, owned by Isabel Eckfeld and shown by Daisy Austad.

Ch. Bellacairn's Bit O'Scotch, owned by Isabel Eckfeld, was a top winner during the late 1960s. Piloted by Daisy Austad to a brilliant career, his record includes a spectacular BIS triumph at the KC of Beverly Hills. *Joan Ludwig.*

of Milbryan), a Group winner and the ultimate breed winner at the 1965 National Specialty show, the Group winning Ch. Caithness Colonel (a Rufus son), Ch. Milbryan Tartan Laddie.

In recent years, Mrs. Bryant's kennel activity has leveled off to a degree due to her judging career which has become increasingly demanding. She judges all Terriers, all Non-Sporting breeds, all Toys and a number of others. However, Milbryan Cairns are still strong competition with a number completing their titles as will be seen from the records, including Ch. Milbryan Delta Dawn O'Connor. Mrs. Bryant had the honor of judging the breed at the prestigious Centennial show of the American Kennel Club held in Philadelphia in 1984, placing Mrs. Hyslop's Ch. Cairndania Sam's Sundew Best of Breed.

Passing to other kennels based in Southern clime, one must notice the "B Cube" effort of Dr. and Mrs. B. B. Bagby, Jr., where a host of champions attest to the sound breeding over the years. The bitch, Ch. B. Cube's Spunky, co-owned with Miss Nancy Thompson, became the first titleholder in Miss Thompson's very successful Gayla Cairn Kennels (1954).

Gayla Cairn

Since then, Gayla Cairn has enjoyed phenomenal success, breeding over one hundred champions, 96 of which were breeder-handled. Ch. Gayla Cairn's O'Tilly captured multiple Groups and a Best in Show to become one of the top winning Cairn bitches while Ch. Gayla Cairn's Gregor McKim, with a show record of 53 Groups and 10 Bests in Show, is another record breaker. Both of these were owner bred and handled. In addition, some seven other Gayla Cairn-bred dogs have captured Groups through the years. Surely, the record made by the dogs of this kennel is outstanding.

In breeding the establishment is equally successful. It has utilized the best stud dogs available, including many of its own that have proven their worth as sires. These include Ch. Gayla Cairn's Davey with some ten champions to his credit, while Ch. Gayla Cairn's Hope holds records as a producing bitch. It is obvious that Miss Thompson knows the formula for producing quality stock and has the bloodlines within her own kennel for proliferating the successes of the past. Chs. Gayla

Ch. Cairndania Sam's Sundew (Ch. Rogerlyn Sea Hawk's Salty Sam ex Cairndania Seaspirit's Seabreeze), owned and bred by Betty Hyslop, made himself an important place in breed history by winning BB at the AKC Centennial under Mildred Bryant. Mrs. Bryant is a Cairn enthusiast herself whose Milbryan prefix was associated with many good dogs. *William Gilbert.*

Ch. Gayla Cairn's O'Tilly, owned and handled by Nancy J. Thompson, established an enviable record in all-breed competition. She is shown winning first in the Terrier group at the Chattanooga KC under the author. *Earl Graham.*

149

Ch. Gayla Cairn's Gregor McKim, owned and handled by Nancy Thompson, is shown here in a 1978 BIS presentation at the Columbus (Georgia) KC under the late Dr. Frank Booth. *Earl Graham.*

Cairn's Gray Knight, Gayla Cairn's Quarles, together with Gayla Cairn's Gregor McKim, Gayla Cairn's Hooligan, Gayla Cairn's Early Bird have all done well, while Ch. Gayla Cairn's Nora (Ch. Gayla Cairn's Gray Knight ex Ch. Gayla Cairn's Forget-Me-Not) is a top producing bitch with thirteen champions get to her credit, seven of these by Ch. Gayla Cairn's Gregor McKim. Most recently Ch. Brigadoon's Tough Guy has been the banner bearer in breed and Group. There is no doubt that this kennel breeds well and shows extensively with excellent results.

Topcairn

The Topcairn establishment of Girard A. Jacobi and William R. Chatham, Spring Valley, New York, was in operation for many years and, while relatively small, it was highly selective and carefully managed to produce quality stock. Unfortunately, Mr. Jacobi died on February 28, 1983, a great loss to his many friends and to the breed. Mr. Jacobi authored the book, *Your Cairn Terrier,* 1976 and was a highly-respected judge. He officiated at the Cairn Terrier Club of America's Specialty at Montgomery County in 1982 and drew a record entry, at the time, of 197 dogs. He was also quite active in club matters, was president of the Cairn Terrier Club of America, and was its delegate-elect at the time of his death. The breed will surely miss Jerry Jacobi, as will his many friends.

Ch. Gayla Cairn's Hooligan (Ch. Gayla Cairn's Davey ex Gayla Cairn's Maggie), owned by Mrs. Sanford A. Lincoln and shown here with breeder Nancy Thompson. *William Gilbert.*

Ch. Gayla Cairn's Kiss My Grits (Ch. Gayla Cairn's Gregor McKim ex Ch. Gayla Cairn's Nora), owned and handled by Nancy Thompson, is one of the numerous homebred champions from this kennel. Shown here winning under judge Joe Gregory *John Ashbey.*

Only a few months before his death, Girard Jacobi was accorded a two-sided honor of tremendous significance. First he was selected to judge the 1982 Cairn Terrier Club of America Specialty and was supported by the fancy with a record 197-dog entry. He is shown with his BB choice, Mrs. Hyslop's Am., Can. Ch. Foxgrove Jeronimo with handler Roberta Campbell. *Gilbert.*

Additional Important Breeders

Other established breeders of the time include the Hal Aspys with a long line of Halkaren Cairns; Don Robbie and his Holemill dogs including Ch. Holemill's MacRodney and Holemill's Barley; Mrs. Nina Matzner and her successful Tina's prefix; Grace Siegler and Vera Hoehn's Cairn Den entries; Bob and Kay Davis' Craigly Kennels with Ch. Shagbark Jody who sired Chs. Craigly Razzle Dazzle, Our Flip and Bogart of Craigly became the nations top sire in 1965 with five titleholders to his credit; Martha B. Baechle, another California entry whose 'O'Southfield suffix is widely known and Mrs. James P. Craco and her sister, Mrs. M. Dalger, whose Cairnwoods Kennels had the honor of breeding two of the leading winners of the day, Chs. Cairnwoods Golden Boy and Cairnwoods Quince. At this point it will be useful to enlarge upon the efforts of the two kennels that owned these two dogs, Mr. and Mrs. Taylor Coleman's Wolfpit Kennels and Mrs. Ralph Stone's Caithness establishment.

Wolfpit

Wolfpit is shared by the Colemans with their daughter, Mrs. Lydia Hutchinson. Begun in Connecticut, and now located in Maryland, it all began in the late thirties when a puppy, Kiltie of Wolfpit came into the Coleman home. She was bred a few times to studs housed at the nearby Eastcote Kennels of Mrs. Platt. In the last litter by Ch. Buff of Eastcote there was a puppy named Foxy of Wolfpit and she in turn was bred to Cherryfield Thistle. The mating brought forth a dark brindle male that was named Mr. Mulroonie of Wolfpit. He was exhibited and made his title in 1949 to change the Colemans from a family with a pet or two to a group of avid dog fanciers.

That they have been successful is an understatement. Over the years Wolfpit has bred and/or owned a host of distinguished champions including Cannonball of Wolfpit, sire of Ch. Bonnie Bairn of Wolfpit who, when bred to Kris Kringle of Wolfpit, whelped the all champion litter of Chs. Bonnie Brae, Bonnie Doone and Bonnie Heather, all of Wolfpit. About the same time, the gray-brindle winner, Ch. Bethcairn David was purchased to strengthen the stud force. In the ensuing years, such winners as Ch. Bonnie Brash of W., his litter sister, Ch. Bonnie Scamp of W., Ch. Bonnie Scoundrel of W. sired by Ch. Bonnie Rogue

This photograph is of great interest from a historical point of view. The lady at the left is Helen Platt of the Eastcote Kennels. The dog with her is Ch. Buff of Eastcote. The other lady is Mrs. Taylor Coleman whose Wolfpit Cairns have enjoyed such great success and who are still winning well. The dog with her was her first Cairn, Kiltie of Wolfpit. Then, as now, Cairns, like most terriers, were never too slow about debating an issue. Kiltie looks as though she'd rather not be between Buff and his kennel-mate Sky Pilot at that particular moment. *Phillipe Halsman from Black Star.*

A FAMILY AFFAIR—The Taylor Coleman family and their Wolfpit affix have been synonymous with fine Cairns since the 1940s. Here Mrs. Coleman (1.) handles the renowned Ch. Cairnwood's Quince as daughter Lydia Coleman Hutchinson and Mr. Coleman pilot the Quince daughters, Ch. Flair's Flirt of Wolfpit and Easter Bonnet of Wolfpit. This photo, taken at the CTCA Specialty 1972, records Quince's win of the Stud Dog class under Mrs. Tom Stevenson. Earlier, Mrs. Stevenson awarded Quince BB at the same event. *Evelyn Shafer.*

Ch. Razzberry of Wolfpit, owned by Mr. and Mrs. Taylor Coleman and shown with Lydia Coleman Hutchinson. *Bernard Kernan.*

154

Ch. Bonnie Tramp of Wolfpit (Ch. Persimmon of Wolfpit ex Ch. Bonnie Vamp of Wolfpit), owned by and shown with Lydia Coleman Hutchinson, is a typical example from this long-established family. *William Gilbert.*

Ch. London Chimes of Wolfpit (Ch. DeWinter's Duncan ex Ch. London Bridget of Wolfpit), owned by Mr. and Mrs. Taylor Coleman and shown here handled by Lydia Coleman Hutchinson. *William Gilbert.*

of W. have come upon the scene. Wolfpit's greatest winner was Ch. Cairnwoods Quince by Ch. Cairnwoods Golden Boy ex Caithness Gracenote. Quince captured the breed innumerable times and had a number of Terrier Group firsts and a Best in Show in tough Eastern competition to his credit. He was the kennel's all-time top winner with national Specialty Bests of Breed in 1971, 1972 and 1973. However, his greatest triumph came when he was 12 years and seven months of age at the 1980 national Specialty. He was entered in the Veteran's class and carried through to a fourth Specialty Best of Breed to become the oldest dog, so far as my records go, to ever gain such prominence. Of even greater interest is the fact that at this same event, Chasand's Yankee Pedlar, a Quince great-grandson owned by Mrs. T. C. Fritz, was placed Best of Winners while (Ch.) Foxy Loxy Vixen of Haverford, a Quince daughter and owned by Daniel Shoemaker, was Best of Opposite Sex; all three dogs were owner-handled. To date, Quince has proved to be an outstanding sire with over 50 titleholders on the record and more in competition. While the breeding program at Wolfpit has naturally been centered about this exceptional dog, there are two others, Chs. Lofthouse Valeta and Craiglyn Christmas Carol who were purchased for breeding to Quince that have done well. Valeta produced Ch. MacMurrich of Wolfpit while Carol is the dam of Ch. Bayberry of Wolfpit. Surely, Ch. Cairnwoods Quince established a record that will be difficult to top. This grand dog died in 1984 at the age of 16 years—he surely left an enduring mark on the breed.

Today, while breeding efforts at Wolfpit have lessened, solid activity continues as evidenced by the owner-handled homebred Ch. Gadget's Gimmick of Wolfpit, winning Best of Breed at the 1985 Potomac Specialty held in conjunction with the Columbia Association of Terrier Clubs in Maryland.

Caithness

The late Mrs. Ralph Stone and her Caithness prefix was another strong factor, with the owner usually exhibiting her own dogs. Few realize that Mrs. Stone's interest in dogs and Cairns in particular dated back to 1926 when she obtained a lifetime registration of her kennel name, Caithness. This activity was fostered by a trip to Scotland which resulted in bringing back a Cairn Terrier to start the entire story. While

Ch. Gadget's Gimmick of Wolfpit (Ch. Persimmon of Wolfpit ex Ch. Sunnyland's Gadget of Wolfpit), owned and bred by Lydia Coleman Hutchinson with whom he is shown here. *William Gilbert.*

Ch. Craiglynn Christmas Carol (Ch. Blencathra Brat ex Ch. Piedwick Drusilla), owned by Mr. and Mrs. Taylor Coleman, was imported from England to add her influence to the Wolfpit breeding program. In addition to being an excellent producer, she could also hold her own in competition. This picture shows her being awarded BOS at the 1977 CTCA Specialty under judge James Reynolds. Handled by Lydia Hutchinson, Carol was seven years old at the time she made this coveted win. *John L. Ashbey.*

Ch. Thistleclose MacGregor of Caithness, owned by Mrs. Ralph Stone, *William Brown*

Ch. Caithness Briar Rose, owned by Mrs. Ralph Stone, was a top producer. One of her sons was the great Ch. Caithness Rufus. *William Brown.*

Mrs. Stone was not active in the show ring until after the war, Caithness always had a Cairn or two to go with the Setters and Dalmatians.

In the late '40s, the activity increased and a Cairn, Cairnvreckan Bedelia was acquired from Mrs. Bacon. This was followed by a trip to England where Eng. Ch. Thistleclose MacGregor was purchased. He was a winner at Crufts and did extremely well in the United States. Both Bedelia and MacGregor completed their American titles in rapid time. MacGregor also did well at stud and produced Chs. Caithness McEwan and Caithness English Accent among others. The turning point of the story came when the import, Foundation Moss Rose of Caithness was obtained. She was bred to another import, Ch. Unique Cottage Mr. Tippy of Caithness and the issue included a bitch, Caithness Briar Rose. This one completed her title quickly and when bred to Ch. Cairndania's McRuffie's Raider produced a litter including Chs. Caithness Rosette, Rosalie and Rosemary together with their litter brother, Ch. Caithness Rufus. The same breeding was repeated and resulted in Ch. Caithness Cathra. Raider also produced Chs. Caithness Chervil and Thurso when bred to Caithness Cinnamon Rose and Ch. Caithness English Accent respectively.

Ch. Caithness Rufus (1963–1972) was a great one. He was sensational in the ring and will stand among the top sires of all times. A red dog, he gained his points quickly including a dramatic and impressive triumph at the 1964 Chicago International. Mrs. Elise Untermyer was the judge and Rufus was but a youngster entered in the puppy class. He showed well and was placed Winners and then Best of Winners. His final test came when he had to compete with 17 champion entries, including the Specialty winner from the previous day. The youngster, in spite of a trying day, never faltered, and showed like a veteran. Mrs. Untermyer was thorough and calm but, as the judging progressed, the tension began to grow. When the final decision was made and the puppy was waved to the Best of Breed position, the ringside gave its unqualified support and approval and "a new star was born."

Rufus continued his winning ways and, while not campaigned heavily, was shown at most of the big ones and always gave a good account of himself. During his rather short career, he captured several Terrier Groups and well over 50 breed wins. He was retired while still in his prime to permit the exhibition of a son, Ch. Cairnwoods Golden Boy purchased by Mrs. Stone.

Ch. Caithness Rufus, owned by Mrs. Ralph Stone, was a leading winner during the '60s. His presence was felt on the breed level where he was a multiple Specialty winner and in keenly-contested Terrier groups, where he prevailed against some of the most heralded show dogs in the country. It is significant to note that he was owner-handled in most of his ring appearances and was a noted producer. *Evelyn M. Shafer.*

		Ch. Redletter McJoe	Ch. Bonfire of Twobees
	Ch. Redletter McRuffie		Redletter My Choice
		Rosefield Rebecca	Ch. Blencathra Sandpiper
Ch. Cairndania's McRuffie's Raider			Jenny's Choice
		Ch. Redletter McBrigand	Ch. Redletter McMurran
	Rossmar's Bronda of Cairndania		Ch. Redletter Miss Splinters
		Rossmar's Ruffican Lass	Ch. Redletter McRuffie
CH. CAITHNESS RUFUS			Ch. Balkaren Cinders
			Ch. Redletter Fincairn Frolic
		Ch. Unique Cottage Sir Frolic	Unique Cottage Golddigger
	Ch. Unique Cottage Mr. Tippy of Caithness		Ch. Unique Cottage McAilenmore
		Unique Cottage Anabladh	Unique Cottage Silver Seal
Ch. Caithness Briar Rose			Ch. Blencathra Elford Chiefton
		Blencathra McBeth of Rhu	Sandrina of Rhu
	Foundation Moss Rose of Caithness		Shieling Patrick of Rhu
		Foundation Mignonette	Foundation Marilyn

Totally, Rufus has sired some two dozen champions including the aforementioned Golden Boy and such good winners as Chs. Bellacairn's Black Bottom and Caithness Colonel. Ch. Cairnwoods Golden Boy has also made his mark as the sire of Ch. Cairnwoods Quince among others while distinguishing himself in the ring with the top win at the 1969 Specialty and several Group firsts. Caithness Kennels permanently closed its doors in the mid-1970s upon the death of Mrs. Stone.

Tidewater

Another establishment of more recent vintage is the Tidewater Kennel of Mr. and Mrs. Charles R. Merrick III which began with Ch. Braecroft's Bobby Burns (Ch. Duncan of Hemlock ex Braecroft's Brindle Bonnie). He was followed by Ch. Cairndania Miss Badness (Ch. Unique Cottage Mr. Bradshaw ex Cairndania McBrigands Holly) who completed her title for Mrs. Hyslop when only six months of age. After acquisition, the Merricks did consistent winning through 1971 when she was retired. Their bitch, Unique Cottage Brigitta, bred to Ch. Lofthouse Davey produced the noted winner, Ch. Tidewater Black Gold. In addition, the stud force at Tidewater included the good dog, Ch. Unique Cottage Mr. Bradshaw, sire of Miss Badness and owned jointly with Mrs. Hyslop. Another important acquisition was the English bitch, Ch. Unique Cottage Phainopepla, dam of Tidewater Brigitta.

Flickwynd

Eleanor Finkler's Flickwynd Kennels, with Chs. Little Pete and Tinker Bell's Son of Flickwynd, deserves good salute. Mrs. Finkler, who obtained much of her foundation stock from Melita Kennels, has bred and owned some two score of titleholders including a big winner of the early 1970s—the black-brindle, Ch. Flicka's Peter Pan, who has also proved his worth in the breeding pen with numerous champions to his credit to date.

Ch. Cairndania Miss Badness (Ch. Unique Cottage Mr. Bradshaw ex Cairndania Mc-Brigand's Holly), owned by Mr. and Mrs. Charles P. Merrick, III, finished her championship at six months and went on to make good wins throughout her show career. *William P. Gilbert.*

Ch. Tidewater Black Gold with owner Charles P. Merrick, III. *Evelyn M. Shafer.*

Am., Can. Ch. Cairmar Amy Amy Amy, a multiple group winner owned by Patricia Broyles and handled by Judy Webb. *John Ashbey.*

Ch. Cairmar Call to Arms is one of the well-known winners from the Cairmar establishment. Shown here with Mrs. Marcum, he is being presented with the BIS award at the 1981 Memphis KC show under Mary Nelson Stephenson. *Bonnie.*

Cairmar

Among the host of establishments that have come into focus since the first publication of this book (1975), Mr. and Mrs. Joe Marcum's Cairmar Kennels, located at Clinton, Mississippi, has compiled an amazing record. Sixty champions since 1969, many of them home-breds, is a record that will be difficult to match. Further, a number of these Cairns have claimed high Group placements and many Best in Show awards.

The kennels started with a homebred, Ch. Cairmar Cantie Croftee who went from puppy class to Winners Dog at the national Specialty. Shortly thereafter, the Marcums had the good fortune to acquire two Cairns from the late Mrs. Stone of Caithness, Chs. Caithness Barnabas and Caithness Cantie Periwinkle. These figure heavily in the pedigrees of today's Cairmar stock. Barnabas sired 31 titleholders while Periwinkle was the dam of seven. Another important acquisition was the bitch, Ch. Tradoroghs Connamarah purchased from Mrs. Mildred Bryant and bred by Dorothy Higgins. This one had already produced three titleholders and went on to add 13 more for the Marcums. Thus, much of the success of Cairmar can be credited to top producing bitches, an old story if one surveys the past, for good producing bitches make a good kennel.

The Marcums have had great success with their Chs. Cairmar Miss Chance and Cairmar Fighting Chance, both Group winners with Fighting Chance taking a Best in Show. Ch. Cairmar Fancy Dresser, a Periwinkle grandson, has also captured Groups and two Bests in Show, while proving to be an excellent stud force with more than 20 champion get to his credit. More recent standard bearers include Chs. Cairmar Call to Arms, a Specialty winner with Groups and a Best in Show to his credit together with the good show bitch, Ch. Cairmar Amy Amy Amy, a multiple Group winner.

There is small doubt that this kennel has the bloodlines required for continued success, while its owners have surely demonstrated that they know how to breed and select quality stock.

Ch. Cairmar Chance Quest, owned by Mr. and Mrs. Joe Marcum. *Van Sickle.*

Ch. Cairmar Fancy Dresser, owned by Mr. and Mrs. Joe Marcum. *Bennett Associates.*

Other Friends of the Cairn Terrier

Additional serious breeders who deserve mention include Miss Kathryn Glick and the Cantycairn dogs; Mrs. D. C. Higgins, owner-breeder of the 1975 Specialty winner, Ch. Tradorogh's Dunstan Claymore, who also had a C.D.X. degree; Mrs. T. E. Lain, a good breeder with such Raelain entries as Chs. Ghillie and Crofter, both of Raelain; Mrs. and Mrs. A. L. Bergeron's Craigly B Cairns with Ch. Craigly A-Bomb, C.D.X.; Margaret Magee's Whistlegate Cairns; Mrs. E. L. McReynolds' Nanlor establishment together with Pauline Hardy and the Brigadoon Cairns, including Chs. Brigadoon Pistol Pete, Pied Piper and Sassy Sue; Mrs. Shiela Bruckley and the Craigly-S dogs including Ch. Craigly Dougal McFlair; Mrs. L. DeVincent and Ch. Shin Pond Cricket; Mrs. Barbara Natarus with a big winner in 1978-79, Ch. Cairndania Sargent's Dalson; Mr. and Mrs. J. R. Kroeger and the Sookota prefix, particularly the homebred, Ch. Sookota Buffalo Bill, who captured Best in Show at the 1970 Fargo-Moorhead event; Virginia Cadwallader who based the fortunes of her Woodmist Kennels upon the abilities and bloodlines of Ch. Wyesider Grey Knight, a 1968 titleholder who did well in the ring and also sired a host of winning get including Chs. Woodmist Violet, London Chimes of Wolfpit, Woodmist Grey Wren and the Best in Show winner, Ch. Coralrock's Boney Maloney, owned and bred by Mrs. R. J. Abhalter; Mrs. Joanne Glodek with a host of good ones including the Group winner, Ch. Mac-Ken-Char's Seasprite; Doris Harris of El Cajon, California, owner of Ch. Buckshot of Melita, a big winner in the middle 1970s; Daniel Shoemaker, whose Waterford Cairns are coming to the fore with the likes of Chs. Foxey Loxey Vixen of Haverford, Waterford Miss Montgomery and Waterford Quintillon; Mrs. Jack DeWitt (Happicairn) with Chs. Foxgrove Mutt and Happicairn Nutmeg; Lt. Col. and Mrs. Terry MacSparran (Littleclan) with Chs. Craiglyn Caledonian and Vinvovium Graham; Kenneth Kauffman (Brehannon) with Chs. Ramblewood Barney Brehannon, Brehannon on the Rocks, and the multiple Group winner Brehannon Graylan Drummer; J. and D. Cantwell's Canadian operation with Chs. Azgard's Johnny Reb and Azgard's Nearly Mist; Pauline Hardy with her Brigadoon Cairns including Chs. Brigadoon Pistol Pete, Pied Piper and Sassy Sasha, together with Charles and Sandra LeClair's

Ch. Ramblewood Barney Brehannon, owned by Kenneth Kauffman, is shown topping the breed at the Ramapo KC show in 1981 under Lydia Coleman Hutchinson.

Ch. Brehannon Graylan Drummer, owned and handled by Kenneth Kauffman, boasts an impressive win record that includes top awards in numerous terrier groups as well as Specialties. *John Ashbey.*

Ch. Mac-Ken-Char's Seasprite, owned by Joanne Glodek. *William R. Lewis.*

Ch. Bonnie Bairn of Wolfpit, owned by Lydia Coleman Hutchinson, was a top winner in the breed during the mid-'50's. She won many Bests of Breed and several Group placements when these were rare for Cairns. A producer of merit, she has approximately thirty champion descendants. *William Brown.*

Chasands entries and many more. Today, there is a host of newer successful breeders and exhibitors who are doing their part for Cairns. Only editorial limitations prevent fuller recognition. Hopefully, they will continue their allegiance to and support of the Cairn Terrier in the years ahead.

Ch. Foxy Loxy Vixen of Haverford, owned by Daniel Shoemaker and handled here by Marjorie Shoemaker, scored a number of impressive wins enroute to her championship. Probably the most noteworthy of these is shown above. Here she is being presented with the BOS award at the 1978 CTCA Specialty under the renowned English judge Margaret D. Wilson (Felshott). *William Gilbert.*

HEAD shorter, wider than other terriers; well-furnished with hair on top, softer than body coat; foxy expression

EARS small, pointed, well-carried, erect, set wide apart; free from long hair, dark desirable

BODY well-muscled, strong, active; neither leggy nor too low to ground; proportions balanced

STOP distinct

EYES wide apart, rather sunken, size medium; hazel or dark hazel; eyebrows shaggy

NOSE black

MUZZLE strong; not too long or heavy; dark desirable; teeth large; neither over nor undershot

SHOULDERS sloping

FORELEGS straight; elbows turning neither in nor out

FOREFEET larger than hind feet, may turn out slightly; pads thick, strong; should stand well up on feet

COAT hard, weather-resistant; outer, profuse close, harsh; inner, short, soft, furry; legs covered with hard hair

BACK level, medium length, strong, not heavy

TAIL well-furnished with hair, not feathery; carriage gay, not over back; set-on at back level

HINDQUARTERS strong, well-muscled

LEGS medium length, not too heavily boned

RIBS deep, well-sprung

SIZE: males, 14 lbs.; 10″ at withers; females, 13 lbs.; 9½″; Body length, 14½ to 15″ from sternum to point of rump (for mature dogs of two years)

COLOR any except white; dark ears, muzzle, tail tip desirable

10

The Breed Standard, Background and Interpretation

THE STANDARD of Perfection for any breed is the specification set forth by proponents of the breed, generally the national Specialty Club, which has been recognized and approved by the American Kennel Club. This Standard sets forth the desirable and undesirable points of structure and temperament and is used as a guide by both breeders and judges.

Importance of a Standard

The Standard is an important factor to the success of the breed. If it is sufficiently specific, it is relatively easy to understand and leaves few points of confusion between breeders and judges. If it is too sketchy, it causes much consternation among tyros and offers the opportunity for a wide variation in personal opinion among the more serious fanciers. Therefore, a clear and concise Standard is a necessity if a breed is to progress. It is believed that the Cairn Terrier Standard falls generally within the category of an adequate specification although several items could be improved for the sake of clarity. This chapter will analyze the present Standard in detail and will elaborate upon several points of importance.

The Standard in Relation to Work

First, is should be remembered that every breed was produced for a specific purpose. In order to carry out the dictates of that purpose, certain basic factors have to be present in any dog of the breed. These do not contribute necessarily to the beauty of the dog but they are required for him to carry out the designated work of the breed and sometimes to protect his very existence.

The Cairn Terrier was originally bred to outlast vermin of all kinds and under all conditions. For these reasons, the factors in the Standard which are required for proper working ability should be considered of utmost importance when breeding or judging. The first of these is temperament. The Cairn has to be of a fearless nature, not quarrelsome but unafraid of man or beast. He must be armed with strong teeth set in powerful jaws so that he can defend himself in a fight to the death. He has to own a good double coat, one profuse with soft undercoat and well-thatched with a tough and harsh outer jacket that will shed rain or snow and will protect against briars, teeth and cold. He has to have a strong back and adequate hindquarters so necessary for any Terrier to aid in holding its prey to the ground and, above all, he has to be possessed of good, strong legs terminating in feet carrying thick, tough pads because a Cairn is an *earth dog,* a digger, and without this equipment, he is useless for his life's purpose. In addition, a Terrier of any breed needs sharp eyes, moderately small and dark and well protected against injury beneath a strong overhanging brow. These are the basic factors without them no Cairn will long survive the work for which he was developed originally.

Interpreting the Standard

Every breed Standard is interpreted differently by different people and that interpretation is influenced to a major degree by their knowledge of and experience in the breed. Because of this condition, it is believed that an analytical breakdown of the Standard will be helpful to all, wherein each point will be viewed critically in light of the use and background of the breed. Possibly such an analysis will help the tyro and may cause some of the oldsters, who have

172

strayed afield because of personal likes, to reorient their thinking for the betterment of the breed.

Unfortunately, too many fashion their breeding programs according to the conformation of the winners of the day, even though these dogs may be far removed from the "classical Cairn" as set forth by the Standard. Breeding to win, as the primary goal, will never improve the breed nor will it maintain the desired type required for the work for which the Cairn was intended. Many will counter with, "we are no longer using them for working purposes, what's the difference?" The answer is always the same: if we breed for personal likes, we shall soon lose all of the identifying features that set the breed apart from its several closely related cousins. It seems just as sensible to breed white Cairns as to breed long-headed ones. In the first case we are losing identity to the West Highland White and in the second to the Scottish Terrier. A survey of the many years spent separating these same breeds to gain their individual autonomy seems to answer the question and offers sound reasons why we should always keep to the specifications set forth by the Standard.

History of the Cairn Standard

The Standard of Perfection for the Cairn Terrier, first adopted and approved by the American Kennel Club, was a substantial copy of the one already in use in England. By 1917 a major difference appeared in color. The English specification made no mention of any color being taboo; it merely offered a listing of the most desirable colors. The American counterpart specifically barred whites. The difference was caused by the American Kennel Club action that barred interbreeding of Cairns and West Highlands, a restriction that antedated British action on the same condition by some eight years. The Standard presently in use in the United States was approved by the American Kennel Club on May 10th, 1938. It may be said, that a Club committee has been at work on a revision of this specification for several years but as yet, no satisfactory substitute has been agreed upon.

Most Important Features

To get to the Standard, there are three major points that must be considered paramount, that must be present in any dog that is to be useful for either show or breeding purposes. These are breed *type,* breed *character* and *balance*. These three points far outweigh the several structural details that are too often given prime consideration. Any dog lacking in type, character or balance, even if endowed with exceptional individual structural features will not be a useful specimen of the breed nor a good animal from which to breed. The dog may have a magnificent head, a grand body, proper hindquarters, etc., but if these attributes do not blend, are not in balance, their presence is of small value. For example, a beautifully formed head that is too large or too small for the remainder of the dog, lacks balance and admittedly does not look well in the ensemble. Similarly, any Cairn that lacks breed character is not a good specimen even though his conformation is well above average. A Cairn that is shy, draws away from people and other dogs, carries his tail down, is not exhibiting true Cairn character. Neither is an overly aggressive dog that goes out of control in the presence of other dogs useful. Of what value would such a fighter be in a pack?

Breed type, character and balance are therefore, of utmost importance if a dog is to become a big winner. The only section of the Standard that deals directly with these fundamentals, (but does not specifically mention them) is the first paragraph.

OFFICIAL STANDARD OF THE CAIRN TERRIER

Approved May 10, 1938

(Comments by the Author shown in Roman type)

General Appearance—That of an active, game, hardy, small working terrier of the short-legged class; very free in its movements, strongly but not heavily built, standing well forward on its forelegs, deep in the ribs, well coupled with strong hind-quarters and presenting a well-proportioned build with a medium length of back, having a hard, weather resisting coat; head shorter and wider than any other terrier* and well furnished with hair giving a general foxy expression.

It is extremely doubtful if many, who are not well versed in the intricacies of the breed, appreciate the fundamentals included in this concise paragraph. This is not an indictment of the language used; it applies equally well to most specifications for other breeds and the

---

* The statement that a Cairn should have a head "shorter and wider than any other terrier" is misleading and inaccurate. The Cairn's head is certainly not as wide as that of an Airedale and it is doubtful whether it is proportionately shorter and wider than that of a Norwich Terrier. It would be better said; head short and wide, etc.

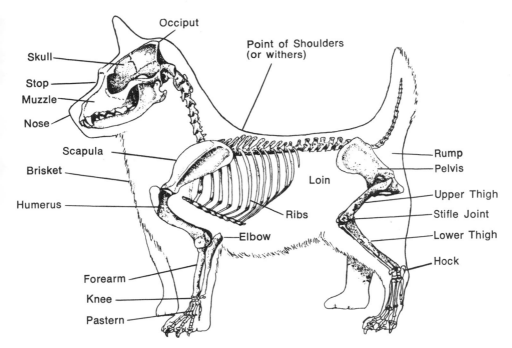

Skeletal Structure of the Cairn Terrier with Reference to Body Contour

shortcomings in this direction are directly traceable to the fact that type, character and balance are all intangible factors, difficult to define positively and seldom understood fully without long and substantial study of the breed, its derivation and its use.

In view of this situation, most standards are drawn to stress strongly the structural points that may be defined more positively. Thus, the tyro, upon reading the Standard, tends to breed for isolated structural factors rather than the whole animal. This is a fatal mistake and may cost the newcomer several frustrating years of effort before any degree of success is attained. It should be remembered that many of the best show dogs do not reach perfection in any single structural detail but if they are typey, are in good balance and exhibit the character of the breed, it may be said that "they carry their faults well." For these reasons, when breeding, always look for the "big three" first and then consider the structural details. I am merely repeating what a great Terrier man, Holland Buckley, said many years ago—"We must first strike for true type of the breed and bring our purely fancy points in afterwards."

"Fancy points" are the structural features that in proper and balanced assembly produce type. For these reasons, these points must

175

be maintained generally within prescribed limits as set forth in the remainder of the Standard, which is quoted here with annotations that may prove useful in understanding its meaning.

Skull—Broad in proportion to length with a decided stop and well furnished with hair on the top of the head, which may be somewhat softer than the body coat.

A broad skull is important and this means broad in proportion to its length. Narrow skulls are to be shunned, they cause the eyes and ears to be too close set. A broad skull separates the eyes and ears properly and yields proper expression with adequate anchorage for the terribly punishing jaw muscles which are a necessity. While not specifically set forth, the skull should be slightly domed in contour.

Muzzle—Strong, but not too long or heavy. Teeth large— mouth neither over or undershot. Nose black.

The muzzle should be pointed to yield the desired "foxy" expression. It should be short, never longer than the skull and preferably a bit shorter. Long muzzles and heavy muzzles are not typical and always yield a foreign expression. The portion dealing with teeth calls for a good mouth, neither over or undershot. In this instance the upper incisors may be either evenly met or join in a scissors bite with the lower incisors, either being acceptable. Generally speaking the scissors bite is more useful since the teeth do not wear as rapidly.

A word of caution is in order here. Many poor mouths are man-made rather than caused genetically. Breeders often do not watch the progress of the second teeth as they appear during the critical teething period, generally around four months of age. At this time, as the new teeth (second dentition) begin to appear, the puppy or milk teeth usually shed or fall out. However, many times this does not occur naturally and the second teeth grow in alongside of their predecessors. This causes the new teeth to come in improperly, sometimes crooked and sometimes in double rows. I have judged Cairns that have had *two full sets* of teeth, never having shed their milk dentition. Such mouths are atrocious and could have been prevented through a little care. Often, some of the milk teeth shed normally and only a few remain. Even in this instance, the permanent teeth that replace them come in improperly. Therefore, watch carefully your puppy's mouth, and if you see a permanent tooth coming in while the puppy tooth remains in place, pull the offender immediately. If you cannot do it yourself, enlist the aid of your veterinarian.

The black nose is a necessity and requires no explanation although there is a tendency in some instances for the pigmentation to lighten

176

Proper size, well-carried

overly large, but properly set on and carried

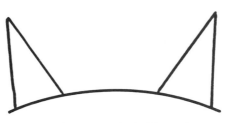
poorly set, undesirable mule-like carriage

Ears and Ear Carriage

slightly in the winter. In West Highlands, this tendency is more prevalent and is termed "snownose." The color returns with more sunlight and probably results from a vitamin deficiency. It is not a cause for alarm unless pronounced and/or permanent.

Eyes—Set wide apart, rather sunken, with shaggy eyebrows, medium in size, hazel or dark hazel in color depending on body color, with keen terrier expression.

The phrase, "set wide apart" is very important since it is vital to proper expression. A Cairn with a properly formed skull will have its eyes set wide apart, one with a narrow skull will not. Invariably, closely set eyes indicate a narrow skull. The eyes should be of a dark hazel color and of medium size. The color will be slightly lighter in Cairns of lighter body colors. On the other hand, dogs with black masks or dark masks require dark hazel eyes even when their body color is light. The eyes must be of a medium size, not too small nor too large. Little, beady eyes yield too hard and piercing an expression while large prominent eyes are equally undesirable. In all instances, the eyes should be deep-set, protected under the brow that is accentuated by the "stop" and well shaded under shaggy eyebrows.

Ears—Small, pointed, well carried erectly, set wide apart on the side of the head. Free from long hairs.

This section of the Standard requires some explanation for proper ears well carried contribute strongly towards proper expression. The placement of the ears is controlled by the formation of the skull, to a major degree. A narrow skull will cause the ears to be too close set, while a typical broad skull will set them apart as required. The wording used in the Standard, "set—on the side of the head" is believed somewhat misleading and probably incorrect. Ears actually set on the side of the head will not be properly carried; they will be "mule-like" in carriage and will contribute to an improper and dull expression. The ears should be set on the *corners of the head* or skull. This will cause them to be widely separated yet carried well to offer an alert expression. The drawings of the several types of ears shown here clarify this statement. The ears must be pointed and not rounded at their extremities. Incorrectly shaped ears are seen now and then. The edges of the ears adjacent to their extremities require close trimming to eliminate long hairs and to accentuate the smallness of the ears. The overall trimming of the head aids this desideratum and will be explained in the chapter on trimming the Cairn.

Before leaving the portions of the Standard that deal with the head generally, mention of several descriptive terms used in connection with the head and expression should be discussed and clarified. This is offered in view of some confusion that has arisen through the use of such terms as "cat-faced," "baby-faced" and "foxy." The first has been variously interpreted and one school of thought suggests that the term means "small-headed" like a cat. This is not believed an accurate interpretation since small-headed Cairns, those with heads not in proportion to their bodies, seldom win and do not make good breeding partners. The term "cat-faced" is believed to refer more accurately to proportions of the head. A cat has a relatively broad skull, and a quite short foreface. The Cairn with proper conformation has the same. Thus, the Cairn's face may be described as "cat-like."

"Baby-face" is a less-frequently-used term and is directed to the same feature as noted heretofore. A baby has a small featured face even as the Cairn. Again, the term does not mean or suggest a very small head but rather one that is not exaggerated, one with a relatively strong skull and small features such as the muzzle, etc. In neither instance is the term suggestive of an overly small head out-of-proportion with the body, and winning Cairns through the years have ably supported these contentions.

The term "foxy" found in the Standard's paragraph on "General Appearance" is quite descriptive of the general appearance of the Cairn's head, although there was strong controversy concerning the

The Cairn Terrier Standard uses the word *foxy* to describe the Cairn's typical expression. It is of interest to study the fox mask shown here and compare it to the dog. The greatest difference between the two is in amount and distribution of facial hair.

use of the term in times gone by. In Kate Stephens' book on the Cairn, the author decries its use while the Rev. Caspersz in his treatise on the breed suggests that the term is probably correct. In this author's opinion, the term is entirely satisfactory. The Cairn does have a "foxy outlook" as caused by the broad skull terminating in a generally pointed and relatively light muzzle. The skull structure is required to support the strong muscles that operate the jaws which are armed with a set of teeth much larger than one would believe possible for such a small dog. Thus, the Cairn, as the Fox, has great punishing power without bulk or bulliness in muzzle. A fox mask is reproduced here to show the similarity in head proportions. Add some furnishings to the Fox's muzzle, supply him with shaggy eyebrows and less prominent eyes and there would be little to choose between the two. Surely, the Cairn has a "foxy expression."

Tail—In proportion to the head, well furnished with hair but not feathery. Carried gaily but must not curl over back. Set on at back level.

This section is rather clear in most respects. The tail is natural, and never docked, should be relatively short and never extend much above the head level when the tail and head are in an alert position. This is the general rule although some tails are shorter and some longer than suggested. Extremes in either instance will cause the tail to be out of proportion with the remainder of the dog. The tail must be well covered with hair and it should be tidied up to remove feathery, flying hair and is preferably tapered to a point at its outer extremity. At the base, the tail should be well furnished with hair so

179

as to appear as an "inverted carrot," a useful description. The set-on should be at back level so that there is no drop off from top-line to base of tail. Proper set-on enhances the top line, makes the back appear a bit shorter and in general offers a more pleasing over-all appearance. The tail should be carried up when the dog is moving and if well-carried naturally, when standing, is a big plus in the show ring. "Heading and tailing" in the ring always detracts to some extent from the overall impression gained by the judge. Most Cairns carry their tail curved slightly towards the head when alert and when moving. This is not the curl mentioned in the Standard which, in reality, refers to a "squirrely" tail, one that has a decided curve or curl. Incidentally, early Cairn Terriers did not carry their tails fully upright but rather at about "three-quarters mast"; such a carriage should not be penalized severely although it surely does not offer as alert an overall picture as a fully upright tail.

Body—Well muscled, strong, active body with well sprung, deep ribs, coupled to strong hindquarters with a level back of medium length, giving an impression of strength and activity without heaviness.

The body of a Cairn is much like that of the West Highlander in that the ribs, while well sprung and deep to offer sufficient heart and lung capacity, are not as rounded as those of the Scottish Terrier. This means that the ribs are more or less heart-shaped in cross section so that the dog appears a bit flat-sided. This is important since the Cairn is a worker that must force his way through narrow rocky crevices where the entry is often limited and without the opportunity to dig it larger. The Cairn requires depth and spring of rib, however, to assure adequate heart and lung room as required by his arduous work. The back is not long nor is it very short. However, overly long backs are just as undesirable as extremely short ones and offer an ungainly weasel-like appearance. The back should be level when standing or moving and should never rise towards the stern. Such a fault is ungainly and generally indicates improper angulation of rear legs.

Shoulders, Legs and Feet—A sloping shoulder, medium length of leg, good but not too heavy bone; forelegs should not be out at the elbows, and be perfectly straight, but forefeet may be turned slightly out, Forefeet larger than hindfeet. Legs must be covered with hard hair. Pads should be thick and strong and the dog should stand well up on his feet.

A "sloping shoulder" is the first statement that needs clarification and expansion. The Cairn Terrier, as any other Terrier breed, requires

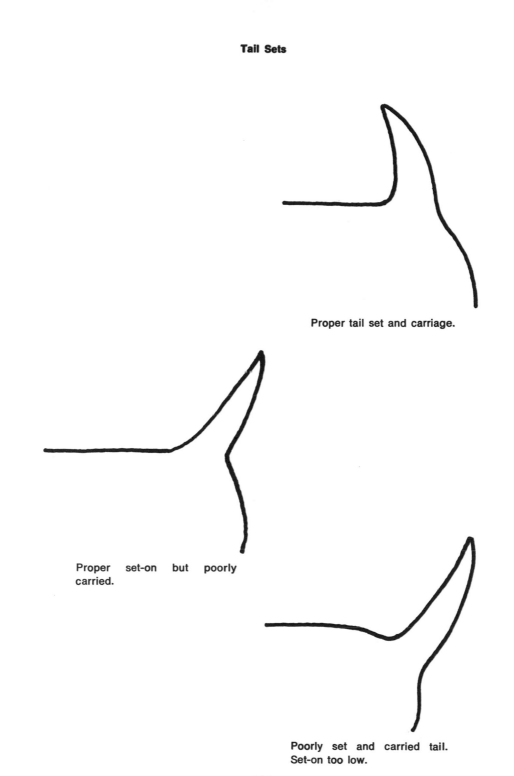

Proper tail set and carriage.

Proper set-on but poorly carried.

Poorly set and carried tail. Set-on too low.

good shoulder placement *and* correspondingly good rear angulation. In front, the angle between the scapula and the humerus should be in the order of 90°, resulting in a "well laid back shoulder." To correspond, the angle between the upper thigh (femur) and the lower thigh (tibia) should be the same. Lack of proper angulation in front results in short necks with the length of back being extended. If too steep behind, the dog may appear to be "built up" or have a high rump. Surely, it will lack drive. Unequal angulation between the front and rear results in apparent lack of coordination, dragging or tracking. In either instance, the movement is poor and impeded. Proper angulation results in a free, long stride, well coordinated in front and rear.

A point not mentioned concerns the width of the front. It should be moderately broad with the front legs separated. They should never "come out of the same hole." Again, moderation is the ideal, since too narrow a front is just as objectionable as too wide a front.

The length of leg for a proper Cairn is a "happy medium" between a short leg and a long one. Reference to the photos of top winners will indicate the desired length of leg. Let it be said that, in general, the tendency is towards too short legs rather than too long ones. The Cairn must be able to scamper over rocks and rough terrain and a dog with legs that are too short will expend much greater energy than one with the proper length of limb. The bone of a Cairn falls into much the same category, not too much nor too little. A proper dog should have sufficient bone to make him sturdy without appearing cloddy. Too little bone offers a "weedy appearance." Obviously the dog should not be out at the elbows and should have reasonably straight legs. I personally have never seen "perfectly straight" legs and a slight deviation does not seem to hamper any dog in its work or in the ring. The forefeet *must* turn out. The term "may" is believed misleading for any short-legged digging dog with feet pointed straight ahead will soon dig himself in. Short-legged diggers must throw the dirt sideways and the only way that this can be accomplished is by having turned out feet. Thick, strong pads are a necessity for digging as are tight feet that will make the dog stand well up on his feet. Splay feet, weak and thin pads are all serious faults for any digging dog.

Coat—Hard and weather resistant. Must be double-coated with profuse harsh outer coat and short, soft, close furry undercoat.

This paragraph will apply to all double-coated Terriers. Texture, density and proper undercoat are all necessities for a proper covering.

Rib Structures

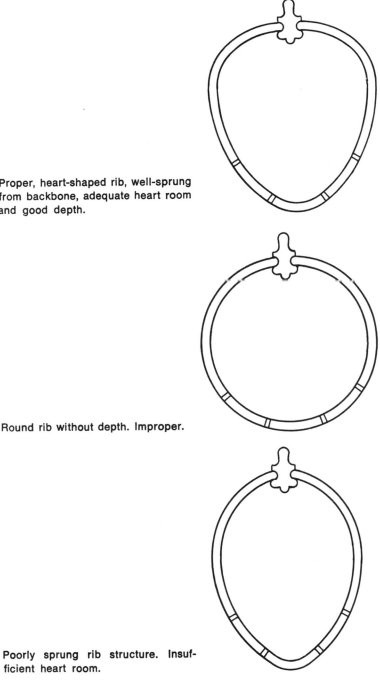

Proper, heart-shaped rib, well-sprung from backbone, adequate heart room and good depth.

Round rib without depth. Improper.

Poorly sprung rib structure. Insufficient heart room.

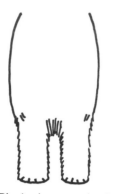

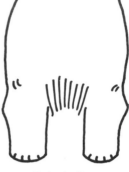

Pinched, narrow front. Fox Terrier-like.

Crooked legs. Out at elbow.

Out at elbow.

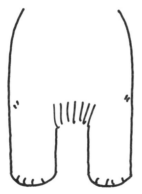

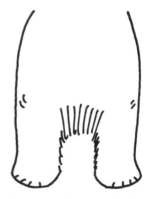

Straight front of proper width. Generally acceptable.

A proper Cairn front. Generally straight legs, proper width and feet turning out slightly.

184

The coat acts as a protection against the weather, teeth of foes and to protect the dog against scratches from brambles and the like.

Color—May be any color except white. Dark ears, muzzle and tail tip are desirable.

Again the item is not well expressed. The wording would permit a parti-colored dog to be shown and this is certainly not within the concepts of the breed. Shadings, such as dark points are permitted and are desirable as noted, but spots are surely not contemplated.

Ideal Size—Involves the weight, the height at the withers and the length of the body. Weight for bitches 13 pounds, for dogs 14 pounds. Height at withers—bitches 9½", dogs 10". Length of body from 14¼" to 15" from the front of the chest to back of hindquarters. The dog must be of balanced proportions and appear neither leggy or too low to the ground; and neither too short or too long in body. Weight and measurements are for matured dogs at two years of age. Older dogs may weigh slightly in excess and growing dogs under these weights and measurements.

This section is self-explanatory but requires some comments in connection with its inflexible height and weight specifications. This author has always believed that weight limits may be inserted as a guide but not as a judging criteria. Two dogs of different bone and substance may weigh a pound or more apart. Also, a dog in top condition will weigh more than one that is in poor condition. Thus, weight is useful as a guide but should not be taken too seriously without considering many other variables. Further, without actually weighing the dog, no one can estimate within a pound with any accuracy. While the Standard does not so state, Cairns do vary as to height and a good dog of 10½ inches in height should certainly not be beaten by a less desirable specimen that measures the desideratum.

Condition—Dogs should be shown in good hard flesh, well muscled and neither too fat or thin. Should be in full good coat with plenty of head furnishings, be clean, combed, brushed and tidied up on ears, tail, feet and general outline. Should move freely and easily on a loose lead, should not cringe on being handled, should stand up on their toes, and show with marked terrier characteristics.

This section covers a great deal of ground and relates to overall general condition with the added admonition that the dog should be unafraid and interested in the general proceedings in the ring. It also touches upon the subject of trimming which will be taken up separately here in the chapter on Trimming the Cairn Terrier.

*Faults—Under this section of the Standard concise statements re-

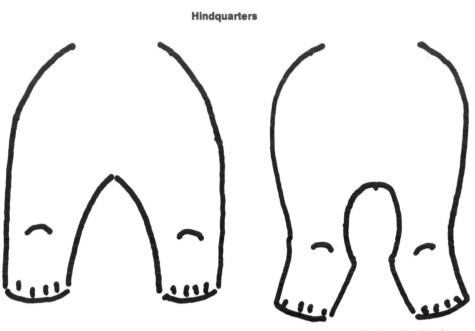

A strong rear structure with hocks parallel.

Undesirable. Cowhocks (hocks turning in, causing weak quarters).

garding faults are listed for each of the structural characteristics as follows:

1. SKULL—*Too narrow in skull.*
2. MUZZLE—*Too long and heavy a foreface. Mouth over or undershot.*
3. EYES—*Too large, prominent, yellow, ringed, are all objectionable.*
4. EARS—*Too large, round at points, set too close together, set too high on head; heavily covered with hair.*
5. LEGS AND FEET—*Too light or too heavy bone. Crooked forelegs or out at the elbow. Thin ferrety feet; feet let down on the heel or too open and spread. Too high or too low on leg.*
6. BODY—*Too short back and compact a body, hampering quickness of movement and turning ability. Too long, weedy and snaky a body giving an impression of weakness. Tail set on too low. Back not level.*
7. COAT—*Open coats, blousy coats, too short or dead coats, lack of sufficient under coat, lack of head furnishings, lack of hard hair on legs. Silkiness or curliness. A slight wave is permissible.*

186

8. NOSE—*Flesh or light-colored nose.*

9. COLOR—*White on chest, feet or other parts of body.*

Summary

This closes the chapter on the Standard and its interpretation. There are many who will disagree with certain of my statements and this is their prerogative. However, the comments offered have been arrived at after many years of observing and judging the best Cairns exhibited in America and observing the best that have been exhibited in England over the past ten or twelve years. Further, these points of argument have been discussed objectively with many of the most successful breeders and exhibitors of the Cairn Terrier, on both sides of the Atlantic. In general, most agree with my conclusions. Whether you agree or disagree, it is believed that a full and complete study of this chapter with careful application of the points discussed to dogs being shown today will be beneficial to both the new and the old breeders. Truly, the Standard is a document that should be studied and understood for:

> When thou seest a closed bag containing
> many things, be not hasty in deciding their
> qualities. Open it, and examine for thyself;
> thou mayest then be enabled to form a just
> opinion.
>
> Anon.

Ch. Cairnwood's Quince enjoyed a brilliant career as a top winner and great producer. He lived to a ripe, old age and the breed is better for his contributions. In this photo, taken at just 20 months, he was already showing some indications of his future promise. *Evelyn Shafer.*

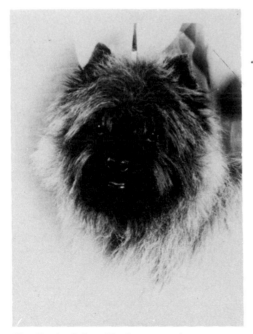

Ch. Gayla Cairns Tucker, owned by Nancy J. Thompson.

11

Raising and Training Show Stock

'T'HE CARE, training and conditioning of good show stock requires a great amount of time and study. Show dogs do not "just grow" like Topsy—they are brought along carefully and many a dog that would otherwise become an average specimen may be groomed and nurtured into a show prospect through intelligent care. I do not mean that a poorly conformed animal can be changed into a winner; but many an average dog has done well in the ring through care and training, while many a good prospect has been ruined for exhibition purposes through lack of diligence in its rearing.

Grading Puppies

The average well-bred litter will include one or two youngsters worth working with for a span of the first five or six months, at which time a more accurate estimate of their potentialities may be made. In choosing the most promising puppies in a litter, it is best to appraise coat, compare length of back to height and study the length to breadth proportions of head. The cutest puppies, those with the profuse and/or fuzzy coats, generally mature with soft open coats requiring untold work to get into show shape and which even then are on the poor side. Of course, if a puppy is otherwise outstanding, the balance may swing in its favor. A proper length of back, strong quarters, and well-balanced, short-muzzled head are necessities when choosing your future champion so give these factors plenty of consideration before disposing of surplus puppies.

It is a good idea to keep your first litter for at least six months in order to get an idea of how various points improve and retrogress. A little attention given the first litter will possess you of valuable information and experience that will pay off in subsequent litters. In this connection, it will aid tremendously in the choosing of promising puppies to watch the litter at play at a sufficient distance so that your presence is not a distraction. By this observation you can find out which puppy is the leader, the one that is "boss." Such an animal is generally an extrovert and will show well in the ring. You will also be able to observe natural tail carriage, ear set and general balance a great deal better than can be accomplished by having the puppies on a table where they are not at ease and are usually very tense.

Added to these tests, find out which puppies like people the best, which ones come to strangers and which keep their tails and ears up when being handled. When these individual characteristics of the puppies have been determined, it will often be easier to decide which you want to keep, for a well-conformed dog that is not easily handled will be of little use in the ring. Of course, no irrevocable decision should ever be made until after six months of age.

Conditioning

Feeding, first of the dam and then of the puppies is important throughout the span of a dog's life, and is of utmost importance during the formative stages. For this reason, feed plenty of animal protein food for substance, muscle and nerves, together with bone building foods and a reasonable balance of carbohydrates, fats, etc. The diet should also contain calcium and vitamin supplements in the form of calcium salts, fish liver oils, preferably fortified, irradiated yeast, etc., although all supplements should be used with reason since too much is often as harmful as too little.

The formation of strong bone and muscle is necessary if the dog is to develop properly. Weak, rickety puppies seldom get the growth required nor do their legs develop well. In fact, most weak puppies end up with bench legs, crooked and sorry looking. Old time breeders appreciated these facts and a poem found in Hugh Dalziel's book on *Diseases of the Dog* written in 1900 is apropos:

> There's some is born with their straight legs by natur,
> And some is born with bow legs from the fu'st—
> And some that should have growed a good deal straighter,
> But they was badly nu'ssed.

The moral is clear—nurse them well, that is feed properly and let nature take its course.

Exercise, too, is required by dogs of all ages and can best be given to puppies in a good sized run either indoor or outdoor according to the weather. As soon as the youngsters can safely be taken outside they should be given the benefit of the sun's rays during hours of healthy play. If you can arrange an enclosed run sheltered with plastic-coated wire netting such as sold for chicken houses, etc., you will be able to give your puppies the benefit of the sun without exposing them to the weather. Such material does not filter out the ultraviolet rays as does ordinary glass.

Developing the Coat

At about eight weeks of age, strip off all flying, fluffy top coat. This will permit normal growth of healthy hair which will develop into a good, tight, straight coat, a great benefit to the dog in later life. Daily grooming of the coat from eight weeks on in the form of brushing will aid immeasurably in improving its density, texture and bloom.

Ears

While working initially on the coat, it is a good idea to remove the hair from the ears. This will lighten the ears and make it possible for them to stand erect. As a rule, a puppy's ears will rise normally to a half-prick position and then go fully erect. This may occur simultaneously with both ears or one may go up followed by the other a few days later. Once up, the ears may drop several times before standing permanently. In general, the ears should go up at from eight to 12 weeks of age. In this connection, there is a definite relationship between teething and ear carriage. When the puppy begins to shed its first dentition, the ears react. Ears that have been tightly erect, may drop for a few days—ears that have never stood erect, may go up. So do not become alarmed if the ear changes during teething. This does not suggest that ears that are not erect or that droop during teething should be neglected—they should not. Watch them carefully and follow the necessary steps, if the carriage does not improve.

Worming

Puppies should be wormed at about six weeks of age for ascarids (stomach or round worms), preferably with the advice of a veterinarian concerning the vermifuge and dosage to be used. If no worms are expelled, do not worm again for about four weeks; if worms are apparent, repeat the treatment in a week's time. Two admonitions are of great importance: first, overworming is the worst thing you can do to a puppy or dog, and may cause arrested development in young stock and a highly nervous condition in a dog of any age; second, never worm a sick dog or puppy. If the animal is not healthy and full of pep, do not worm without a veterinarian's advice. After a puppy has attained the age of four to five months, no worming should be done unless you actually see evidence in the stool and can identify the type of parasite. If you cannot identify the type or see no worms, do not dose without consulting a veterinarian. He can make a microscopic examination of the dog's feces to determine whether worms are present and the type thereof, and then prescribe the proper vermifuge and dosage, for the weight of dog involved. A prominent veterinarian once said "promiscuous worming has killed more dogs than the worms" and any experienced dog breeder will bear out this statement. Therefore, do not over-worm or promiscuously worm your dog but consult some one who knows the answers and will have a happier and healthier dog.

Further, all puppies should be protected against distemper at an early age. First by isolating them from any dogs that have been in contact with dogs outside of the kennel, and second by prophalaxsis and/or immunization administered by a competent veterinarian.

Teething

At approximately four months of age, the average puppy commences to lose its puppy teeth and acquires a permanent set. This teething period continues from one to two months according to the individual puppy. During this time, special attention should be given to the mouth. Experience has shown that the puppy teeth do not always fall out or shed normally. For this reason, if you see a permanent tooth crowding in alongside a puppy tooth, quickly extract the

192

offender and give the permanent tooth a chance to grow in straight. If you cannot remove the tooth yourself, enlist the aid of a veterinarian—although milk teeth generally come out easily since they have very little root. Many poor mouths can be attributed to failure to care for the teeth during teething, when the mouth was made poor by the owner's dereliction. As a breed, the Cairn has a good mouth so keep watch over the teeth and there is little to offer further concern.

Ear Carriage and Teething

As mentioned heretofore, during the teething period, ears do funny things. Some ears will not stand erect before the puppy teethes, while others that have been up will drop. Personally, I prefer to help ears that are not erect at four months or which have dropped during teething. This may be done by either rolling them and taping them together at the desired distance or by forming a tape backing for the ears and then taping them together. Either method is satisfactory. Another approach is to brush the ear at its inside and outside surfaces with collodion. When this hardens, the film offers sufficient support to cause the ear to stand. In general, taping, etc., strengthens weak ear cartilage and helps set the ears. Some ears may not stand for a long time and the taping must be repeated. The tape should be left on for a week or ten days and then removed before the ears become sore. Boric acid powder dusted around the base of the ears helps to prevent soreness.

Lead Breaking and Handling

At about five months of age, the puppy is ready for preliminary show training. Lead breaking is the first step. This may be most easily accomplished by first permitting the puppy to wear a light show collar for a day or two. The next step is to attach a lead to the collar and try gently to lead the dog. If he has a mind of his own, and most have, merely hold the lead and let the puppy balk and pull for about ten minutes. Repeat the lesson daily, for a few days, and you will notice that the dog's distrust of the lead lessens and that you can finally lead him around. In about a week's time, the puppy will permit leading for a walk. This should be short at first, as young dogs tire easily, gradually increasing in length until at eight months, the puppy is walked about a mile a day in two periods. This early lead training means much in later show experience. You will have a dog that does

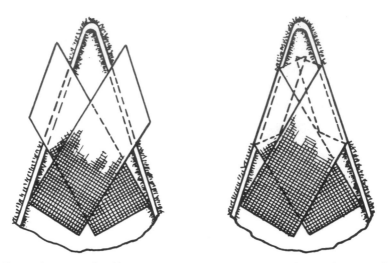

To apply a tape backing on an ear use two or more pieces of tape and apply to each ear as shown. Criss cross the tape and apply at front of ear. Cup the tape so that ears are upright and then tape ears together as shown on facing page.

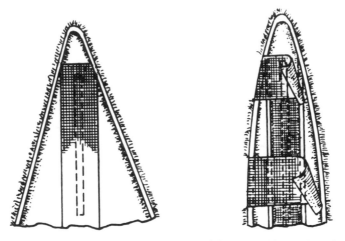

To roll ears use a portion of a toothpick as a splint and apply to front of ear as shown with adhesive tape. Next, roll ear by wrapping two strips of tape as shown. Finally, tape ears together as shown on facing page.

not fight the lead, moves easily and without fear, and is under complete control. Teach the pup to move on either a loose or tight lead, at your left side, without pulling. Endeavor also to keep the ears and tail up by constant talking and periodic bribing with small pieces of liver or other choice tidbits. This makes the puppy a good showman and many an inferior dog has beaten a better specimen on showmanship alone. A good dog that does not make the best of itself is a hard animal to judge and is a complete disappointment to its owner while a good showman is always the "judge's friend."

Let the puppy run about the kennel or house while you are around and always keep tidbits in your pocket. Let the dog take a nibble occasionally and, before long, you will have the youngster looking up at you even when being walked. This makes his exhibition a pleasure. During all walks with your puppy stop periodically and pose him as you would in the ring, make him stand with tail up and ears erect and with his neck well up. This gets him used to ring procedure and adds immeasurably to his showmanship.

It is also useful to have someone not known to the puppy examine him now and then. This merely requires overall handling of the puppy and does not require knowledge; anyone can do it. At the same time, have the lips lifted and gums and teeth examined; this will eliminate future antics when the judge wants to examine the bite.

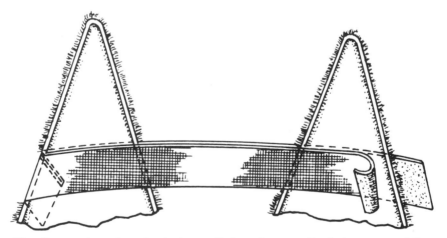

After the ears have been backed, or rolled as shown on the facing page, set them the proper distance apart with a longer strip of tape as shown above. Apply another strip on other side of ears so that tapes are adhered together. Be sure that ears are free to move and that tape is not adhered to head hair.

195

Lead breaking should be followed by walking your hopeful in congested areas where cars and people pass. This accustoms the puppy to the very atmosphere of a dog show with its excitement, noise and many strangers. A dog that does not shy at such things out-shows one that does.

Car and Crate Training

It is also a good idea to train young dogs to ride in a car and in a crate for several weeks before starting to show them. In this manner, much of the excitement of their first few shows is eliminated as they ride like veterans and are comfortable and used to riding and crating. When first breaking a puppy to this experience, teach him to sleep in a crate by substituting it for his regular sleeping box. After a week of this, and when he is perfectly comfortable in the crate, take him for a short ride in it. Take him to the store or village several times for short rides. After a while he may be taken for longer rides until such time as he is perfectly broken to riding in a crate. By following this course of training, the puppy arrives at this first show fresh, not sick and scared as would have been the case had he not been properly trained.

In the event that he tends to be car-sick, you may administer a sedative prescribed by your veterinarian before you start out. This will calm his nerves and relieve car sickness to a marked degree. After several rides, you will probably not have to worry since most dogs are good travelers and like to ride.

All of the foregoing may seem like a great deal of trouble and work—and it IS—but few, if any, dogs ever become top show animals without exhaustive training prior to reaching the ring. This is one of the reasons why professional handlers do so well — they generally spend time with their charges *before* they begin to show the animals.

Grooming

Grooming your dog is the most important single item towards good show condition. This chapter will discuss general grooming techniques and requirements exclusive of show trimming, which will be expanded upon in a chapter to follow on "Trimming the Cairn." Grooming should begin at about two months of age and continue throughout the dog's life. Five to ten minutes vigorous brushing every day will do more good for the texture and growth of a dog's coat than any other treatment. It will also stimulate the skin and cause a flow of natural oils thereby creating a healthy skin condition. At each grooming period, loose flying hairs should be plucked out and very little combing should be done since this tends to remove too much undercoat.

Encouraging Coat Growth

In order to further stimulate the growth of hair at selected points, warm olive oil massaged into the skin is good. This is especially helpful around the muzzle and on the legs as it softens hard furnishings and, thus, prevents the whisker and feather from breaking off. Rain water lightly brushed into the hair is also a growth stimulant and will aid in bringing out the bloom.

Care of Nails

Another frequent task concerns nails; these should be cut back with nail clippers and then filed a little each day or two to keep them very short. This is especially true on the front feet since the nails on the rear feet wear off more rapidly than those in front. Short nails improve a dog's feet and make them more compact, while long nails tend to splay the foot and break down the pasterns. This task should start early, at about eight weeks and continue throughout the dog's life. Further, once the "quick," or vein in the nail, has retracted, the process is quickly and easily accomplished.

Teeth

Teeth should also be cleaned periodically and this may be paced by the time required for a noticeable build-up of tartar on the teeth. This appears on the canines and molars near the gum line and is the reason that it is necessary to remove it before the build-up becomes sufficient to cause a receding of the gums. Periodic brushing of the teeth with a regular tooth brush dipped in bicarbonate of soda and/or salt will do a great deal towards maintaining healthy gums and clean teeth. If the tartar does not come off it may be necessary to scrape or chip it off with a dental pick using great care not to injure the gums. In this operation, if you are not proficient, let your veterinarian do the work.

Ears and Eyes

Ears and eyes should also be carefully watched. Bloodshot eyes may be eased with an ophthalmic ointment if the condition is caused by local irritation such as dirt, or by wind. If the eyes do not clear up within a day, the aid of a veterinarian should be enlisted promptly. Ears generally do not require any attention other than a periodic superficial cleaning but they should be watched carefully so that canker does not gain a foothold. If the dog either scratches his ears constantly or continually shakes his head, the ears may be in trouble and careful examination should be accorded with prompt remedial treatment if indicated.

These are the major items of care that come under the general heading of this chapter. Early training, conditioning and general hints on physical care are useful and will become a habit after you have raised a few litters. Knowledgeable dog people do the many things set forth in this chapter as a matter of course and if asked what to do, they would be hard pressed to tell you. In any event, following the suggestions here will cause your puppy to grow into a better dog, physically and show-wise and certainly will eliminate many of the difficulties that may arise had you not followed the prescribed course of action.

12

Breeding Rules and Axioms

$\mathbf{W}$HEN a person becomes interested in breeding
Cairns the usual question is, "What is the best way to start?" Such
a query has a multitude of answers, many of which may be good
counsel. However, I believe the soundest advice that can be given
the tyro is to obtain a good, high-quality, well-bred bitch. With this
start, years of heartaches and disappointments can be avoided. To
investigate the problem further, it should be understood that the
breeding of show dogs, show horses, and, in fact, any livestock is
never easy. Persistence is generally rewarded and to those who have
tasted this reward, the work is worthy of the effort. To quote a successful English breeder—"To attain continued success needs patience and
endurance and the optimistic temperament of never-ending hope."
Many new converts to the sport of showing Cairns, buy a good specimen, show it with better than average success and then start to breed
with the thought that this success will carry over to the progeny. This
is not always the fact.

Most persons seeking breeding success begin in the wrong way and,
thus, delay their ultimate goal many years. There is no short-cut to
high quality and, therefore, the use of inferior stock only prolongs
the time required to produce winners. Of course, there are instances
where a fine dog has come from parents of mediocre type but these

cases are indeed rare and such dogs seldom reproduce their own quality.

The Foundation Matron

The surest and quickest way to be successful, which is attested to by all leading breeders of any kind of livestock, is to acquire the best matron obtainable, one of high quality and unquestioned pedigree, and then line or in-breed her to the best stud dog available. Offspring of this mating may not be the ultimate but the choice of the litter will generally be good foundation stock. No successful kennel has ever perpetuated the breed without an abundance of top quality bitches. Good stud dogs are many and are available to all, but a good bitch is a rare asset whose value cannot be overestimated.

Thus, honest and sound advice to anyone endeavoring to begin breeding operations is to get a *good* bitch. This does not mean a puppy, but preferably a proven brood bitch (not over five years old) of successful bloodlines. Breed her well and if only one litter is whelped she has done her part in the long term program. From this litter, select the best one or two female puppies, if there is a choice, and breed them in the same family, as suggested in more detail hereinafter. The offspring of this second generation breeding will usually be of quality and will stand a chance in the show ring if properly "put down," trained and shown.

Evaluating Breeding Stock

Don't be "kennel blind." This affliction is defined as the inability, or *lack of desire,* to see faults in your own stock. *No dog is perfect.* Be critical, for to paraphrase Pope:

> Whoever thinks a faultless dog to see,
> Thinks what ne'er was, nor is, nor e'er shall be.

Look for and see the faults in your dog. Without knowing these shortcomings, you can never overcome them by intelligent breeding. On the other hand, appreciate good points and use this appreciation objectively in the choice of young stock. Study the pedigree of your bitch and learn as much as possible about her forebears, their family good points and their family faults. With this information, you can breed away from these faults by proper selection of a stud dog.

Choosing a Stud Dog

Family failings are of great importance and generally overshadow individual faults. A dog from a family of poor-coated dogs, even though its coat is passable, will throw poor-coated dogs more often than not. Conversely, a dog with a mediocre coat from a good-coated family will usually pass this fault to only a small number of its offspring. Family faults are difficult to overcome and intelligent breeding is the only means of rectifying the mistakes of previous breeders.

This does not mean that you should only breed families, for at the same time you should not overlook individual faults. In selecting two individuals for breeding purposes, try not only to select dogs that do not exhibit family faults, but who are also free from glaring individual faults. Endeavor to complement your breeding stock—try to use a stud that is strong in the weak points of the bitch and vice versa. In this manner, you are combating faults from two or three different approaches. Never perpetuate a fault by breeding in a manner likely to strengthen that fault.

Character is all-important when selecting a stud dog. Bitchy dogs rarely produce well, nor do weedy, weak-boned dogs make good sires. A dog that is masculine, of good size and full of fire, with proper bone and substance has the best chance to pass on his good points. Such a dog is said to have "plenty to give." An excellent example was the dog Harviestoun Raider; he was too much dog for show purposes but he surely left his mark as a sire.

Prepotency

Some stud dogs have the elusive quality of prepotency. Definition of this term is difficult; suffice it to say that it is the ability to reproduce good qualities. A prepotent stud, when used with the same bitches will sire, on an average, more good puppies than a dog of equal type that is not possessed of this quality. Certain dogs seem to have it while others do not. Therefore, when choosing a stud, endeavor to find one that is prepotent and this may best be determined by his success as a sire. Champion dogs are not always the best studs; many fine dogs never enter the ring but produce as well or better than some of the "popular" studs of the day. Again, Raider is a good example. Therefore, evaluate the situation and choose a dog that meets specific requirements, rather than the champion of the moment who may not be the best niche for your bitch.

Complementing the Bitch

Another point of great importance is to always use the dog that will best complement your bitch. Too many breeders, use their own studs because of convenience. By so doing they are frequently perpetuating faults that could be overcome by a more objective approach. Remember, the real expense in raising good dogs is the time consumed; the months and sometimes years that must be expended to up-grade your stock. A stud fee is but a fraction of this cost and a worthy investment if you want to move forward. So never use your own dog if he does not offer the greatest benefits to the bitch involved. This does not mean that if you have a suitable stud that he should not be used but it does suggest that convenience is not a short-cut to improved quality.

Age of Breeding Stock

Age is another consideration. It is generally conceded that old bitches produce better when bred to younger dogs and vice versa. Animals within the range of two to five years old may be bred together but older animals are best bred to young, virile mates while very young animals niche better with consorts of greater maturity.

The Bitch's Type

The bitch's type and character is also of great importance. Many astute breeders say that a bitchy or feminine bitch is best but no less an authority than A. G. Cowley (one of the most successful breeders of Scottish Terriers) allowed that a doggy bitch was the best producer. The argument could be enlarged upon but with little gain so, to repeat, the bitch should be as good an individual as you can afford and can obtain. It is an absolute fallacy to keep bitches for brood purposes that are not good enough to show. Wise breeders have for centuries followed the course of using only the best. The true strength of any kennel resides in its bitches. Somerville, more than two hundred years ago, gave this counsel:

> Watch o'er the bitches with a cautious eye,
> And separate such as are going to be proud.

This is as good advice today as it was then for seldom does a bitch amount to much that is not "proud" as exemplified by temperament, bearing and courage.

Line Breeding and Inbreeding

Certain breeding formulas have proved to yield the most satisfying rewards. Breeding in a line and inbreeding, as a rule, produces the quickest, best and surest results.

Line breeding may be defined broadly as breeding within the same family and it has been used in this context heretofore. Specifically, however, and according to most authorities, line breeding is concerned with the mating of two individuals, one of which is an ancestor of the other: for example, grandsire to granddaughter. *Inbreeding,* on the other hand, is defined as the breeding of two related individuals, neither of which is an ancestor of the other and, generally, not over two generations removed. For example, half-brother to half-sister, first cousin to first cousin, etc. Both inbreeding and line breeding bring out recessive as well as dominant factors and it is for this reason that family background is so important. Line breeding accentuates recessives to a lesser degree than inbreeding. Both types may be practiced with great success if careful selection of the mating partners is practiced together with careful choice of the progeny for subsequent breeding operations.

Out Breeding

A third type of breeding formula, is known as *out breeding.* This is concerned with the mating of two unrelated, or distantly related individuals. The latter is generally the case. Even here, it will be found that most modern Cairns are related in the sixth or seventh generation. All of these formulas have produced well with the first two being the most successful for obvious reasons.

Random Breeding

There is one other type of breeding formula which is used more frequently than any other and this may be termed "random breeding" for want of a more appropriate term. Unfortunately, this is the path followed by the majority and the reason there are so many poor specimens of every breed seen on the streets. This is directed to the practice of breeding a bitch to the dog that is available at the lowest cost in spite of faults, bloodlines or what have you. The results are nearly always the same—poor stock, generally poorer than either of the parents, which downgrades the breed with each successive generation.

It has another unhappy result; when one of the bitches from this progression falls into the hands of a sincere person who wants to breed properly, it will generally require generations to straighten out the past mistakes. This is the reason that it is recommended that any person starting as a breeder buy as good and as well-bred a bitch as possible. It will cut years off the tedious road to success.

Points to Consider

When practicing line and inbreeding the breeder should keep close check on the size and virility of the stock produced. It has been found that, when too close breeding of this character is carried on for several generations, a tendency does sometime develop towards loss of size, and loss of virility. These tendencies have been proved by experiments conducted with mice and rats. For example, Weisman and Von Guaiti in-bred mice for 35 generations and found that the average per litter dropped from an initial 6.1 to a final 2.9. Ritzema Bos when experimenting with rats found that inbreeding was also responsible for loss in size. Average figures showed a 20% decrease in weight of offspring at the end of six years of breeding.

Of course dog breeders would not repeat these techniques for as extended periods as did the researchers but the trend has been proved and when the evidence of these problems becomes apparent, it is best to breed out of the line. This does not necessarily mean a complete out-cross, even if one is available, but the use of a rather distant relative. The progeny of this mating may be bred back into the original line.

This word of caution is to allay the fears of many concerning the alleged "evils" of line and inbreeding. Selective breeding close up has always been the surest and quickest way to "set" good points and since no moral issues prevail in nature, every breeder should take advantage of these formulas, tempering their zeal with a constructive and critical eye on the results of their efforts.

Why Line and Inbreeding Work

The reasons behind the success of line and inbreeding may be explained by the theories expressed in the laws of heredity. Study of these theories will help explain many factors which are otherwise difficult to understand. Heredity is, however, a very extensive study. Many excellent books are available that delve deeply into the subject. For this reason, only a very short resume of the theories will be stated here.

The hereditary influence may be broadly surveyed by the application of the Law of Ancestral Influence. This law may best be defined as the diminishing influence of each successive generation of ancestors upon the inherited traits of a given dog. The parents are said to contribute 50% (25% each), the grandparents 25% ($6\frac{1}{4}$% each), great grandparents $12\frac{1}{2}$% ($1\frac{9}{16}$% each) and so on ad infinitum.

Arithmetically broken down as to the influence of each ancestor in pedigree form, we find the following chart to be illustrative,

Parents (50%)	Grandparents (25%)	Great Grandparents ($12\frac{1}{2}$%)
	Grand Sire ($6\frac{1}{4}$%)	G.G. Sire ($1\frac{9}{16}$%)
		G.G. Dam ($1\frac{9}{16}$%)
Sire (25%)		G.G. Sire ($1\frac{9}{16}$%)
	Grand Dam ($6\frac{1}{4}$%)	G.G. Dam ($1\frac{9}{16}$%)
	Grand Sire ($6\frac{1}{4}$%)	G.G. Sire ($1\frac{9}{16}$%)
		G.G. Dam ($1\frac{9}{16}$%)
Dam (25%)		G.G. Sire ($1\frac{9}{16}$%)
	Grand Dam ($6\frac{1}{4}$%)	G.G. Dam ($1\frac{9}{16}$%)

From this graphic representation, it will be seen that the more distant the ancestor, the less its influence on the dog. This also explains why line and inbreeding is useful. Either type of breeding reduces the number of individual relatives, increases their influence and thereby cuts down the variables with which we must deal.

Mendelism is the specific application of the laws of heredity as applied to a given factor or factors. Dominant and recessive characteristics may be charted so that when breeding two individuals having known backgrounds, the results may be predetermined within limits. It is generally impossible to obtain the known background of many characteristics of a given dog so that the application of the theory is sometimes difficult and often impossible to follow.

In color determination, however, it is very successful since the color of a dog is usually a known quantity and, thus, may be traced back through generations of breeding. For this reason, the color of progeny from two individuals may be forecast in many instances.

Other breeding factors are not as easily predetermined by Mendelian formula due to unknown quantities in the backgrounds of the stock. The complexity of the problem is further increased by the fact that the same laws apply with equal force and effect to all characteristics for all puppies in a litter. If an experimental breeding can be made, and, if a breeder is patient and willing to sacrifice two or three breedings, he may predetermine certain factors which will be of benefit in future matings as well as in subsequent breeding operations. In general, however, the broad theory (so far as dogs are concerned) finds its greatest success in color determination.

Breeding Axioms

Much of the foregoing advice is succinctly offered by a series of four axioms set forth by the late W. L. McCandlish, author, judge and breeder. He proposed the following as rules to be followed, to which I have added some explanatory remarks:

"Like begets like". McCandlish says that this is more of a law than an axiom. The closer two animals are to one another in appearance and temperament, the greater the likelihood of the offspring being like the parents. Thus, if the parents are top specimens, the get should be good; if the parents are poor, the get will be poor or poorer.

"Breed to breed". Meaning never breed with a mere litter in mind but rather with *subsequent breedings* from the offspring being of *paramount consideration*. Proceed with the view that the progeny will have improved breeding value over either of the parents.

"Never breed from a second generation fault". Second generation faults are generally family faults and will continue to reproduce with ever-increasing strength. Conversely, second generation virtues indicate a dominant influence that is desirable.

"No animal is well bred unless it is good in itself". The axiom points out the fallacy of breeding to pedigree alone. The great majority of pedigreed animals are not show specimens. The axiom stresses the necessity of using only those with the best of conformation and temperament for breeding purposes.

13

Trimming and Conditioning the Cairn Terrier

THE ART of trimming a Cairn Terrier or any other double-coated, hard-haired dog, involves a great deal of ability and knowledge. It is not impossible to learn this art but it will take time and more than the usual tenacity of purpose to do so.

It must always be remembered that the Cairn *is not* a heavily trimmed breed. The Standard specifically says, *"tidied up on ears, tail, feet and general outline."* Of course the inclusion of the words, *"general outline"* brings in the whole dog and often causes the uninitiated to over-trim.

Trimming makes a dog look smarter and improves its general appearance just as a haircut or "hair do" improves the appearance of a man or woman. This operation takes a little time each day and the best trim may be decided upon by observation and comparison. In all cases, a dog's trim should be personalized. Trim to make the dog look *its* best by bringing out good points and hiding faults as much as possible; never use a stereotyped pattern.

Trimming to the Dog

In general, it should be understood that no two dogs are trimmed alike by the expert. One requires heavy trimming, another's coat should merely be thinned, while a third needs more coat with greater density. With this wide range of variables, it is apparent that proper trimming must be customized to suit each animal under consideration. Further, trimming may be used to minimize faults and bring out virtues. For example, if a dog is heavy in shoulder and too wide in front, the shoulders should be well trimmed down and the feather at the outsides of the front legs kept quite short so that the fault is minimized through eliminating unnecessary hair. If the dog is too narrow in front, the reverse treatment is accorded and a heavier coat is carried on the shoulder and at the outside of the legs. If a dog's tail is low set, hair should be taken off its underside and more hair should be cultivated on its frontside as well as on the hindquarters to offer the appearance of a better set-on. Large-eared dogs need more attention and closer trimming of the ear edges and more coat around and between the ears than small-eared ones. In other words, there can be no set trimming formula since the actual work on any dog must be carried out to present *that* dog in the best light, to accentuate good points and minimize known faults. For as Carlyle said:

> The greatest of faults I should say,
> is to be conscious of none.

Actually trimming is an art, there is no easy way to learn. Experience and knowledge are the only teachers. First, one must know how a good specimen of the breed should look and second, one must be able to properly fault one's dogs. With these two situations in hand, the trimming commences. Even now, if you are not adept at using stripping combs, thinning scissors and other paraphernalia you cannot do the work. Thus, it is apparent that it requires background and knowledge—tempered with more than average experience—to do a really good job.

These factors are among the reasons why professional handlers often do better in the ring than those who are not so experienced. The professional's dog is generally well put down while the novice-trimmed animal is often poorly presented. This should not cause discouragement but rather it should create the challenge to learn and to do better.

That all good dogs of the breed bear a resemblance to one another is a tribute to the trimmer's art, since these same dogs if stripped bare would often not look alike. Faults would appear that are entirely hidden by expert trimming. A good judge can find these faults, for

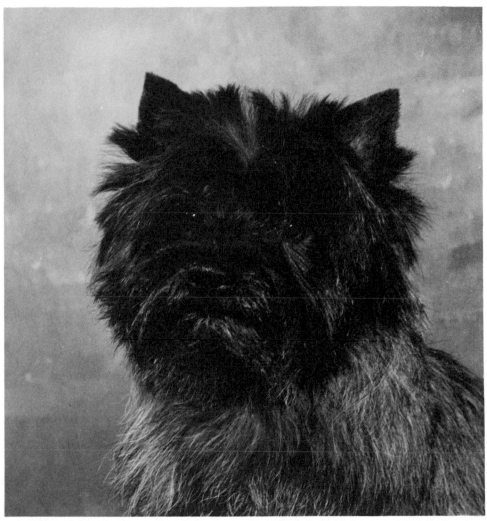

This attractive headstudy of Ch. Bellacairn's Bit O'Scotch illustrates good head trimming that enhances the desired "foxy" expression of the Cairn, but still honors the tradition of keeping the breed a natural, unspoiled terrier. *Missy Yuhl.*

he not only knows what he is looking for but he knows the devious ways used to hide faults and, by use of his hands, can quickly discover them.

Often one finds a straight stifled animal, almost "chow-hocked," that appears to have good angulation. Upon inspection, it will be found that much hair is trained to stand away from the hock. At the same time, hair has been grown on the thigh to round out an otherwise straight stifle. The overall picture is good but the bone structure is just as bad as before the expert went to work. So it goes—faults are minimized, good points are accentuated until the dog appears at his best.

Learning to Trim

The trimming charts offered here are about all the help anyone can give. The rest comes with experience, appreciation of conformation and a knowledge of what is required by the specific animal under consideration. The fine points of trimming can only be mastered by hard work, mistakes, observation of experts at work and experience—the same formula that is applied in every other breed that requires trimming.

In this connection, some learn slowly while others have a capacity to learn more quickly. Trimming of feet in itself is an art seldom mastered. Yet neat feet do more to set off a dog than any other single factor. Much the same is true of tails and ears. These are all important in the presentation of the breed and the ability to trim properly. These portions of the dog should be mastered first. The rest will come with experience, if you are patient and willing to learn.

Presentation

A good dog poorly presented has its chances of winning cut tremendously. This is not because the judge does not know faults of the dogs in competition but rather because the overall appearance of a dog generally has a strong bearing on the outcome of the placements. Type is of major importance and a dog poorly set down often appears to lack type due to the faulty trim. On the other hand, a reasonably good dog properly put down exemplifies the proper type and even when hidden faults are found, it is difficult to beat him, for the most important act in judging is to pick dogs that look like Cairns.

For this reason, faulty trimming often spoils the chances of an otherwise good dog.

This commentary on trimming does not answer the question of "how should a Cairn Terrier be trimmed?" because such a question cannot be answered by a general statement. However, any exhibitor who will pick up the challenge can learn through experience, study and intelligent observation. One comforting thought, you can never ruin a dog by trimming, for your mistakes will soon be obliterated by new growth of coat.

Coat Management

In general, all puppies should have the top coat removed at about four to six months. The softer puppy coat will fall out eventually and it is better to strip it off and then begin to condition the new coat with daily brushing and/or gloving (grooming with a hound glove). In this manner a youngster's coat may be brought along so that it is in acceptable condition if and when you decide to show him in the puppy class. Thereafter, if the coat is properly maintained as noted hereinafter you may be able to keep it "rolling" for many months and in acceptable show condition. If you cannot roll the coat, it should be removed, stripped off, when the top coat "blows." This means, when the coat becomes overly long and/or blousy. Loss in density of coat detracts from the dog's overall appearance and makes it difficult to keep the coat looking neat. Removing the coat at this time allows a new, lively jacket to grow and it should reach its prime in from six to 10 weeks after removal of the dead coat.

Grooming Tools

Tools used for trimming vary with different people but usually include combs, brushes and gloves together with scissors, thinning scissors, and stripping or plucking combs or knives. Scissors may be used for trimming around the ears and feet, if used with caution, although some adept individuals use the knife for all of these operations. When using scissors, never leave telltale scissor marks.

Trimming Methods

Thumb and forefinger plucking is nearly a lost art but the few experts that remain prove that it is still the best means for bringing along a coat. Using the plucking knife is the next best approach since both methods eliminate dead hair while leaving live strong hair in place with the former being the more effective of the two.

The use of clippers and thinning shears is probably the most often used means of trimming and is obviously the poorest since neither remove dead coat but cut it off along with the live coat, leaving the dead roots in the dog's hide. These tend to slow the growth of new hair and in some cases actually stop it with the net result that the dog's coat suffers badly. It is true that thinning a coat with thinning shears has its advantages but clipping has very little in its favor except speed.

The harmful part of clipping the coat revolves around the double coat of the Cairn. Clipping cuts off all hair at the same length. This means that the under coat as well as the harsh outer jacket is shortened. Since no hair is eliminated from its roots, the dog's coat is now shortened without proper conditioning. For this reason, if you do use clippers as a fast method of taking a dog down, be sure to grub out the under coat and comb thoroughly before clipping so that a portion, at least, of the dead hair is eliminated. This method may be used for kennel dogs and old pensioners but *should never be used on show stock*.

Getting back to plucking by hand or with a comb or knife, take only a few hairs at a time. Grip the hair rather loosely and pull. Dead hair comes out quite readily and live hair draws through your fingers or knife according to the method used. This leaves the live hair in place and it in turn can be shortened later, if desired, by means of a plucking knife held a bit tighter to cause some cuting of the live hair or more appropriately by singeing. This last seems to be a forgotten procedure but it is very useful. A lighted barber's taper drawn across the dog's coat in the direction of the lie will singe off the unruly hairs and will also, if desired, burn or singe back the longer hairs to a more desirable length. Singeing should not be used until the coat is in condition as it is not a good means for trimming from the rough since it, like clipping does not remove dead roots from the skin.

Spot Trimming and Rolling

Many experts begin trimming a dog in the rough by the "spot" method. That is, they take off the hair at the spot or spots that it grows the slowest. A week or so later they take off another spot or spots and so on until at the end of about four weeks the entire dog

212

Trim ears to a point and keep hair short on upper third only. Leave full on remainder of ears.

Level out top line and remove only enough hair to outline neck and shoulders.

Even hair around ruff, remove wild hairs only.

Shape tail like inverted carrot. Never make it appear thin or weak.

Trim lightly under lower jaw, leave full apron.

Shape legs to make them appear straight, blend body into legs in a generally smooth line.

Shape neatly with plenty of hair over hocks and legs.

Trim around feet so they appear neat. Clean out all hair between pads and file toenails short, front and back.

Even skirt along bottom line, keep long but well above ground.

You don't need much equipment to get the job done. A steady table, tack box or bench at which you can sit or stand comfortably is your first essential. An adjustable leash hanging from the ceiling or a metal bar attached to your tack box or grooming table will be invaluable in keeping your dog in position while you work on him. With your tools handy and a good light on your dog you are ready to begin.

YOUR BASIC EQUIPMENT NEEDS

A wire brush mounted in rubber or a stiff bristle brush.

A fairly coarse metal comb of good quality is essential.

A coarse and a fine stripping knife especially for terriers

Thinning shears and barbers scissors for finishing touches.

A good toe nail clipper and a coarse metal file are musts.

Using the wire brush, start at the back of the
head and go over the entire body, brushing with
the lay of the hair, including the chest, legs and
tail, until all tangles, knots and clumps are
cleaned out. When your brush meets no resistance you are ready for the metal comb.

Follow the same procedure with the comb until
the coat lays flat. Brush and comb the head
and face whiskers last as dogs will sometimes
resent this. Don't be rough but do be firm and
he will get the idea and learn to like it.

Use stripping knife or thumb and forefinger to remove just enough hair from neck so that it blends into shoulders smoothly.

Use stripping knife to even out top coat to make top line (back) level. Be sure that there is no apparent build-up adjacent the tail.

Shape tail to look like an inverted carrot. Do not trim drastically but even up the hair. Blend into back and rump. Remove more hair from back of tail than from the front. Blend into hips.

Comb hair on front legs downwardly, then study to determine where it should be thinned and/or removed to make legs appear straight when viewed from front and side. Even up feather and remove any flying hair at elbows. Trim *very lightly* Leg hair grows extremely slow.

is trimmed down and the first trimmed areas are beginning to regrow. Thereafter, the coat is worked frequently, thinning and shortening where required and grooming all the time to keep the coat at its peak.

Once the dog is in show coat, periodic work may be done to keep him in show coat. This is best accomplished by "rolling the coat," that is, taking off some of the coat while leaving sufficient long hairs to maintain the coat lying correctly. In time, three distinct coats will be carried by the dog, one coming, one prime and the other "going." When this is accomplished, the "going" coat is taken off at a time that another week's growth will cause the prime coat to pass over, the coming coat to go to prime and permit new coat to "come." When this condition is attained, the dog may be kept "in coat" for months. True, there may be periods that the coat is not as good (as dense) as others but it will always be presentable and may be brought to its peak at any time with about two weeks' work.

The "spot" trimming technique may be all right for the expert but the novice is best served by overall trimming at the start. This means taking off all of the top coat and grubbing out some of the under coat on the body, neck and tail. The hair on the "drop" or "skirt" should never be taken off since it requires months to regrow. The same is true of the leg feather and head furnishings.

Trimming the Head

The head, particularly, should always be well covered with hair. The sides must have a "frame" or ruff of abundant hair to complete the picture. The eyebrows should be more or less shaggy to offer the proper expression while the muzzle has some whisker but not so much as to cause it to appear "blocky" and heavy and thus spoil the expression. The ear tips (no more than $\frac{1}{3}$ down at any time) are the only portions of the head to be relatively free from long hair. These should be velvety smooth and closely trimmed at the edges to enhance the smallness of the ears. All of this is very important for all of these furnishings in proper trim and perspective enhance to a large degree the expression, and a Cairn without a Cairn's expression loses much of its identity and charm. It is suggested that the tyro study carefully the head portraits of several top winners offered throughout this treatise in order to appreciate this important and elusive point.

The head furnishings are best brought along by selectively trimming

Comb hair on top of head forward and upward. Comb the ruff from behind the ears out and forward. Study the effect before doing any trimming in this area. Trim hair inside of ears close for about $\frac{1}{3}$ of the way from top of ears. Trim hair on outside of ear close for the same distance.

Trim ruff in moderation always keeping a heavy "frame" well furnished with rough hair, as shown below. This can be accomplished with thinning scissors or by thumb and forefinger in plucking.

The effect of proper trimming of the ruff and ears is noted in this drawing. The head appears neat but not heavily trimmed.

the ends to bring them to a proper length and a more or less uniform density and by brushing the hair to keep it lively and to remove any dead coat.

All the while the trimmed body coat is being "worked" to maintain proper lengths at various parts of the dog. See the charts for more detailed information concerning the trimming pattern which, as explained, should be varied for individual dogs to bring out good points and minimize faults. Throughout the life of a show dog the coat should be worked constantly. This means daily "picking" to remove loose hairs and to keep the coat as lively and tight as possible. Truly, a dog is never in such condition that a few minutes work will not improve him. For this reason, work on your dog's coat each day with a critical attitude. Such work pays big dividends in the length of time the coat is useful. Of course, if you are keeping a rolled coat in condition, these remarks are superfluous since they are the order of the day.

Additional Helps

A good trimming bench or table is an invaluable aid when working on your dog and also helps to train him for show. The table should be of the proper height so that you may stand comfortably while working and should not be too large in area. A table about 25 inches long by 18 inches wide is adequate. Mounted on the side of the table near the front should be an adjustable upright from which can be suspended a slip collar adjustable to the proper height for each dog. This not only aids you in your work but will keep the dog's head up and teach it to stand properly. Instead of an adjustable upright you may hang a collar from the ceiling directly over the table. Either expedient is satisfactory. Another addition, used by most experts, is a large mirror mounted behind the work bench so that you may observe the reverse side of the dog. This gives you "the judge's view" while you trim and reveals many imperfections that would never be discovered without the mirror's aid.

Cleaning Without Bathing

When getting your dog ready for the show ring it is best to wipe off the body coat with a damp sponge or Turkish towel in the direction of the lie, for cleaning purposes. This is all that is generally required since the fine double coat of the dog protects the skin from dirt. Overall washing is neither required nor desired. Washing lessens the harshness of the top coat and causes it to become "blousy." Thus, washing is detrimental to the overall coat condition. It is far better to keep your dog in a clean run and on clean bedding so that superficial wiping off does the trick. Under these conditions, only the feather, feet and head will require washing. These should be thoroughly washed and dried, the process makes the hair appear more full and abundant and enhances the overall appearance of the dog.

Now cut the hair around the feet close to the pads to give feet a round, full look. This is best done with the dog's weight on the foot. You can make him stand by raising the opposite foot during the trimming. Also trim the hair between the toes.

Using your toe nail clippers cut just the tips of the nails about ⅛" being careful not to cut into the quick.

Then use your file to smooth and round off. Dogs don't mind the filing as much as the cutting. Toe nails should be filed as close as possible once a week to keep in shape.

Correcting Faults

While you can't actually correct physical faults, you may be able to hide some of them by careful trimming. So, if there is an undesirable curve or dip, leave hair full there to cover.

220

Front view: Here is the transformation compared with the untrimmed dog, side by side. Note how tidying up helps outline and improves neatness.

Rear view: Here is the transformation viewed from the rear. One side tidied and the other side rough.

Getting Ready for the Ring

After cleaning the dog as noted, the coat should be brushed and combed thoroughly and the furnishings, when completely dry should also be brushed and combed. If the coat is the proper length, little more is required until the final grooming with comb and brush before entering the ring. If the coat is overly long or tending to "blow," it is a good idea to towel the dog before the final grooming. This will make the coat lie and a slight dampening will help also. Before going into the ring, it is useful to use a little Brilliantine or Vaseline well rubbed into the hands and then onto the dog's coat. This will help hold it in place and bring out the gloss. Very little is required and it should be thoroughly brushed after application. The coat may be given a final combing and the dog is ready for the ring.

221

When the coat is overly long or when unruly hairs are present, a hair spray is useful and this may also be used on the feather and whisker. Lightly sprayed on it will hold the coat in position. Some use "sugar-water" as a means for holding the coat and in a few cases for stiffening the hair. This is, as the name implies, a solution of sugar in water, boiled until dissolved. It may be of varying degrees of concentration according to the use. Rubbed onto the coat, it should be permitted to dry before combing. It will cause the individual hairs to adhere together and in some cases, if not thoroughly combed out will lend texture to the coat. Any judge that knows can feel this and other coat stiffeners so the only real benefit obtained is in holding the coat close.

Summary

One last admonition, *the Cairn is not a heavily trimmed breed* and exaggerated trimming to make the dog appear "molded" should never be used. The Cairn is a delightful breed that should appear more or less natural without that over-trimmed appearance of several other members of the Terrier group. However, selective and careful tidying can go far to improve the performance of your dog in the ring and you should avail yourself of this advantage to the utmost.

This is about all of the advice on trimming that can be offered. The rest is up to the exhibitor. Remember, however, you cannot help losing if your dog is inferior anatomically to another exhibit but losing because of poor condition or showmanship are factors controlled by you and you alone. Apropos is a remark accredited to the late George Steadman Thomas, well known Anglo-American terrier expert, handler, and judge, who said, "The best looking dog will often beat a better dog put down indifferently," and truer words were never spoken.

14

Dog Shows, Their Value and Procedure

WHAT is the value of a dog show? This question is frequently asked when discussing the advisability of entering a dog in one of these events. The answer is simple and the reasons for showing your stock are logical and sound. The only true measuring stick of your breeding progress and success is by comparison of the best you have with the best of other breeders.

Dog Shows as Proving Grounds

If your dog or dogs win consistently, you can rest assured that the type of dog you are breeding is desirable and that you are progressing in your program. If you do not win or win infrequently, you should reevaluate your stock and your program.

Furthermore, showing dogs keeps you on your toes. The results of the shows are a constant challenge to your ability. If your dogs do not win, or win very seldom, do not be "kennel blind," but begin to look for shortcomings and when you find them, start to breed away from these faults and so improve your stock. Dog shows are the only opportunity you have for comparison, the obtaining of an unprejudiced criticism as represented by the judge's placement of your dog with reference to other dogs. If, after attending three or four shows, you find that all judges have similar reactions towards your entries, rest assured that their opinions, good or bad, are correct and be guided accordingly.

History of Dog Shows

Dog shows have had a long and varied history and are conducted on different plans in different countries. In England, shows have been in existence for a long time. The first event of the bench type was held for sporting dogs at Newcastle-on-Tyne in 1859. Sixty pointers and setters made up the entry. Shows of varying success were held from that time until April, 1873, when the Kennel Club (England) was organized and caused a stabilization of the events and created their first real bid for prominence.

In the United States, early history of shows is obscure but honor for the first bench show in our country is credited to Hempstead, Long Island, near which place a show was held in 1874. Westminster was the first of the better organized clubs to hold a show and its initial event was staged May 7 to 11th, 1877, in New York City, where it has been held continuously ever since.

The American Kennel Club was organized September 17, 1884, in Philadelphia, Pennsylvania. Until that time, registration for dogs in the United States was with one of two early organizations. The National American Kennel Club whose Stud Book was first published in 1878 by Dr. W. Rowe and which became the forerunner of the American Kennel Club Stud Book, and the American Kennel Register (Field and Stream). This last effort only lasted a few years. In any event, we may take the 1884 date as the real beginning of organized interest in bench-type dogs.

The organization of the American Kennel Club did in the United States what the Kennel Club accomplished in Great Britain; it established dog show practices by enforcing uniform rules and provided an impartial governing body operating for the best interests of pure-bred dogs and for the benefit of no individual or group of individuals.

Championships

Dog shows in different countries, under the authority of different kennel clubs, operate in varying manners and award championships after different requirements have been met. English shows are divided into several classifications, depending on their importance and scope. The only shows that have any bearing on championships are those events termed, "championship shows." The remaining fixtures, which are numerically superior, may be likened to our sanction matches. The English championship shows are analogous to our licensed or members' shows, in that a dog, by winning in its sex at one of these events is awarded a Challenge certificate. No relation exists between the number of entries and the certificate awards; this is taken care of by the fact that relatively few championship shows are held each year, thereby assuring a good entry with worthy competition. It requires three such certificate awards under three different judges to qualify for the title of champion.

In the United States, a different system prevails. Only the Winners Dog or Winners Bitch at a show can earn championship points. How many they earn at any given show is in accordance with a point rating system set up by the American Kennel Club, which uses as base the number of dogs of each sex of the breed exhibited at the show and the geographical division in which the show is located.

To become an American champion of record, a dog must win 15 championship points. These must be won under at least three different judges, and must include two major point shows. (Major shows are those at which 3 points or more are awarded to the Winners Dog or Winners Bitch.)

In an effort to keep competition strong and to equalize changing conditions of popularity, the American Kennel Club continually reassesses the point requirements for the breeds.

In 1917, when the point rating system first went into effect, the ratings for both sexes were the same, and there was no distinction between geographical divisions. The requirements for Cairn Terriers at the time were:

> 1 point ... 1 dog in competition
> 2 points .. 2 dogs
> 3 points .. 3 dogs
> 4 points .. 4 dogs
> 5 points .. 5 dogs

At the present time, for the purposes of determining the allotment of championship points, the American Kennel Club has divided the continental United States into four regions, or divisions. Division #1 covers the east and north, division #2 has the south and west. California, by itself, comprises division #3, and division #4 is made up of nine states in the plains, the Rockies and the Pacific Northwest. Alaska, Hawaii and Puerto Rico each have their own point rating.

Show entries and point ratings are reviewed annually and adjusted up or down as conditions warrant. Ratings for each year are published in the April issue of *Pure-Bred Dogs / American Kennel Gazette* and in the front of every dog show catalogue. A quick check will tell you just how many Cairn Terriers are required for a given number of points at the shows you attend.

In general, the American Kennel Club endeavors to keep the number of 3, 4 and 5 point shows to about twenty percent of the total shows in a given division. This means that major shows (3 points or better) will be available but will not be so numerous that the average exhibitor can normally finish a dog in three shows. It also means that in a small registration breed, where competition is hard to find, it will not be impossible to finish a champion, which would be the case were all breeds to have the same rating.

Prior to 1917, the American system was entirely different. At that time, the point rating at any show depended upon the total number of dogs exhibited at the show. Thus, it was actually possible for a dog to win 5 points without any competition. The ratings for shows were as follows: 1000 dogs and over—5 points; 750 to 1000 dogs—4 points; 500 to 750 dogs—3 points; 250 to 500 dogs—2 points and 250 dogs and under only one point. The obvious unfairness of this system revolved around the fact that at a one-point-rating show, a winning dog might beat more dogs of the breed than at some other show where a five point rating prevailed. The present system eliminates these inequities and permits the maximum point rating at any show regardless of overall size providing the required number of dogs in the sex of the breed are present.

Canadian championships are acquired in much the same manner as American championships except that only ten points are needed. The other requirements are substantially the same and ratings vary in accordance with the numbers being shown in each breed.

Show Procedure

The method of procedure of a dog show is relatively simple to comprehend. It is nothing more than an elimination contest where

There are several thousand dog shows held all across the United States every year. They vary from small informal fun matches to giant spectacles that attract dogs from the opposite coast and even other countries. This aerial view shows the giant Santa Barbara Kennel Club show. It is a one-day, outdoor, unbenched event and one of the leading shows in the country. R. Batoo.

A view of the benching area of the Detroit Kennel Club show. Like Santa Barbara, this too, is a one-day affair, but the dogs are required to be on their benches for most of the time they are in the show building. This is to enable the spectators to see most of the dogs entered. Almost all benched shows are held indoors in large cities at the present time. *Evelyn M. Shafer.*

dogs with specific qualifications compete in relatively small groups or classes. The winner of each elimination round progresses to the next higher competition for further evaluation until only one dog remains, and that dog is designated Best Dog in Show.

Every dog show is broken down into breed competitions which are usually further subdivided by sexes with at least five regular classes being provided in each sex. These classes together with their official definitions may be found in Chapter 6, Sections 3 to 8 inclusive of *Rules Applying to Registration and Dog Shows* (American Kennel Club), and may be obtained from the American Kennel Club, 51 Madison Ave New York, N.Y. 10010. The context of which is as follows:

The Puppy Class shall be for dogs that are six months of age and over, but under twelve months, that were whelped in the United States of America or Canada, and that are not champions. The age of a dog shall be calculated up to and inclusive of the first day of a show. For example, a dog whelped on January 1st is eligible to compete in a puppy class at a show the first day of which is July 1st of the same year and may continue to compete in puppy classes at shows up to and including a show the first day of which is the 31st day of December of the same year, but is not eligible to compete in a puppy class at a show the first day of which is January 1st of the following year.

The Novice Class shall be for dogs six months of age and over, whelped in the United States of America or Canada, which have not, prior to the date of closing of entries, won three first prizes in the Novice Class, a first prize in Bred-by-Exhibitor, American-bred, or Open Classes, nor one or more points toward their championships.

The Bred-By Exhibitor Class shall be for dogs whelped in the United States of America, or, if individually registered in The American Kennel Club Stud Book, for dogs whelped in Canada, that are six months of age and over, that are not champions, and that are owned wholly or in part by the person or by the spouse of the person who was the breeder or one of the breeders of record.

Dogs entered in this class must be handled in the class by the breeder or by a member of the immediate family of the breeder

For purposes of this section, the members of an immediate family are: husband, wife, father, mother, son, daughter, brother, sister.

The American-bred Class shall be for all dogs (except champions) six months of age and over, whelped in the United States of America, by reason of a mating which took place in the United States of America.

228

The Open Class shall be for any dog six months of age or over except in a member specialty club show held only for American-bred dogs, in which case the Open Class shall be only for American-bred dogs.

All class entries except in the open class, require careful study of the dog's eligibility for that class. In general, young dogs over six months and under a year old that were whelped in the United States or Canada should be entered in the puppy classes for experience. After they pass one year of age, they are generally eligible for three wins in the novice class. They should then be sufficiently seasoned for entry in the upper classes. Before making an entry for any show, be sure to check the requirements of the class in which you are entering, since if the dog is ineligible for a class in which it is entered and competes, it will be disqualified after the win is checked by the American Kennel Club.

The championship points in each sex of each breed are contested for by the winners of the five above mentioned classes (blue ribbon winners). These dogs compete in the Winners class and the ultimate winner is designated Winners Dog or Winners Bitch (purple ribbon) as the case may be. The two winners are the only dogs in the breed to receive championship points. A Reserve Winner (purple and white ribbon) is designated in each sex and may be any dog who has not been previously defeated except by the winner. The Reserve Winner is the recipient of the championship points in the event that Winners is later disqualified.

The next step in the process of elimination is for the Winners Dog and Winners Bitch to meet with any dogs entered for Best of Breed competition. These entrants are dogs that have qualified for the title of champion and this group then competes for the honor of Best of Breed (purple and gold ribbon) and the winner of the class is so designated. Judging of this class also determines the Best of Opposite Sex to Best of Breed and the Best of Winners.

In the United States, champions are seldom entered in the classes in competition for the championship points. This is not true in England where champions are entered in the open class and compete for the Challenge certificate. Many arguments have been made pro and con concerning this deviation from American practice for it is apparent if the practice were the same in the United States, as it is in England that fewer champions would be made and possibly the urge to show dogs would be dulled among the less ardent exhibitors.

All-breed shows are further subdivided into seven variety groups, set up by the American Kennel Club, which consist of arbitrary classifications of breeds that have some general relation in point of use, etc. Thus, Sporting dogs (Group 1) includes such breeds as spaniels, setters, pointers, and retrievers. Hounds (Group 2) includes Beagles, Greyhounds, Dachshunds, etc. Working dogs (Group 3) are represented by Doberman Pinschers, Great Danes, Boxers, Samoyeds, Akitas, etc. Terriers (Group 4) are all dogs that go to ground and includes the Cairn. Toy dogs (Group 5) are self-explanatory with Pekingese, Pomeranians, Chihuahuas, Toy Spaniels and Pugs being representative breeds. The sixth of these groups is known as the Non-Sporting group and includes a more heterogeneous collection of breeds than any of the other six groups. Bulldogs, Boston Terriers, Dalmatians, Poodles and Chow Chows are some of the members of this group. The seventh and final group is known as the Herding group. An offshoot of the Working group, it was initiated in 1983 and consists of breeds originally developed to help move and control livestock. Collies,

Ch. Heathcairn Hector, being placed first in the Terrier group at the Lexington Kennel Club, 1954, by the author. Hector is owned by Mr. and Mrs. Carl E. Brewer and was handled to the win by Mrs. Brewer. *Norton of Kent.*

German Shepherd Dogs, Welsh Corgis and Shetland Sheepdogs are among the most familiar Herding breeds.

The final judging at any all-breed show revolves around the variety group judging, and in this phase, the Best of Breed winner of every breed within each group competes for the honor of best in that group. In this manner, the show has been finally narrowed down to the six group-winning contestants for the judge to go over for the Best Dog in Show. The ultimate winner has eliminated every dog in the show to gain the coveted position.

Incidentally, if a class dog wins a group, or Best in Show award that dog becomes the recipient of the highest number of points available in the group or show as the case may be. In this manner, if only one point is available in its breed and a dog ultimately wins a group or Best in Show including a five-point-entry breed, that dog acquires five points instead of the original one. This only applies to dogs that have come up from the classes.

The foregoing is a brief explanation of show procedure. The same general plan is followed at Specialty shows (shows for one breed only) except that group judging is eliminated.

Sanction Matches

Sanction matches are shows held for experience, and no championship points are awarded. These matches may be of the specialty or all-breed variety, for puppies only or for all-age dogs. They are a great deal of fun and an excellent training ground for dogs and exhibitors since they are conducted in substantially the same manner as point shows.

Benching Rules

All-breed shows, specialty shows and sanction matches may be held indoors or out-of-doors and may be benched or unbenched. New rules make it mandatory for a club to state on their premium list (for point shows) whether or not the show is benched. If benched, it is required that the dogs remain on their benches throughout designated hours of the show except when being exercised, readied or shown. This does not apply to puppies which need not be benched until after they have been judged.

Premium Lists

Premium lists are the prospectus of the show issued by each show-giving club. They set forth the approved judges and their assignments, show hours and rules and include prizes, entry forms, etc. Having exhibited at a show or two you will automatically be placed on the exhibitors' mailing list and will receive subsequent lists for shows in your locality. If you are not on these lists, the show dates and super-intendents' addresses are carried by all dog magazines and by the *American Kennel Gazette* months in advance of the shows. A letter to the proper official will bring a list promptly.

Joining a Dog Club

If you plan to exhibit dogs, endeavor to join a local dog club. Most cities have such an organization and it generally includes a majority of the active breeders and exhibitors in the vicinity. Contact with these persons will help you over many rough spots and you can also gain much knowledge through this association.

A Rewarding Hobby

In general, dog shows are wonderful places to gain knowledge of your breed and dogs in general. Professional handlers and experienced exhibitors may be watched as they prepare their dogs and their actions in the ring should be noted. Much can be learned in this manner. Most of these persons are willing to assist the novice if asked courteously and at a time they are not rushed to show or prepare another dog. They were all novices at one time or another since there is no means yet devised of skipping this phase. Intelligent observation and courteous questioning will aid more than anything else in acquiring the knack of showing dogs.

One more word on the subject of dog shows. These events while awesome the first time, get under your skin. There is no more fasci-nating hobby than showing dogs. The bustle of the shows, the rush to get your dog ready and the thrill of winning cannot be equalled elsewhere. To all this add lasting friendships built up through associa-tion with congenial companions met everywhere you exhibit, and you will appreciate why so many persons follow the shows with unrelenting interest, year after year.

15

Trends and Observations

THE CAIRN Terrier at this time stands in its best position in the history of the breed. More dogs are being registered and exhibited than ever before. More people have interest in the breed than ever before. While both situations have many meritorius aspects, they also offer food for thought.

The Influence of the Novice

This tremendous increase in interest has brought into the fancy a host of newcomers, the large majority of whom have little or no background in dogs. They may be termed novices for want of better terminology. On the other hand, the strong bulwark of experienced fanciers lessens progressively as time passes.

This will eventually create a condition where the majority of the fancy lacks the experience and background that in past years has stabilized the breed. Newcomers establish trends that are often taken as the rule rather than the exception. These trends are exhibited mainly by excessive trimming, poor exhibition techniques, and weak temperaments. None of these is desirable nor proper.

Trimming and Coat Management

Many dogs being exhibited lack coat length and density. The Cairn is a natural breed—trimming should be carefully carried out to make the dog appear tidy but not heavily trimmed. The development of knowledge of the proper trimming technique is an art that cannot be accomplished in a day, a week or a month. It requires deep study and careful effort to bring the dog to perfection. Certainly, stripping off the top coat and exhibiting the animal with little or no covering is wrong and should be heavily penalized. It is true that the shorter the coat the easier it is to keep the animal going but conversely, the less it looks like a Cairn. While the chapter on trimming goes into great detail on the methods to be used, it does not even infer that a Cairn should be exhibited without a good double coat with substantial length in the outer jacket. Exhibitors should understand this before they exhibit their dogs.

I might say, in the early days of the breed, when it was shown substantially in the rough, it did not do well in Group competition. Terriers, in general, are a heavily trimmed group of dogs and therefore the untidy animal in a ring with the others did not offer a good impression. However, tidying up a dog means just what it says; making the animal appear tidy, feet and tail trimmed to eliminate straggling hair and the coat in a reasonably tight condition with a clean and tidy apperance. Such a dog can win in any competition and this is the desideratum.

Exhibition Techniques

Poor exhibition techniques are also a drawback to winning. A dog that has to be propped up for examination, that must have its tail held up and head strung up will seldom do as well as the animal that shows well on a loose lead. Of course this takes hours of training with most dogs and few exhibitors seem to have the time to work daily with their exhibit until perfection is attained. Those that do, reap the rewards for a natural show-er is difficult to beat with one that requires "propping up."

Temperament

Weak temperament is probably the most important of the listed faults. The Cairn Terrier was bred to run in a pack. For this reason, Cairns must not be fighters. They should be willing to spar with other dogs out of curiosity but should never be vicious nor overly argumentative. On the other side of the coin are the shy ones, those that just will not get their tails or ears up and who refuse to spar or even look at other dogs. Another type of weak temperament is found in the animal that wants to bite the judge, the exhibitor or anyone else within reach. This problem generally occurs among shy dogs but sometimes is apparent in those that are overly aggressive. In either case the dog should not be shown nor used for breeding purposes as his temperament is weak and a goodly portion of his get will carry this offensive characteristic.

Cairns in general have fine temperaments and make excellent pets and show dogs. Their fine, double coats can take all kinds of weather and the variety of colors, from a light cream to a black, offers a range that meets any personal preference. The breed is outgoing and lovable, it is active and above all it is a sturdy dog brought up in the Highlands where resistance to weather, disease and hardships of all kinds were absolute necessities. The Cairn Terrier of today carries all of these inherited attributes and makes a wonderful companion, show dog or worker (today's representative can go to ground just as well as its ancestors when the opportunity is presented). It is for this reason that we all must preserve the working characteristics of the breed and the physical traits that contribute to those characteristics; without them we lose type and character, the very charm of the breed.

A Final Word

So ends this treatise on the breed. It has been a pleasure to write as it has enabled me to renew many friendships that had been interrupted by time. Cairn fanciers, as with most of the Terrier-oriented clan, are dedicated and interested people who love their breed and who strive to improve its position, a worthy objective fully repaid by the love and devotion of their dogs.

The Terrier From The North

Losh' Bogie man haud off your han';
  Nor thrash me black and blue.
Frae fools and foes I seek nae praise,
  But frien's should aye be true.

Nae silky-haired admirer I
  O'Bradford Toys, Strathbogie;
Sich thoughts, I'm sure cam' in your head,
  While dribblin' o'er the cogie.

I ken the Terrier o'the North,
  I ken the towsy tyke—
Ye'll search frae Tweed to Sussex' shore,
  But never find his like.

For pluck and pith and jaws and teeth,
  And hair like heather cowes,
Wi' body lang and low and strang,
  At hame in cairns or knowes.

He'll face a foumart, draw a brock,
  Kill rats and whitteritts by the score,
He'll bang tod-Lowrie frae his hole,
  Or slay him at his door.

He'll range for days and ne'er be tired,
  O'er mountain, moor, and fell;
Fair play, I'll back the brave wee chap
  To fecht the de'il himsel'.

And yet beneath his rugged coat
  A heart beats warm and true.
He'll help to herd the sheep and kye,
  And mind the lammies too.

Then see him at the ingle side,
  Wi' bairnies roond him laughin'.
Was ever dog sae pleased as he,
  Sae fond o'fun and daffin'?

But gie's your hand, Strathbogie man'
  Guid faith' we maunna sever.
Then 'Here's to Scotia's best o'dogs,
  Our towsy tyke for ever!' ".

(By Dr. Gordon Stables,
The Live Stock Journal, Jan. 31st 1879)

Foumart—A Polecat
Brock—A Badger
Whitteritts—A Weasel
Tod—A Fox

BIOLOGICAL FACTS AND DATA

Vital Signs for Adult Dogs Under Generally Normal Conditions

Normal Temperature taken rectally: 101.5°–102°F

Normal pulse rate: 80 to about 120 per minute

Normal respiration: 10 to 30 per minute

Age of Maturity and Mating Facts

Sexual maturity in dogs occurs at from about seven to nine months of age but this may vary. However, the American Kennel Club will not register puppies by a sire less than seven months old at time of mating.

Bitches normally have their first Oestrous cycle (period of heat) at about nine months of age although it may come earlier or later. The American Kennel Club will not register puppies born out of a bitch less than eight months old at the time of mating.

The Oestrous cycle lasts about three weeks. The most appropriate time for planned mating is after the discharge has become generally colorless, between ten to fourteen days. A bitch will come in season normally two times each year at six month intervals.

The period of gestation for puppies is normally 63 days from the breeding date. This may vary slightly and puppies are frequently whelped at from four days early to one or two days late.

Puppy Facts

Eyes open between nine and twelve days from whelping date.

Weaning should begin at from five to six weeks of age, depending upon the strength of the puppies and the extent of teething.

Teething begins at from four to five weeks of age, while permanent incisors with the shedding of milk teeth starts at from two to five months of age. The canine (large tusk-like dentition) and cheek teeth (Premolars and

237

molars) come in from about four-and-a-half to seven months of age. Dogs vary one from another in all of these and the foregoing ages are approximations offered solely as a general guide.

In any situation that appears to be abnormal, the best procedure is to consult immediately with your veterinarian. Many problems that have become serious could have been averted by following this admonition.

Ch. Catescairn Rogue (Cairnvreckan Oscar ex Cairnvreckan Kaffir), owned by Mr. and Mrs. H. B. Stewart, Jr. *Rudolph Tauskey.*

Yearly American Kennel Club
Cairn Terrier Registrations

Year	Number	Year	Number
1913	1	1949	482
1914	5	1950	535
1915	None	1951	501
1916	8	1952	585
1917	32	1953	632
1918	34	1954	632
1919	70	1955	622
1920	91	1956	752
1921	59	1957	776
1922	67	1958	872
1923	107	1959	929
1924	120	1960	982
1925	124	1961	1076
1926	208	1962	1270
1927	217	1963	1401
1928	181	1964	1899
1929	205	1965	2369
1930	348	1966	2883
1931	347	1967	3968
1932	311	1968	4532
1933	344	1969	5677
1934	431	1970	6698
1935	562	1971	7738
1936	580	1972	7753
1937	556	1973	7497
1938	498	1974	7339
1939	419	1975	6365
1940	427	1976	6432
1941	411	1977	6359
1942	341	1978	6369
1943	252	1979	6262
1944	170	1980	6561
1945	340	1981	6346
1946	426	1982	6108
1947	516	1983	6154
1948	392	1984	5892

British Breeders
Past and Present

John Alexander	Ugadale
Misses Allen and Turner	Crockshed
A. Arrowsmith	Thimswarra
Mrs. Bassett	'of Frimley
W. N. Bradshaw	Redletter
Miss Bengough	Twobees with Mrs. Butterworth
Mrs. C. M. Bird	Placemore
Miss M. E. Bunbury	Shieling
Baroness Burton	Dochfour
Messrs. Cammish and Williams	Camcairn
Mrs. Alastair Campbell	Brocaire
Miss Campbell	Craiglyn
Miss B. Bentley-Carr	Attic
T. W. L. Caspersz	Turfield
Miss B. M. Dixon	Rossarden
Mrs. Charles H. Dixon	Gunthorpe
Mrs. E. H. Drummond	Blencathra
Mr. and Mrs. A. Firth	Cairngold
Alex Fisher	Fimor
Mrs. N. Fleming	'Out of the West
Mrs. H. M. Forbes	Ross-shire
Miss M. D. W. Gibson	Mistyfell
Misses M. and D. Hall	Felshott
Miss F. Hamilton (later Mrs. S. Somerfield)	Oudenarde
Misses Hall and Wilson	Felshott
Mrs. J. E. Harding	Brucairns
Hon. Mary Hawke	Lockyers
Mrs. A. Heery	Wimpas
Misses Homes and Winsley	Davmar
Mes. D. Howe and C. Clark	Courtrai
Miss J. M. Hudson	Clanranald
Miss M. Irving	Beechacre
Mrs. M. Jagger	Vinovium

Mrs. M. Johnson	'of Keycol
J. E. Kerr	Harviestoun
Mrs. D. H. Leigh	Thistleclose
Mrs. E. Leverton	Merrymeet
Mrs. D. D. Lewis	Cairncrag
Mrs. A. Loader	Gayclan
Miss Lucy Lockwood	Cloughton
Miss H. Longmore	Unique Cottage
(later Mrs. Parker-Tucker)	with Miss J. Marshall
Miss Hilda L. Manley	Lofthouse
A. Mackenzie	Moccasin
D. Maclennan	Carngowan
Mrs. Marsh	Toptwig with Mr. Danks
Mrs. M. Mawson	Glenmacdhui
Mrs. Mirrlees	Shinnel
Miss A. D. Moody	Rhosbridge
W. Moyes	Bogton
Mrs. N. R. Newton	Strathinvar
Miss O. I. Nicholls	Michelcombe
Mrs. Sally Ogle	Pinetop
Mrs. Prichard	Donnington
Miss E. M. R. Reoch	Valiant
Errington Ross	Glenmhor
George J. Ross	Firring
Mrs. T. Rudland	Trashurst
Lady Sophie Scott	'of Harris
Mrs. B. Shea	Redstacks
Mrs. M. Shuttleworth	Monary
Mrs. H. M. T. Small	Avenelhouse
Mrs. K. Stephens	Hyver
Mrs. N. Swires	Crowtrees
Capt. H. A. Townley	Carysfort
Miss C. Viccars	Mercia, often with others
Miss and Mrs. Viccars	Elford
Lt. Col. H. F. Whitehead	Guynach
A. J. Wilkinson	Foxgrove
Mrs. E. M. Yeend	Yeendsdale

American and Canadian Breeders
Past and Present

Mrs. Robert Abhalter	Coralrock's
Mrs. R. T. Allen	Craigdhu
Elizabeth H. Anderson	Down East
Mrs. H. G. Aspey	Halkaren
Miss M. Baechle	O'Southfield
Mrs. Nina Bentler	Tina's
Mrs. Amy Bacon	Cairnvreckan
Dr. and Mrs. B. B. Bagby	B Cube
Mrs. Donna Bebeau	Misty Isle
Mrs. A. L. Bergeron	Craighly-B
Miss Elizabeth Braun (Mrs. Paul B. Ernst)	Bethcairn
Mr. and Mrs. Carl Brewer	Heathcairn
Mrs. B. E. Brouillette	Crandrum
Mr. and Mrs. F. C. Brown	Pinegrade
Cedonia Browder	Cedar Farms
Mrs. Winans Burnett	Quinatisset
Mrs. David Bryant	Milbryan
Mr. and Mrs. J. M. Butchkoski	Innesfell
Mrs. Virginia Cadwallader	Woodmist
J. and D. Cantwell	Azgard
Mrs. John Carpenter	Kencanis
Mrs. Vernon Carpenter	Braecroft
Mr. and Mrs. Taylor Coleman	Wolfpit with Mrs. J. D. Hutchinson
Mr. and Mrs. J. R. Corbitt, III	Kutisark
Miss Margaret Coulson	Cairnmailen
Mr. and Mrs. Roger Cox	Rogerlyn
Mrs. Ray F. Crump	Kencairn
Mrs. L. DeVincent	Shin Pond
Jack and Susan DeWitt	Happicairn
George P. Davies	Kindon
Mrs. S. K. David	Craigly
Mrs. C. F. Dowe	Dowsfort
Mrs. Isabel Eckfield	Bellacairn

Mrs. G. and Miss Mary Jane Ellis	Killybracken
Eleanor Finkler	Flickwynd
Mrs. LaVerne Fiorella	Metcourt
Mrs. T. C. Fritz	Brightridge
Miss K. Glick	Cantycairns
J. A. Green	Loch Katrine
Mr. and Mrs. L. O. Griffith	Braelog
Marianne Ham	Maricairn
Pauline Hardy	Brigadoon
C. and G. Harkins	Kim-E-Cairn
Doris and Baker Harris	Tail's End
Jean and Buell Herrick	Crestcairn
Miss Jean Hinkle	Port Fortune
Miss Isabel Hoopes	Hickoryside
Lydia Hopkins	Sherwood Hall, Sherwood
Elizabeth Horton	Crofters
Miss Helen Hunt	Shagbark
Miss Celeste Hutton	Greysarge
Mrs. G. W. Hyslop	Cairndania
C. R. Jackson	Koskosing
Girard Jacobi	Topcairn
B. and F. Jenkins	Wee Acres
Mrs. Amy Katz	Kandykate's
Kenneth Kauffman	Brehannon
Allan P. Kirby	Graymar
Miss Luanne Klepps	Cairnwoods
(later Mrs. James Craco	
and Mrs. M. Dalger)	
Mr. and Mrs. J. R. Kroeger	Sookota
Bertha Rae Lain	'of Raelain
Miss Clara LeVene	Tanacairn, Tana
Mrs. Edward Loomis	Knocwood
Mr. and Mrs. Donald Lynch	Cathmhors
Rosalie K. Lynch	Cricklade
M. V. Magee	Whistle Gate with S. E. Evans
Kenneth MacBain	Cabrach
Miss Edith MacCausland	Kedron with Miss A. P. Ross
Col. and Mrs. G. W. MacSparran	Littleclan
Mr. and Mrs. Joe Marcum	Cairmar

Mrs. George McDonald	Gamac
Kay and James MacFarlane	Badenoch
Miss M. McGee	Whistlegate
Miss F. J. McGregor	Kihone
Mrs. and Mrs. M. K. McLeod	Tartan
Mrs. E. C. McReynolds	Nanlor
Mrs. Nina Matzner	Tina
Mrs. Ballinger Mills	Bayou Haven
Mr. and Mrs. Charles R. Merrick III	Tidewater
C. and A. Norris	Bairdsain (Baird's)
Mr. and Mrs. Ross A. Obenauer	Kildrummy
Miss Claudia Phelps	Rosstor
Mrs. Howard Lee Platt	Eastcote
Mrs. Henry Price	Robinscoft
Mr. and Mrs. Paul Renshaw	Hollow Tree
Don Robbie	Holemill
Mrs. Byron Rogers	'of Misty Isles
J. and K. Rokaitis	Paisley
Miss A. P. Ross	Kedron
Mrs. E. Salotti	Ramblewood
Miss Elsie Shanks	Fula
Mrs. L. M. Shirkie	Balkaren
Mr. and Mrs. Daniel Shoemaker	Waterford
Mr. and Mrs. P. L. Shoop, Jr.	Shoop's Isle
Mrs. Grace Siegler	Cairn Den with Vera Hoehn
Mr. and Mrs. Henry Slack	Rosscamac
Jerry Sloan	Clangatha
Mrs. N. B. Smith	Cragwood
Mr. and Mrs. Thomas Stamp	Countryside
Mrs. Henry Stephens	Grosse Point
Mr. and Mrs. H. B. Stewart, Jr.	Catescairn
Mr. and Mrs. Richard Stix	Cairmore
Mrs. Ralph Stone	Caithness
Laura and Roy Strong	Glencairn McNeill
George and Nell Stumpff	Lakewood's
Mr. and Mrs. L. Tappin	Tapscot
W. Bryden Tennant	Glenconnor
Mrs. Nancy Thompson	Gayla Cairn

Mr. and Mrs. Philip Thompson	Braemuir
Mrs. F. G. Thomson	Brookmead
Mrs. Martin Tidd	Lochnor
Vera A. Timm	Tanacairn, Tana's
Mrs. A. D. Turnbull	Lannock
C. J. Walls	Clachnacuddin
Mrs. Norman Ward	Cornor
Mrs. Payne Whitney	Greentree
Mrs. Phillip Wilder	Whetstone
Mr. and Mrs. Robert B. Williams	Wildwood
Mrs. L. M. Wood	Melita
Dr. and Mrs. W. G. Wrenn	Cairnhame

American Champions and Obedience Degree Winners 1974-1984

THE LISTING that follows includes titleholders for the period noted above. In most instances, the listing by year includes those Cairns whose names were published during that year. This does not mean necessarily that these dogs completed title requirements during the year concerned. A sincere effort has been made to include all title recipients for the period but there may be some few omissions and these are regretted. The published records are difficult to follow and are not always fully accurate.

1974

Champions of Record

Accalia's Munchkin
Accalia's Red Wizard
Alison Macbrigdov's Aberdeen
Almin's Blondee
Almin's Mr. Tuffy Tue

Ambejo's Ten Ol' Klei Mop
Anlin's Tinka Jo Jingo
Ascolo Kochikola
Bellacairn's Bit O' Fire
Bellacairn's Junior

Bellacairn's Mollie Magee
Bit-A-Croftee of Raelain
Bodibo's Orson
Bonnie Scalawag of Wolfpit
Brightridge Caper's McMindy
Brightridge Love Bug
Brightridge Sparkle Plenty
Brightridge Sugar Plum
Cairmar Colonel Peri
Cairmar Fancy That
Cairmar Stormie Dawn
Cairmar Storm Warning
Cairncrest Tuffy
Cairndania Brigrey's Dorey
Cairndania Brigrey's Dunbar
Cairngorm's Appolo
Cairngorm's Midnight Raider
Cairnwood's Margaree
Caithness La Nostra Minnie
Caithness Piper of Bagpipes
Casey's I'm A Lover
Countryside's Sea Coral
Crag Valley Thistle
Craigly-B Smart Alcc
Croftee's Captain Chris
Cuttie Sark's Dapper Dan II
Dixie's Rebel Rascal
Dorquette Merry Whistle
Dundane's Menehune Mac
Felshott Copper Coin
Flickwynd's Alphie of Meghill
Foxgrove Susanella
Furzeleigh Fergus
Gaffner's Gala Applause
Gaffner's Wally Wallbanger
Gamac Cantie Scot
Gamac Tartan Miss Wags
Gayla Cairn's Bridget McKim
Gayla Cairns Honest Abe
Gayla Cairns Idiots Delight
Gayla Cairns Quiet Hope
Gayla Cairns Zachary
Greggden Brandywine
Greg's Great Pepi
Greta Melita of Staten

Greysarge Mr. Christian
Heatherbrae's Misty Mac Hugh
How-Bee's Doonrae O'Scotia
How-Bee's Gracette O'Scotia
Hurray Murray of Tu-Lane Acres
Innisfree's Red Baron
Justcairns Jubilee of Lochwood
Kim-E-Cairn's Rufus
Kisncairn Hannibal Hayes
Kisncairn Michaela O'Mine
Kisncairn Top O' The Morning
Laird's Sunset Kisncairns Mr.
Lakewood's Grey Boy
Lakewood's TigerTank
Leilani's Chip-of-Bit O'
MacMurrich of Wolpit
Maricairn Apollo's Caspar
Meghill's Governor McTuff
Melita's MacTavish of Auvern
Metcourt's Orange Blossom
Milady Milinda of Cairn Den
Mitchan Donna of Heshe
Moonsweep of Sclwyn of Thimswarra
Nahtsees Nagus' el Ut Toogunee
Nightfalls Minute Maid
Oliver's Sandy
Paisley's Duke of Burbank
Paisley's Kernel Pepper
Redletter Moonstar Turn
Red Robin Zoomie
Rossmoor's MacLeod
Rossmoor's Nickle Silver
Salmonbrook Glen Garry
Serendipity Rose Red, C.D.
Sulinda Samson of Worrindale
Tartan's Gingersnap Macduff
Tearincairn Spartan
Too Max Redwing
Topcairn Billy's Find
Ugadale Futurist
Ugadale Hallmark
Vinovium Tuscan
Whistle Gate Grizzel
Willy's Twinkle of Flickwynd
Windy Way's Molly Meg Me

Woodmist Grey Heath

Obedience Degrees

Angus the Pooh, C.D.
Ch. Arways Georgy Boy, C.D.
Arway's Red Muffin, C.D.
Bartoli's Mac Ennis, C.D.
Bruce McPherson, C.D.X.
Buffy Belle McHaney, C.D.
Ch. Cairndania Brigrey's Dorey, C.D.
Cluny's Mary Hawke, C.D.
Dasoma Scruftish McBrier, C.D.X.
Dylon of Melita, C.D.
Fletcher O'Stonehaven, C.D.
Galagallant Suede Jaffey, C.D.

Gen Del's Angel Victoria, C.D.
Glo's Jolly Jay Bimbo, C.D.
Lambrusco's Wendy, C.D.X.
Leibchen O'Callen, C.D.
Merry Christmas Stuart, C.D.
Romunda's Drift-O-Smoke, U.D.
Romunda's High Fashion, C.D.
Ch. Shag Farus of Iowa, C.D.
Ch. Tradorogh's Dunstan Claymore,
    C.D.X.
Tuffy MacWright, C.D.
Williams' Brandy Shawn, C.D.X.

Ch. Woody McRuff of Highhedges, C.D.

1975

Champions of Record

Abracadabra Sans Souci
Alison Kenbeau Edinburgh
Arlwyn Red Baron
Auverne's Pilgrim of Tail's End
Avenelhouse Nutcracker
Bagpipe Greypegs Gilligan
Barnaby of Flickwynd
Barnstormer of Barberi Hedge
Bellacairn's Big Shot
Braelog Tuscan's Tammy
Brightridge Buckley
Brightridge Busy Lizzie
Brightridge Cedar Chips
Brightridge Duncan's Joker
Bright Spark of Petersden
Cairmar Barberry Lass
Cairmar Chance Quest
Cairmar Christmas Storm
Cairmar Royal Brandy
Cairmar Stormie Dream
Cairndania Brigrey's Barkley
Cairndania Davey's Delilah
Cairndania Davey's Dellis
Canonach Kilkelly
Carindales St. Nick
Cathmhor's Gay Toptwig

Craigly-B Angelica
Craigly-B Tiffany
Craigly-B Vixen
Craigly Dan Dee McFlair
Craigly Fergus McFlair
Craigly Stumpy McFlair
Darroch of Bonnie Brae
Donimar Scoggin Thig
Dundane's Menehune Pickles
Duntiblae Top Secret of Toptwig
Flickwynd's Captain Hook
Flickwynd's Rumpelstilskin
Foxgrove Jester
Gayla Cairn's Dixie Darling
Gayla Cairn's Forget-Me-Not
Gayla Cairn's Gregor McKim
Gayla Cairn's Happy Owen
Gingerbred's Rocky Candy
Ginger Snap of Flickwynd
Glencairn Neile McNeill
Glenrichard Sauncie Fiona
Glen Shiel Ired
Glynncuri's Canty Jig
Greysarge Tough Cookie
Heathcairn Gunther
Hilltop Scarlet Contessa

Kamidon's Juniper Jennifer
Kim-E-Cairn's Bonnie Lad
Kim-E-Cairn's Druidsgate Tryst
Kisncairn That's My Girl
Kobils Cleo of Flickwynd
Kyleila of Cairmar
Lakewood's Barnstormer
London Bridget of Wolfpit
Mac-Ken-Char's Seafinn
M.A.C.'s Mister McCrae
May Morning of Wolfpit
Metcourt's Bill Bailey
Metcourt Good Golly Ms Molly
Miss Appropriate O'Misty Isle
Morris-Heim's Ebullient Elmer
Morris-Heim's Mr. Chips
Murdock McFlair
Nahtsees Bitoogunee Gees'ook
Nahtsees Xoots Dadzee Tsah
Nightfalls Harry-O
Norton's Royal No Way
Norton's Royal Robbie

Patrick Peppercorn of Staten
Red Banner O'Kisncairn
Regimental's Amy-O-J
Rockwell at Ridgley
Rossmoor's Loner
Sabal of Overlook
Salem Hill's Little Hobo
Sandlapper's Teddy Bear
Scot's Heather of Ymir
Shaja's Red Rosie O'Brae
Society's Raleigh of Cairn Den
Sookota Geronimo
Tartan's Jolly G MacDuff
Telfer Roadrunner
Tu-Lane Acres Bryan Bishop
Vinovium Caius
Wee Acre Cahoot
Whistle Gate Red Falcon
Wiscairn Golden Harvest
Woodmist Firefly
Woodmist Jonquil
Woodmist Replica of Echo

Woodmist Starfire

Obedience Degrees

Ch. Alexander MacRuff O'Southfield,
T.D.
Annie Laurie's Moppet, C.D.
Baker's Maggie May, C.D.
Brandy Haaheo Hauoli Love, C.D.
Camelot of Crag Lochan, C.D.
Ch. Clary's Sound Off, C.D.X.
Ch. Cragcastle Tartan, C.D.
Ch. Craigly-B Peter Piper, C.D.
Golden Ailsa, C.D.
Haggis McTavish, C.D.

Heatherbrae's Susie Cutes, C.D.
Lakewood's Indian Summer, C.D.
MacAphee The Toad, C.D.
Mandett's Molly of Lyn-Del, C.D.
Misty Briget, C.D.
Pickett's Toto, C.D.
Red Pepper of Deltona, C.D.
Romunda's High Fashion, C.D.X.
Sandy Man MacNevitt, C.D.
Wee McBrindy of Hillndale, C.D.
We-Hi-Te Miss Buffy, C.D.

Whistle Gate Bit O'Folly

1976

Champions of Record

Alison Burr Kenkin Blenheim
Bit O'Kandy O'Windy Pines
Blynman Just A Bit

Bobbie's Friar of Prestwick
Bonnie Belle of Prestwick
Brankt of Prestwick

Brightridge Cadence
Brightridge Hanke Bannister
Brightridge Misty Heather
Brightridge O'er Creekstone
Brightridge Ruffian
Brandy Tam O'Shanter
By's Dr. Pepper of Prestwick
Cairmar's Brandywine
Cairmar's Connecticut Yankee
Cairmar's Fighting Chance
Cairmar Grand Chance
Cairmar Happicairn's Becky
Cairmar Misty Storm
Cairmar Tartan Taffy
Cairncrest Tuppence
Cairndania Brigrey's Dumbeg
Cairndania Seaspirit's Keal
Cairndania Tammy's Targon
Cairn Gorm's Bleck Gold
Cairn Gorm's Gabriella
Cairnworth Molly of Brindle
Caithness Reginald
Carborn of Melita
Cessnock Ghilly's JJ Johanna
Clandara's Solataire
Clan Makaws Gay Mike of Melita
Coral Rocks Sparky Maloney
Craigly Dougal McFlair
Craigly Jamie McFlair
Craigly Maggie McFlair
Craiglyn Christmas Carol
Craiglyn Culture
Dapper Cairn's Barnaby
Dapper Dan of Wildwood
Dees Wee Babe
Flickwynds Andyboy of Leeway
Flickwynds Hidi O'Hillerdale
Gingerbred's Triscuit
Gold Miner of Tail's End
Galagallant Suede Jaffey, C.D.
Gayla Cairn's Big Bertha
Gayla Cairn's Et Cetera
Gayla Cairn's Holligan
Gayla Cairns Hubert
Gayla Cairns Millie McKim
Gayla Cairn's Nora
Gayla Cairn's Yittle Sister
Glenwoulfe Merry Mousetrap

Happy of Cairn Den
Hearn Thunder Thighs
Huggy Bear O'Misty Isle
Kamidon Sky Hawk of Cairmar
Kencanis Prince Errol's Rogie
Kim-E-Cairn's Mac O'Mist-N-Mac
Kim-E-Cairn's Red Fox
Kisncairn Scarlet Jezabel
Kutisark's Deefer
Lakewood's Foxy Lady
Lakewood's Raggedy Ann
Lakewood's Top O'The Mornin
Lillabeth of Dunburn
Lochreggand Rubetta
Lord Ian McVie
Macdaffin of Wolfpit
Mac-Ken-Char's Sea Captain
Macmischief of Wolfpit
Macspacek Wee Bonni O'North
McPooh's Ringleader
Metcourt's Butcher Boy
Metcourt's Magnolia Blossom
Milbryan Kmart of Cairmar
Mingala O'Windy Pines
Morrisheim's Satin Sandy
Nahtsees Gijook Goon Tuyees
Nahtsees Gijook Sagee Teeyah
Nightfalls Sundance
Nortons Royal Pickie
Oudenarde Sea Hawk
Persi Redthol Jay-O
Redletter Marco
Regimental's Meg of Tyree
Renart's Tinker Bell
Rex The Robber of Cairnden
Roc Mar's Winter Wind
Roderick Dru of Crondall
Ronanjo Heather of Cessnoch
Roylaine's Reginald
Salty Sea of Shoop's Isle
Sandy Cairmar Keyes
Shirlong's Flying A
Spunky of Whistle Gate
Tartan's Tipsy Tavish
Teacher's Regal Fagan
The Gunner of Flintridge
Timberlake's Red Baron
Toptwig Cathmhor's Jason

Twinlaw Honeysuckle
Tycan's Ready-Or-Not
Woodmist Grey Cavalier
Wocdmist Hollyhock

Woodmist Meadow Hawk
Woodmist Melody
Woodmist Persimmon
Woodmist Willow

Woodside Bell

Obedience Degrees

Ch. Alexander MacRuff O'Southfield,
   T.D., C.D.
Arways Johnny Belinda, C.D.
Archibald Kerri-Onkow, C.D.
Annie Christie, C.D.
Angus Paladin, C.D.
Bellian's Shaded Sadie, C.D.
Blue Hill Great Gatsby, C.D.
Caremar Missy Truffles, C.D.
Checker's Tartan Trailer, C.D.
Cheri's Lucky Penny, C.D.
Christopher's Toby, C.D.
Cinric's Barnaby, C.D.
Colltrag Dandi Sandi Andi, C.D.
Ch. Craigly-B Dusky Enchantress, C.D.
Ch. Craigly-B Wizard, C.D.

Eaton's Misty Heather, C.D.
Genie, C.D.
Gypsy's Robbie The Devil, C.D.
Inverary Morag, C.D.
Lord Duffer McBriar Rose, C.D.
Lura O'Killybracken, C.D.
Oudenarde Truly Scrumptous, C.D.
Philrays Aprilfool of Gatsby, C.D.
Pintar's Tobias, C.D.
Rudolph Gschwind, C.D.
Sir Winston Greenfield, C.D.
Sunny Pepper Gypsy-O, C.D.
Timberlake's Rudy-Baker, C.D.
Arway's Red Muffin, C.D.X.
We-Hi-Te Miss Buffy, C.D.X.
Dasoma Scruftish McBrier, U.D.

Blue Hill Great Gatsby, C.D., T.D.

1977

Champions of Record

Alison Kened Adel
Alison Mahbam Tuppence
Bagpipe's Bandit O'Lay Dee Ayr
Bagpipe Windfall of Wolfpit
Balcoven Bracken
Bellacairns Bonnie Bruce
Blynman Bewitching
Bonnie Vamp of Wolfpit
Brightridge Debutante
Brightridge Midnight Special
Brightridge Rocket
Cairmar's Chamberlain
Cairmar's Colonel Sam
Cairmar Fancy Dresser
Cairmar Flaming Brandy

Cairmar's Trump Card
Cairndania Chiperall
Cairndania Sargent's Dalson
Cairndania Sea Hawk's Heron
Cairn Gorm's Goldfinch
Cairn Gorm's Lady in Red
Cairnwood's Fiver
Cairnwood's Nighean
Cairnwood's Starshine
Case O' Scotch of Shoop's Isle
Castlerock's Sir Angus
Channing MiLady Anne
Chriscay's Heavens to Betsy
Chriscay's I'm Toto Too
Clan Makaw's Merry Marcietu

Coolin of Melita
Copperglen's Highwayman
Coral Rock's Bonnie Maloney
Craigly B Brynde of Glencairn
Craigly Katherine McFlair
Craigly-S Rebel
CountrySide's Holly Hi
Dand's Lord Bucford O'Cairn Den
Dandy Dan the Varmit Man
Douglas Macrog of Staten
Duncan IX
Elfstone's Hi-Jinx
Explosion of Melita
Flickwynd's Buzz Saw Barney
Gamac Country Squire
Gayla Cairn's Buncombe
Gayla Cairn's Earthquake
Gayla Cairn's Mister McKim
Gayla Cairn's No No Nannette
Gayla Cairn's Virtue
Gingerbred's Power House
Glencairn Molly McNeill
Gypsy's Ragtime Ruffie
Happicairn Nutmeg
Haverford's Becky O'Waterford
Hearn Bourbon
Jean Brodie O'Misty Isle
Justcairn Stormy Knight
Kathleen's Candy O'Southfield
Kenbraw's Macho MacDuff
Kil-Kenny of Raelain
Kiku's Lochmors Lucky Lad
Kim-E-Cairn's Drummer Boy
Kim-E-Cairn's Mighty Shamus
Kipper KiJa Son
Kinloch Honey Babe
Kisncairn Too Good To Be True
Kobil's MacDuff of Flickwynd
Lachdale Smokey Bear
Lady Kathryn O'Montclair
Lakewood's Bonnie Lass
Lakewood's Suzy Q
Lakewood's Tiger Lady
Lesmars Miss Lori

Little Dab'l Doya of Cairn Den
Mac's Maggie May
Maricairn Tobi of Ramblewood
Mary Wilf's Sir Lancelot
McDuff's Song of the South
McPooh's Flaming Star
McPooh's Sand Burr
Meriwynd's Pinch O'Pepper
Metcourt's Buckwheat
Metcourt's Cherry Blossom
Midnight of Prestwick
Moonbeam of Redletter
Nahtsees Maxi S'Isan Xoots
Nightfalls McDuff
Norton's Royal Misty
Norton's Royal Trouper
Oliver's Lucky Mac
O'Southfield's Trouble Galore
Our Little Joy Timothy
Piccairn's Mia
Ragamuffin's Pojo
Ragamuffin's Sugar Bear
Recless Angus
Recless Wendy's Girl
Redletter Maharajah
Regimental's Laird Rob
Rockwell's Quicksilver
Rossarden Harvest Gold
Rossmoor's Princess Pat
Roylain's Cheeta
Samantha of Cairncrag
Sulinda Rufus of Blyman
Sultan's Red Satan
Tartan's Tuppence MacDuff
Taylor's Mr. Ed of Raelain
T's Sprout O'Heather Wildfire
Topcairn Imp
Toptwig Fly by Night of Oudenarde
Tradorohgs Cluny Connamarah
Whistle Gate Abbie Shoon
Wiscairn Dixie
Woodmist Grey Wren
Woodmist Windjammer
Woody McRuff of Highhedges

Obedience Degrees

Angus McDuff XIV, C.D.
Christopher's Carrie Lin, C.D.
Dapper Cairn's Wee Murphy, C.D.
Heather Noel of Kerry Lane, C.D.
Kathcairns Razzdazzle, C.D.
Little Minch's Carrie, C.D.
Love's Feathers Mactavish, C.D.
Mab Glatisant Andy MacAndrew, C.D.
Mab Glatisant Nutmeg Tansy, C.D.
Mab Glastisant Arthur Rex, C.D.
Rag Muffin Annie, C.D.
Ms. Samantha Aynn, C.D.

Simpson's Bridget, C.D.
Stephen's Lady, C.D.
Von Stohr's Scottish Lad, C.D.
Windward's Colin Glencannon, C.D.
Golden Ailsa, C.D.X.
Lord Duffer McBriar Rose, C.D.X.
Lura O'Killybracken, C.D.X.
Wee McBrindy of Hillndale, T.D.,
   C.D.X.
Clary's Mab Glatisant PWCA, U.D.
Philray's Aprilfool of Gatsby, C.D., T.D.
Wobbleit Aboot-Abit Brook, T.D.

1978

Champions of Record

Accalia's Hutch
Albanoch Jalice
Albanoch's Swashbuckler
Almin's Trudi Tuebeg
Avenelhouse Royal Scot
Bagpipe Londons Oliver
Barberi Hedge Garry Owen
Bayberry of Wolfpit
Bold Oaks Play It Again Sam
Boysenberry of Wolfpit
Braebriar's Brody
Brehannon's Wee Bit of a Brogue
Briana's Aunt Jodi of G-N-J
Brightridge Benji
Buckshots Rory of Cessnoch
Cairduil Pendle Witch
Cairmar Angel On Her Nite Off
Cairmar Brandy Alexander
Cairmar Cara of Wildwood
Cairmar Cassandra
Cairmar Fancy Is as Fancy Does
Cairmar Pistol Peri
Cairmar Stormie Surprise

Cairncrest Danyell
Cairndania Davey's Darter
Cairndania Tuscan's Tanger
Cairn Gorm's Brigadier
Cairnworth Bit O'Macho
Chriscay's Iz She Windy
Chriscay's Wind in the Willow
Clan Makaw's Merry Myrt Tu
Clary's Charity
Copperacre Angus of Sarnat
Copperglens Blackwatch
Coralrocks Boney Maloney
Countryside B's Barrister
Crag Valley Isabelle
Creekstone Captain Crunch
Crichton Stars 'N Stripes
Dan D's Barnabas Ben Shalom
Echo of the Chimes O' Windy Pine
Flickwynds Rosalee
Flickwynds Terrytown
Flickwynds Whiskey of Halo
Foxy Loxy Vixen of Haverford
Gayla Cairn's O'Ruffie

Gayla Cairn's O'Suffie
Gayla Cairn's Quite Like Davey
Gayla Cairn's Rosscraggen
Gayla Cairn's Xylophone
Gayla Cairn's Zanzibar
Gingerbred Oh Henry
Glencairn Lovely McNeill
Greetavale Golden Vow of Courtrai
Hapi's Prissy Bear of Quixote
Heathcairn Miss Tammy
Heather's Harvest Storm
Heshe Hilarious
Heshe Lilly Langtry
Innesfree's Bryan's Song
John Paul JP Brandys
Kaerstie O' Montclair
Karendale Davey's Darger
Kenbraw Red Spark
Kim-E-Cairn's Shadrack
Lakewood's Charming Betsy
Lakewood's Indian Witchcraft
Lakewood's Mean Joe Green
Lakewood's O C
Lakewood's Sir Echo
Lakewood's Teddy Bear
Lochwood Black Watch
MacBriar of Wolfpit
MacJess' Bonnie Jean
Magic Midnight O'Southfield
Marma's Max
Mister Mac of Raelain
McDuff's Happy Annie-versery

McPooh's Forever Yours
McPooh's Peter Cracker Jack
McPooh's Timberlake Stardust
Meriwynd's Glenfree Sprite
Metcourt Great Balls of Fire
Metcourt's Magnum Opus
Milbryan Pepper Pot of Almin
Mister MacDuff De Dan D
Mountview's Clear as Crystal
Nahtsees Gunyul'Xoots Tootum
Persimmon of Wolfpit
Ragamuffins Casey
Ragamuffin's Silversmythe
Ramblewood Stormy O' Moonstar
Rockwell's Artful Dodger
Rockwell's Jubal Early
Rogerlyn Sea Hawk's Salty Sam
Ruby Love of Melita
Scots Mist Thistle Rakos
Shajas Fay of Glenkaren
Shaja's Teenie Tish O'Haven
Strike Up the Band of Wolfpit
Sundune's Misty McFirth
Tammy's Sarah
Topcairn Ferelith
Tulane Centenial Budd Wizers
Whetstone Whimsy of Cairmar
Whistle Gate Glen Feddich II
Wicked Witch 'O Cairn Cove
Wiscairn Echo of Donnrich
Woodmist Violet
Ymir's Kris Kringle of Kishorn

Obedience Degrees

Angus McDuff XIV, C.D.X.
Arways Johnny Belinda, C.D.X.
Cairmar McMillan Ceilidh, C.D.
Camelot of Crag Lochan, C.D.X.
Casey Mac Blackbeard, C.D.
Countryside's Debutante, C.D.
Glengarry of Dalhousie, C.D.
Kathcairns Razzdazzle, C.D.X.
Kathleen's Scottish Taffy, C.D.
Katno Tiger, C.D.

Majestic Mist, C.D.
Master Charge LaRoche, C.D.
Miss Spunky Bunky, C.D.
Moppet's Misery Maxie, C.D.
Mr. Bilbo Baggins of Gatsby, T.D.
Mr. Chips XXI, C.D.
Tipsy Tim of Trestle Glen
Tradorohgs' Daniel Dhu, C.D.
We-Hi-Te Miss Buffy, U.D.
Wilcairn Caraway Emmacorn, C.D.

Champions of Record

Accalia's Inkster
Accalia's Orkney
Alison's Duntup Arran
Aonghas Breac of Achnaruie
Avenelhouse Plain Jane
Balcoven Marksman of Wolfpit
Bellacairn's Ragtime Bonnie
Bellacairn's Seumas
Biljonblues Beguine
Blynman Fire Eater
Blynman Reddy O'Kihone
Bonnie Gidget of Wolfpit
Bonnie Tramp of Wolfpit
Braw Clan's Gypsy Fiddler
Brightridge Caper's Penny
Brightridge Deran Murfe Lad
Brightridge Minute Man
Cairland Afternoon Delight
Cairland Bobby Dazzler
Cairmar Amy Amy Amy
Cairmar Carrousel Charme
Cairmar Duncan Phyfe
Cairmar Misty Christmas Morn
Cairmar Critic's Choice
Cairmar Muzzle Loader
Cairmar Parade at Dawn
Cairmar's Angel After Dark
Cairmar's Charisma
Cairmar's Infernal Angel
Cairmar's Leslie
Cairmar's Summer Mist
Cairndania Hawk's Debbie
Cairndania Jester's Jingles
Cairndania Jester's Joy
Cairndania Targon's Thomas
Cairndania Sea Hawk's Harcon
Cairndania Sea Hawk's Hendy
Cairngorlynn Red Ruffie
Cairn Gorm's Ima Pistol
Cairnhill Gamekeepers Toby
Cairnhoe Fireworks O'Wolfpit
Carnoustie of Wolfpit
Chriscay's Joy in the Morning
Clarepat's Dan D's Fancy Dan

Cliffcairn Graegirl's Fionna
Copperglen's Sunstone
Coralrocks Georgia Bell
Cray Valley Juniper
Craigly Kevin McFlair
Cricklade's Merril Rae
Criscairn Toto Too
Donimar Scottish Mist
Duke Clancy McScavenger
Ecum Secuh of Wildwood
Flickwynds Fancy Nancy
Flickwynds Halo of Hearts
Foxgrove Jeronimo
Foxgrove Mutt
Gamac Night Hawk
Gayla Cairn's Bang Crash
Gayla Cairn's Brotherton
Gayla Cairn's Eaststar
Gayla Cairn's Gray Knight
Gayla Cairn's Hi-Hopes
Hearn Hogmaney
Heathcairn Charlie
Heather-Dee-of-Rocky-Clan
Heather's Harvest Buff
HelenReady O' Southfield
Highhedges Skipper of Badenoch
Jauntibelle Gaelic Cairndania
Jeremy McFlair of Staten
Kamidon's Jubilee Jasmine
Karendale Classic O'Meri-Leigh
Kelly Bridgit
Kiku's Andrew O'Capscot
Kim-E-Cairn's Sandpiper
Kim-E-Cairn's Whistle Binkie
Kisncairn Polly Flinders
Kisncairn Tommie Tucker
Kobils Bonnie of Flickwynd
Lachdale Red Bandit
Lachdale E. F. Hutton
Laird Jamie O' Southfield
Lakewood's Jameson Maloney
Lakewood's Leo
Lakewood's Moon Mist
Lakewood's Pistol Pete

Lakewood's Red Raider
Lakewood's Stormy Weather
Lakewood's Talking Tilda
Lochreggand Yogie Bear
Lucky too of Cairn Den
MacBrian of Wolfpit
Marbelhill's Pep of Geynncuri
Meriwynd's Brock O'Gibralter
Meriwynd's Sand Storm
Miss Muffin O' Southfield
Ms. McD
Nomands Beau of Cessnoch
Oudenarde Flying Flirt
Pennyland's Kare Kim-E-Cairn's
Pinetop Piccadilly
Quince the Piper of Cessnoch
Ravensworth Arran of Wolfpit
Recless Fantasia
Recless Tristan Himself
Regimental's Lucy in the Sky
Rockwell's Hello Dolly
Rockwell's Littlechap
Rossarden Choral

Roylaine's Red Ritchie
Schellairn Mischevious Kate
Shajas Wee Bonnie Obrae
Stewart's Joshua of Atholl
Teri's Taffy
Timberlakes Gal Glenrichard
Tina Louise of Bellacairn
Toptwig Cathmhor's Toby
Toptwig Norman
Twigbent Deagal
Twigbent Fail
Wee Tam's Bonnie Tyke
Whetstone Annie Hall
Whetstone Halston
Whetstone Miss Dior
Whetstone Tommy Hawk
Whitsle Gate Tam O'Shanter
Wiscairn Heather
Woden of Wildwood
Woodmist Greyling
Woodmist Penelope
Woodmist Vixen
Woodside Midnight Bell

Obedience Degrees

Ch. Alexander MacRuff O'Southfield,
   T.D., C.D.X.
Mr. Bilbo Baggins of Gatsby, T.D., C.D.
Blynman Sea Mist, C.D.
Ch. Brehannon's Wee Bit of a Brogue,
   C.D.
Cairmar PDQ of Lakewood, T.D.
Carlson's McDuff, C.D.
Debs Wandern Rebel O'Royland, C.D.
Duffy XXI, C.D.

Ginger Girl of Wildwood, C.D.
Kim-E-Cairn's Bonnie Melissa, C.D.
Kintail Ivanhoe, C.D.
Ch. Lakewood's O C. T.D.
Little Minch's Carrie, C.D.X.
Philray's Aprilfool of Gatsby, T.D.,
   C.D.X.
Schneiders Gregory MacPeck, C.D.
Tiffany's Toy Tiger, C.D.
Wee Mac Hardy, C.D.

1980

Champions of Record

Aesop Tails Bandit O Meriwynd
Almin's Chance For Tue
Bellemere's Captain Rowdy
BI

Brehannon On The Rocks
Brightridge Millie's Mitzi
Broc's Bain Kelpie
Brucairn Drummer Boy

Cairland Bagpipes
Cairmar Centurion
Cairmar Coco Chanel
Cairmar Colonel Fairway
Cairmar Devil's Advocate
Cairmar Fancy Stepper
Cairmar Music Box Dancer
Cairmar's Quartermaster
Cairmar's Taste of Honey
Cairncrest Duncan's Delight
Cairndania Douglas Detree
Cairndania Keal's Kealter
Cairn Gorm's Rags to Riches
Cairn Gorm's Shamus
Cairnlea's Robson
Cairnmoor Salty Sams Sallie
Cairnwoods Inghinn
Caries T C Jester
Cessnoch Ghilly's JJ Jessica
Chasands Miss Bryanna
Chasands Yankee Peddler
Chauncey Boy O'Southfield
Cliffcairn Mr. Sanderz
Craigly Sir Prize of Viran
Criscairn MS Munchkin
Daveleigh's Kelley
Dees Happie Amanda
Dorlyn's Easy Livin'
Dugan Aberystwth of Benway
Emerald Valle Shaun
Feldspar's Druscilla Penny
Ferniegair Tara
Flickwynd's Black Magic
Flickwynds Impossible Pip
Flickwynds Magic Halo
Gayla Cairn's Edward McKim
Gayla Cairn's Elmer
Gayla Cairn's Jedadiah
Gayla Cairn's Josie
Gayla Cairn's Yarborough
Glencairn Bobby McNeill
Glencairn Carrie McNeill
Glencairn Neil McNeill
Happicairn Frolic
Heathcairn Grayson
Jodian's Bonnie Prince Charlie
Jodian's Iron Duke
Karen's Miss Sassafras

Karengary's New Spirit
Kim-E-Cairns Gerolf
Kim-E-Cairns's Macho Man
Kingstones Bonny Heather
Kirriemuir O'Windy-Pines
Kirkwalls Rocky Glenrichard
Kisncairn Topnatch O McLaren
Lachdale Red Ruffles
Lakewood's Bristol Moon
Lakewood's Buffalo Bill
Lakewood's Moon Dust
Lakewood's Moon Flower
Lakewood's Moon Tripper
Lakewood's Raisin Cain
Lakewood's Terrific Triffle
Lakewood's Thespian
Lesmars Star Baby
Loch Katrine Lady Ellen
London Chimes of Wolfpit
Lucky Lady O'Misty Isle
MacKenzie of Overlook
Maidenlees Bonnie Lass
Maricairn Sea Anemone
McLin's Piper of Loch Morar
McPooh's Midnight Serenade
Meriwynd Finnigan Beginagin
Meriwynd Macuchla
Milbryan Trucairn Tornado
Misty Morn's Bold as Brass
Moran's Shadow of Oakie
Nahtsees L'Eiw Wus Ts'Itskw
Nahtsees Teeyadoosee Ponica
Nahtsees Teeyah Geesook Shih II
Nightfalls Chance Encounter
Norton's Royal Sammie
Pennylane Kim-E-Cairn's Lady M
Pennyland Kim-E-Cairn's Oliver
Petunia O'Kisncairn
Rag A Bash Jenifer Twinkle
Ragamuffins Tomma Tweed
Ravensworth Ninia Luv
Recless Aberdeen
Redletter Marvo Killybracken
Ridgewood Wee Willie Winkie
Rossarden Gipsey Rover
Seascape Bet Your Britches
Shadow's Weekend Warrior
Shin Pond Cricket

Skyover French Connection
Tagalong of Wildwood
Taylors Happy New Year
Terrytowns Topper O'Kenbraw
Thimswarra Regal Laird
Thornwoods Foxfire
T' is Gramp's Sweetstuff
T's is Squiget McBess

Topkick Boss Tweed
Tu-Lane Acres Gutsy Bush
Uniquecottage Galah
Uniquecottage Gold Ortolan
Warpaints Devil of Cessnoch
Waterford Miss Montgomery
Whetstone Wild Heather
Whetstone Wild Oats
Woodmist Scarlet Star

Obedience Degrees

Alfie Mac Scooter, C.D.
Black Beard II, C.D.
Bramble of Millwood, C.D.
Casey's Shadow, C.D.
Craigly Quoiche McCrippen, C.D.
Golden Ailsa, U.D.
Kavei's MacTiger, C.D.
Majestic Mist, C.D.X.
Miss Spunky Bunky, C.D.X.

Mr. Whiskers of Dover, C.D.
Prescott's Tartan Flash, C.D.
Priddy Bonnie Red Lady, C.D.
Red Oak's Prince Phillip, C.D.
Rheny's Little Buster Brown, C.D.
Scotch Mist's Golden Girl, C.D.
Scots Mist Thomas, C.D.
Scotch Mist XIV, C.D.
Sweetbriars Merry Muffin, C.D.
Toto Payne, C.D.

1981

Champions of Record

Alison's Mytup Bruaria
Annwood Kings Highwayman
Ar-cee El Chico
Argyle of Shoop's Isle
Attic Leandros
Azgard's Johnney Reb
Azgard's Nearly Mist
Bellacairn's Bit'O Blarney
Bellemere's Sassy Shell
Bennel's Black Pepper
Bennel's Brandaleena
Big Ben of Wolfpit, C.D.
Bold Oaks Acorn O'Worrindale
Bold Oak's Redneck
Braemar's MacGregor
Braw Clan's Gypsy Fife
Brehannon Cinnamon Sugar
Brehannon With A Chaser

Brigadoon's Adam's Apple
Brigadoon's Pied Piper
Brigadoon's Pistol Pete
Brigadoon's Sassy Sasha
Brightridge Wendy's Jewell
Cairland Center Fold
Cairland Count Me In
Cairland Prime Contender
Cairmar Barnabas Collins
Cairmar Caramel Candy
Cairmar's Depth Charge
Cairmar Flying Colors
Cairmar's Fortune Hunter
Cairmar Scot Free
Cairmar's Touch of Class
Cairndania Jeronimo's Jaunty
Cairndania Sailor's Kate
Cairndania Sargent's Dinnitty

Cairndania Sargent's Strutter
Cairndania Sea Hawk's Hance
Cairnwoods Haverford Oh Wo
Capricorn's Collin Ridge
Carnedds Unheard Melody
Cessnoch Ghilly's Aarron
Cessnoch Ghilly's Angus
Chasands Mighty Avenger
Chriscay's More the Merrier
Clan Makaw Myrt's Brat
Coralrocks Clancy Maloney
Coralrocks Kiti Maloney
Coralrocks Nelly Maloney
Coralrocks Pippin Maloney
Copperglen British Sterling
Copperglen Cinnabar
Courtrai Spun Silver
Crag Valley Georgiana
Craigly B Bergie
Craigly B Rory of Mcriwynd
Creekstone Cinderella
Criscairn Wizard of Oz
Dan D's Heather of Cairn Den
Danny Boy of Wildwood
Dapper Cairn's Duncan Dan
Druidsgate Gadaboot
Feldspar's Butterscotch
Ferniegair Fearnought
Ferniegair Kristy
Flickwynds Crystal Valle
Flickwynds Feisty Robyn
Flickwynds Scotch Heather
Flickwynds Super Jock
Foxgrove Jaunty
Foxgrove Jessica
Gairlock's Rascal O'Ragtime
Gayla Cairn's Early Bird
Gayla Cairn's Elsie
Gayla Cairns Enof-O-That
Gayla Cairns Kojak
Gleneagle of Wolfpit
Halo's High Society
Howdy's Serendipity Weewin
Jean of Staten
Jo Jo McDuff of Barret
Karen's Miss Silly Puddy
Kengraw's Brash Bart

K'Hurst Razzle Dazzle McPooh
Kim-E-Cairn's Scotch Rebellion
Kim-E-Cairn's Shannon Cairnehl
Kinncayre's Grey Gilligan
Kirkwall's Jessica Jocosa
Kisncairn Night Hawk
Kisncairn Shilegh O'Mine
Lakewood's Indian Legend
Lakewood's Snapshot Studley
Lakewood's Thaddeus
Leeways Acapulco Gold
Loch Katrine Iain Gregarach
Lochreggand Gabriel
London House Toasted Muffin
MacLogan Berry of Wolfpit
Marblehill's Gold-N-Rust
Maricairn Sea Booty
McLin's New Decade-Diamond Lil
McPoohs Valle Tifany Star
McTaggart of Raclain
Meri-Leigh's Star Blazer
Merriwynds Graystone Pebbles
Missy of Worth-Mor
Nahtsees Teeyah Geesook Shih
Nightfalls Goodcookie
Norton's Royal Sparkle
Old Orchards Big Shot
Piper's Anges of Blynman
Prestwicks's Uno
Quixote's April Fool
Ragamuffin's Cassidy
Ragamuffin's Trace O'Bagpipe
Ragtime's Smitty Smith
Ramblewood Barney Brehannon
Ravensworth Zip of Donnrich
Recless Tartan San O'Tavish
Red Oak's Salty Sea Spray
Reds Scottish Bandit
Robbie's Second Hand Rose
Rock'in Chimes O'Windy Pines
Rogerlyn Sailor Cairndania
Rowdy's Rough Rider
Sam's Little Miss Nutmeg
Schneiders Ginger MacRogers
Scots Mist Tinker
Seacross Stargazer
Spiceberry of Wolfpit

259

Sundune's Salty Sadie
Sunnyland's Gadget of Wolfpit
The Unsinkable Mollie Brown
Uniquecottage Glint of Gold

Uniquecottage Gold Kinglet
Uniquecottage Phainopepla
Whetstone Fair'N'Warmer
Whetstone Weatherman

Woodmist Copper Bracken

Obedience Degrees

Ch. Big Ben of Wolfpit, C.D.
Bonnie Bess, C.D.
Ch. Cairnmoor Salty Sams Sadie, C.D.
Carol's Christie, C.D.
Coletownes Betsy, C.D.
Countryside Barkley's Taffy, C.D.
Countryside's Mr. McGregor, C.D.
Ginger Girl of Wildwood, C.D.X.
Kim-E-Cairn's Bonnie Melissa,
   C.D., T.D.
Kirstie Dhu O'Southfield, C.D.
Kirstie Dhu O'Southfield, T.D.
Kisncairn What The Sam Hill, C.D.
Lura O'Killybracken, U.D.

Mab Glatisant Arthur Rex, C.D.X.
Ch. Miss Muffin O'Southfield, C.D.
Morrisheim's Rusty MacDonald, C.D.
Nahtsees Tuyeeseek Xigah Kah, C.D.
Pennylane's Rude Valentino, C.D.
Reager's Scrappy Bearsden, C.D.
Red Oak's Prince Phillip, C.D.X.
Rocky McKeag, C.D.
Sandy MacDuff III, C.D.
Sequoia's Wee Bonnie Lassie, C.D.
Tammara of Twisted Oaks, C.D.
Toby of Cairn's Heather, C.D.
Trapper John II, C.D.
Tu-Lane Acres Millie Hi-Life, C.D.

1982

Champions of Record

Albanoch Saturday Nite Fiver
Almin's Golden Nugget Tueson
Andrew Kris of Terror
Audrey's Misty Samaircin
Avenelhouse Partridge
Avenelhouse Sixpence
Billy Bob of Raelain
Binnie O'The Brae
Blynman Melody
Bold Oaks Booker T
Bold Oaks Cover Girl
Brehannon's Graylan Drummer
Brigadoon's Road Bandit
Brightridge Benjamin Benny
Brightridge Big Ben
Brightridge J C Penny
Cairland Atom Action

Cairland Talent Scout
Cairmar's Boss Man Almin
Cairmar Cachet
Cairmar Caldonia
Cairmar Lil Gambler
Cairmar Captivation
Cairmar Courteson
Cairmar Simply Smashing
Cairncove's Camilla
Cairndania Jeronimo Jass
Cairndania Thomas Jarrie
Cairnehl Riff Raf Kime-Cairn's
Cairnehl's Noah Nonsense
Cairngold Crackerjack
Cairngorlynn Bunty O'The Brae
Cairngorlynn Ruffies Radar
Cairnhoe Chantyman

Cairnhowse Morning Star
Cairnhowse Sargent Pepper
Canorwoll For-Get-Me-Nought
Chasands Show Stopper
Chasands Travelin' Man
Chriscay's Luke Skywalker
Coiltrag Master MacGregor
Coralrocks Foxy Maloney
Coralrocks Mini Maloney
Copperglen Pendleton
Courtrai Tommy Tucker
Craiglyn Caledonia
Creekstone December Disaster
Crofter's Gate Calma
Crofter's Gate Dana
Croydon Sea Chanty
Fillkatoms' Sir Winston
Flickwynd's Elizabeth
Flickwynd's Roderick
Flickwynd's Susannah
Gabrielson's Chipper Laddie
Gayclan Watchit
Gayla Cairn's Kiss My Grits
Gayla Cairn's Sadie
Gayla Cairn's Simon
Glencairn Barnabas McNeill
Glencairn Britannia McNeill
Glencairn Ducky II O'Meriwynd
Glencairn Sally McNeill
Harobed Hill Butterscotch
Holly Hill Highland Mary
Holly Hill Top Of The Line
Jodian's Fourteen Pounder
Jodian's Virgo Brindle
Kamidon Sandpiper
Karengary's Indian Spirit
Kathleen's Stormy Amber
Kenbraw's Apache
Kisncairn Lulu
Lady Sharoon O'Misty Isle
Lakewood's Buffalo Gal
Lakewood's Comet
Lakewood's Derringer
Lakewood's General Sherman
Lakewood's Moon Lady
Lakewood's Suzy Sippin Soda
Lakewood's William O'Charbe

Lakewood's Winsome Witch
Littleclan Sadie
Liza Jane of Raelain
Loch Katrine Falcons Kirstie
Loch Katrine Jennie Marie
Lochreggand Sir Vivor
Maricairn Noel of Ramblewood
Meriwynd Finnigans Rainbow
Mandarin's Andy McDandy
McMaggie
Milbryan Delta Dawn O'Cairmar
Misselwaithe's Bit O Honey
Mister Hi MacCair
Naiad of Kihone
Nightfalls Prime Time
Patter's Tigger of Cairmar
Piccairn's Cailinn
Pop Music of Shoop's Isle
Prescott's Venture in Ragtime
Quick Trick of Wolfpit
Quixotes April Love
Raelain's Fighting Tiger
Ragamuffins Laird O'Braemar
Ragtimes Easy Lovin Ember
Ramblewood Maricairn Teasel
Recless Gaelic
Rheny's Little Buster Brown, C.D.
Rocky McLin Of Pearland
Rowdys Earl Of Fitzroy
Seneley Capt Poldark-Uniquecottage
Shajas Gaeya Obrae
Sherry Berry of Wolfpit
Shin Pond Denny
Shoop's Isle Highland Piper
Shoop's Isle Mermaid's Song
Sky Rocket of Raelain
Teddy T Terrier
Topcairn Oliver
Topcairn Ovation
Uniquecottage Blackbird
Waterford Quintillion
Weeknowe Walsing Susan
Wildwood's Orkney Scuff
Wiscairn Buccaneer
Wiscairn Starshine
W W Wilbur
Worrindale Lara's Crystal

Obedience Degrees

Angus McDuff XIV, U.D.
Bellian's South-Down Sophie, C.D.
Ch. Big Ben of Wolfpit, C.D.X.
Chriscay's Soda Pop Kid, C.D.
Black Beard II, C.D.X.
Bonnie Bess, C.D.X.
Brigand of Gatsby, T.D.
Cecilia of Braemar, C.D.
Cristy of Heatherdale, C.D.
Duffy XXXII, C.D.
Fiesty MacDuff, C.D.
Graymist's Zippy Duncan, C.D.

Happicairn Cinnamon, C.D.
Hyper-Heather, C.D.
Ch. Laird Jamie O'Southfield, C.D.
Mab Glatisant Andy MacAndrew, C.D.X.
Mab Glatisant Nutmeg Tansy, C.D.X.
Muf-N-Den Misty Morn, C.D.
Our Girl Kibbles, C.D.
Piccairn's Wandle, C.D.
Prescott's Tartan Flash, C.D.X.
Sir Balfour of Blynman, C.D.
Stonebriar's Shona, C.D.
Ch. Whetstone Fair N' Warmer, C.D.

1983

Champions of Record

Almin's Liberty
Annwood Memerlin
Annwood Only Odalisque
Avenelhouse Sabrine Gull
Barich Cinnamon Toast
Biljonblue's Big Time Brucie
Blynman Abigail of Piper
Bon-A-Star Barnaby Rufus
Bondette of Ferniegair
Braelog Seahawk's Reagan
Brehannon Chocolate Madness
Brehannon's Codbank Summer
Bridgette The Midget
Brigadoon's Meg of Sugar Pine
Brigadoon's Tough Guy
Brigadoon's Twig of Sugar Pine
Brightfields Captain Billy
Brightridge Bandit's Barney
Brightridge Dear Abby
Brightridge Ruff 'N Ready
Cairland Highlands Bombadil
Cairmar Angel In My Pocket
Cairmar Angel's Morning After
Cairmar Angel On My Shoulder
Cairmar Boo Boo Bear
Cairmar Commodore
Cairmar's Fallen Angel
Cairmar Light My Fire

Cairmar Party Chaser
Cairnacre's Lord Angus
Cairndania Jeronimo's Jet
Cairndania Sam's Sandral
Cairndania Sam's Simon II
Cairndania Sam's Sundew
Cairnhill Delight
Cairnhoe Carronade
Cairnland High and Mighty
Cairnhaus Xerox Copy
Cairnwoods Rumble De Thump
Carie's Just Ernie
Caryshader Seriema
Casacoray Jamie Boy
Cessnoch's Polish Princess
Chassands Escape Artist
Chelsa Caprice of Raelain
Clandara's Starbuck
Clayridge Braw Broc
Col-Cairns Ruffy Righinn
Columbus Day Pint O'Brandy
Copperglen Tartan Tweed
Coral Rocks Loney Maloney
Coral Rocks Stoney Maloney
Cragcastle Tartan's Teddy
Craigly Sparkle McPercy
Creag-Mhor Stormy Weather
Christy

Cedar Farms Sizzle at Allegro
Dees Sugar Kandi
DeRan No Can Do
Denbryl's Lochan Ora
Devil Cairn Andromeda
Don Quixote's Fashion Plate
Dorlyn's Easy Lovin'
Elfin Princess Szhiska
Elfin Shamrock Charlie O'Kiku
Fanci Gilliflower of Raelain
Farley's Case
Feldspar's Felicity
Feldspar's Noteworthy
Ferlie
Flickwynds Foxy Freddie
Flickwynds Mac of Andyboy
Gadget's Gimmick of Wolfpit
Gayla Cairns Kaz
Gayla Cairns Martha Wurst
Gayla Cairns Sam
Gayla Cairns Sue
Gingerbred's Tuttie Fruitie
Glencairn Rob Roy McNeill
Golden Sherry of Shoop's Isle
Graystone Gambit
Graystone Gauntlet
Greetavale Super Lad
Harcon's Sea Wolf of Macnan
Heathcairn Brains
Heiland's Bit O'Cairmar
Het's Christie of Cairmar
Huckleberry of Wolfpit
Kamidon Ensign Osprey
Karendale Salty Sam's Toto
Karengary's Indian Giver
Kishorn's Stake Acclaim
Kisncairn Tidbit O'Holly Hill
Lakewood's Barwillagin
Lakewood's Foxfyre
Lakewood's Minnie Pistol
Lakewood's Moon Tugger
Lakewood's Sattelite
Lakewood's Spellbinder
Lakewood's Wareagle
Leeways Rosebud of Flickwynd
Loch Katrine Bit O'Scotch
Loch Katrine Highland Laddie
Macjess Glengarry

MacNan Knight of Nottingham
MacNan Sea Holly of Lochbuie
Marblehill's Kelly Girl
Mary Wilf Jeronimo's Moon Rock
McPooh's Hat Trick
McPooh's K'Hurst Silver Salute
Meri-Leigh's Sweetbrier
Meriwynd's MacRigsby
Meriwynd's Quincy
Meriwynd's Twink
Misty Moor's Bridget
Misty Moor's Gleneagles
Misty Moor's Wee Mopet
Morihas Special Surprise
Nightfalls Cool Change
Norton's Royal Election Eve
Pattwos Martell Cognac
Pattwos Too Tuff McDuff
Penystone's Mist O'May
Piccairn's Muffett O'Brocair
Pilis Willie of Image
Pinetop Gold Dust
Piper's Beatrice Lilly
Ragamuffins Shaugnessy
Ragtimes Wee Lady Kathryn
Ramblewood Tansy O'Maricairn
Recless Druidsgate Markson
Redcoat's Colonel Buckshot
Regard of Kihone
Sagittarius' Isle of Skye
Saint Nicholas of Staten
Schellairns Brier of Wolfpit
Seascape What A Pip
Shajas Foxy Fergus
Shajas Gordy Obrae
Shajas Stormhaven Jaunty Jo
Sharolaine's For Pete Sake
Shin Pond Rhodes
Shin Pond Tradition
Spicy Mr. Bumble O'Southfield
Spring Valle Josie Bon
Stanedykes Angus
Stanedykes The Laird
Stebru's Arthur D. Macarthur
Stebru's Todd's Macruff
Taffy Dacey Bagpipe
Taylor's Cheeky of St. Lea
Tidewater Brigitta

Tidewater Master Gold
Tiffany's Sparkle Twist
Tinker Belle of Bannockburn
Tosh of Hillerdale

Trixie Howd's Serendipity
Trufre's Streussel
Wee Gaelic Todd Cairndania
Weeknowe Waising Gold Tophat

Woodmist Bold Badger

Obedience Degrees

Corky, C.D.
Bellian's South-down Sophie, C.D.X.
Brigand of Gatsby, T.D., C.D.
Ch. Cairmar Cachet, C.D.
Ch. Cairmar's Christmas Storm, C.D.
Ch. Cairn Moor Salty Sams Sadie, C.D.X.
Ch. Chriscay's Iz She Windy, C.D.
Clayridge Priddy McBryce, C.D.
Ch. Glencairn Neil McNeill, C.D.
Gleanloch Sandy, T.D.
Heather's Brindled Misty, C.D.
Karon Mactavish, C.D.
Kintale Mak-B Clan MacGregor, C.D.

Kirkwalls Dust Devil, C.D.
Littleclan Sarah Jane, C.D.
Meriwynd Finnigan's Fling, C.D.
Ch. Piccairn's Cailinn, C.D.
Priddy Bonnie Red Lady, U.D.
Ragamuffins Morgan O'Braemar, C.D.
Red Oak's Prince Philip, U.D.
Scotchmist's Golden Girl, U.D., T.D.
Scotchmist XIV, C.D.X.
Shadow Chaser, C.D.
Squire McDuff, C.D.
Suzy of Windsor, C.D.
Tam-O-Shanter Bonny Lasse, C.D.

Ch. T'is Gramps Sweet Stuff, C.D.

1984

Champions of Record

Annwood Nosey Parker
Annwood Pitcairn
Annwood Pitchblende
Arn-Mar's Lady Cassandra
Barich Tc's Black Raspberry
Bellacairn's Dear Gussie
Benway's State Of The Art
Blackbird of Wolsingham
Blynman Can-Do
Blynman Melinda
Bold Oaks Bombadier
Bold Oaks Maxwell Macgregor
Bonnie Hoyden of Wolfpit
Brigadoon's Mighty Joshua
Brigadoon's Razzle Dazzle
Brightridge Daisy's Dolly
Cairland Hit Parade

Cairmar Andrew of Raelain
Cairmar's Bobby Mc Lin
Cairmar Calamity Jane
Cairmar Countdown
Cairmar Kitten On The Keys
Cairmar Red Alert
Cairmar Scarlet Ribbons
Cairmar Shadow Boxer
Cairmar Shadow Box Image
Cairmar That's Tuff
Cairncrest Irina
Cairndania Jeronimo's Devlin
Cairndania Rufus Razzle
Cairn Glen's Copper Top
Cairngorlynn Joy Cairndania
Cairnhill Wellington
Cairnhowse Starfire

Carnival's Mary-Go-Round
Cairnlea Midnight Nutmeg
Cairnlogs Seventy-Sixer
Caithbea's Addlebery A Gra
Camelu's Highland Mcred
Canorwoll Dusty Miller
Canorwoll Head Over Heels
Cedar Farm Pizzaz At Allegro
Chasands Chantilly Lace
Chriscay's All That Glitters
Coralrocks Sharon Maloney
Cragcastle Chivas Regal
Croydon's Bit O'Sage
Deran Angel of Fire
Deran Westminster Abbey R
Druidsgate Thalassa
Duffy McDuke of Campbell Loch
Dunvegans Tullock O Blantyre
Foxairn Little Miss Marker
Foxairn Ruffnready
Flickwynd's Foxy Freddie
Gaelic' Haggis Macbasher
Gay Tayls Benedict Brigadoon
Gay Taylis Bridget Brigadoon
Gayla Cairn's Endora O'Cairmar
Gayla Cairn's Question Mark
Gayla Cairn's Zippi
Glencairn Benny McNeill
Glencairn Meghan McNeill
Glencairn Missy McNeill
Glencairn Ruggles McNeill
Graystone Fairborn Flame
Happicairn Firecracker
Highland's Quick Chatter
Hollyberry of Bannockburn
Karen's Mr. King Brinney Boy
Kenbraw's Corker
Khurst Cairnehl Tigger McTay
Khurst Tata Bunky Car'Omik
Kileen's Kiku's Bugsy Elfin
Kilkeddan's Chief Justice
Killarney's Image of Wildwood
Kim-E-Cairn's Burly Billy
Kim-E-Cairn's Exceptionale
Kishorn's Halston's Honeycomb
Kishorn's Rush Hour
K-Z's Sea Spirte Samantha
Lachdale Red Flare

Lakewood's Ginger Snap
Lakewood's Gold Trinket
Lakewood's Heather
Lakewood's Pac Man O'Farus
Lakewood's Whippersnapper
Littleclan Robin
Loch Katrine Christmas Joy
Loch Katrine Fiona Gregarach
Lochreggand Gamekeeper
London Chorister of Wolfpit
London Crier of Wolfpit
Macbramble of Wolfpit
Mac Nan Sir Arthur's Alex
Mac Rufus Calico
Marblehehill's Solid Gold
Mentmore Courtesan O'Wolfpit
Meriwynds Waltzing Matilda
Meybriars Poper O Sanndpiper
Milbryan Magic Dawn
Morihas General Casey
Muf-N-Den Misty Morn, C.D.
Nightfallo Famous Amos
O'Grady's Argyll
Pattwos Sherry Brandy
Pollyanna O'Kisncairn
Recless Fortitude
Recless Jaunsama
Recless Leroy
Redcoat's Colonel Buckshot
Renart's Mickey MacPhee
Rosette O Kiscairn
Roylola Rose of Alwmana
Shajas Rufus Obrae
Sharolaine's Just Jodi
Shin Pond Target
Shoop's Isle Fifth of Scoth
Sherryvore Ceilidh O'Kaird
Spring Valle Qunicy Bru Jo
Stutz The Hiwayman of Meybriars
Tidewater Biggy's Miracle
Tillietudlem's Duffus
Ugadale Stormchild
Ugadale Scotch Thistle
Waterford Brightfield Brita
Whipshe Witchcraft
Woodmist Bold Badger
Woodmist Meghan
Wundrvu's Mytee MacKennish

Obedience Degrees

Bit O'Scotch II
Blynman Sea Breeze
Bonnie Bess
Bridgette The Midget
Chocolate Chips
Copperglen Brite N' Sassy
Dee Dee Lass
Ginger Girl of Wildwood
Ch. Glencairn Barnabas McNeill
Kim-E-Cairn's Rugged Ronald
Kim's Spunky of Branchburg
Kirkwood New Girl In Town
Ch. Kisncairn Lulu
Love's Feathers MacTavish

Lucky's Boo-Boo of Tru Fre
MacGregor of Orcas Island
Marquardts Highland Heather
Marquardts Katrinka Tiffany
Ch. Misty Moor's Bridget
Mr. Scooter II
Mr. Whiskers of Dover
Our Girl Kibbles
Schneiders Brookfield Karen
Scotch Mist's Golden Girl, T.D.
Tamra of Alamawa
The Red Knight of Misty Moor
Tuff Enuf Tina
Vegacairn Mary's Toto O'Q

Bibliography

THE FOLLOWING listing of books and articles will offer the serious fancier useful ground in which to study dogs in general and Cairns in particular. The articles offer considerable information on background and in many instances are directed to histories of the old kennels with mention of breeders and outstanding dogs. In general, study of the material listed herein will add much detailed information to the data set forth in this book.

Books of General Interest

Thomson-Gray, D.J.:   *The Dogs of Scotland.* Dundee, 1887, 1891

Leighton, Robert: *The Complete Book of the Dog.* London, 1922

Ash, Edward: *Dogs, Their History and Development.* London, 1927, 2 Vol. 1936

Hutchinson's Dog Encyclopedia. London, c. 1935. 3 Vol.

Smith, A. Croxton: *Terriers, Their Training,* etc. London, 1937

Marvin, John T.:   *The Book of All Terriers,* N.Y., 1976

The Complete West Highland White Terrier. N.Y. 1977

Ch. Cannonball of Wolfpit, owned by Mrs. Taylor Coleman.

American Kennel Club: *The Complete Dog Book.* New York, 1985

Books on the Cairn Terrier

Rogers, Mrs. Byron: *Cairn and Sealyham Terriers.* New York, 1922

Ross, Florence M.:   *The Cairn Terrier.* Manchester, c. 1925, 1933

Stephen, Kate L.:   Cairns, a chapter on the breed in Dorothy Gabriel's book, *The Scottish Terrier.* London, n.d.

Jacobi, Girard A.   *Your Cairn Terrier,* Fairfax, Va., 1976

Johns, Rowland: *Our Friend The Cairn.* N.Y. 1932

Ash, Edward: *Cairn Terriers.* London, 1936

Beynon, J. W. H.:   *The Popular Cairn.* London, 1929 Same with Alex Fisher, London, 1950 et seq.

Caspersz, T. W. L.:   *The Cairn Terrier Handbook,* London, 1957

Whitehead, Hector F.:   *Cairn Terriers.* London, 1959

Cairn Terrier Club,   *Various Yearbooks* (Eng.)

The Cairn Terrier Association, *Various Yearbooks* (Eng.)

The Southern Cairn Terrier Club, *Various Yearbooks* (Eng.)

The Cairn Terrier Club of America, *Various Yearbooks*

Pedigree Studies—The following pedigree studies offer to fanciers of the Cairn one of the most complete listings of its kind to be found in any Terrier breed.

Caspersz, T. W. L.: *English Pedigrees and Families.* 1932

Anderson, Elizabeth: *Pedigrees of American Bred Cairn Terrier Champions.* 1920-1933, N.Y. 1934

Porter, Frances with LeVene: *Pedigrees of American Owned Cairn Terrier Champions.* 1934-1942
Pedigrees of American Owned Cairn Terrier Champions. 1943-1952

Fisher, Alex: *List of Cairn Terriers (English) 1953-54.* A 59 page list of Cairn Terriers with Line and Family, Sire and Dam noted, over 4,000 dogs in listing, corrected.

Magazine Articles of Interest

Cairn Chatter (Amer.) Obit, re Walter Bradshaw: Nov. 1982.

Country Life in America: Turnbull, Eva. H.: The Canny Cairn, June, 1924, pp. 72, 74, 76.

Watson, James: The Terriers From Scotland, Feb. 1915, pp. 56-57.

Williams-Campbell, Mrs. E.M.: The Cairn Terrier, Jan. 1912, P. 40.

Country Life (London): Cairns, Hon. Douglas H.: Cairn Terriers. July, 1920, pp. 112-113.

Smith, A. Croxton: The Terriers of Scotland, Sept. 2, 1922, pp. 267-268.

American Kennel Gazette: Anderson, Elizabeth: Win or Lose, It's a Great Game. Jan., 1933, pp. 12-16.

Jones, A. F.: How A Sky-Line Kennel Makes Good (Tapscot). Aug. 1928, pp. 9-13, 94.

How Cairmore Blazed a Trail, Apr. 1929, pp. 9-14, 104.

Tapscot Moves To An Ideal Home, June 1930, pp. 9-14, 55.

Cairndania Wants Its Finest Dogs of the Show Ring To Be True Pals. Nov. 1936, pp. 18-22, 175.

Pinefair Believes Its Cockers and Cairns Should Create Happiness. May, 1938, pp. 24-28, 179.

Why Bayou Haven is Famous. July, 1938, pp. 23-26, 177.

Noted Cairndania Danes and Cairns Have New Home. May, 1939. pp. 17-21, 179.

Ch. Kiltie's Foxglove of Cairndania, owned by Mrs. G. W. Hyslop. *Rudolph Tauskey.*

Lloyd, Freeman: Some Terriers of Other Times. June, 1928, pp. 14-18; May, 1928, pp. 21-24; April, 1928, pp. 23-26.

The Bonnie Terriers of Scotland. Nov. 1932, pp. 22, 26, 73: Jan. 1933, pp. 24-28: March, pp. 12-16.

Macpherson, C. Brewster: Cairns Are Working Terriers. June, 1933, pp. 24-27, 123.

Porter, Frances: Breed Column, Sept. 1938, p. 30: May 1940, p. 46.

Rogers, Alice and Corrine S. W. Ward: Why We Need A New Standard For the Cairn. October 1934, pp. 17-21, 152.

Tappin, Lindsley, Biography, Nov. 1933, p. 28.

Our Dogs (Eng.): Caspersz, T. W. L.: The Evolution of the Cairn. Dec. 13, 1935, pp. 893-894.

Azor (Amer.): Porter, Frances: King's Choice. Aug. 1937, pp. 10, 56.

Dog World (Eng.): Beynon, J. W. H.: The Cairn, March 6, 1942, p. 145 et. seq.

Obit, re Alex Fisher: June 23, 1972

Obit, re Walter Bradshaw: July 9, 1982, p. 1 et seq.

BIBLIOGRAPHY

ALL OWNERS of pure-bred dogs will benefit themselves and their dogs by enriching their knowledge of breeds and of canine care, training, breeding, psychology and other important aspects of dog management. The following list of books covers further reading recommended by judges, veterinarians, breeders, trainers and other authorities. Books may be obtained at the finer book stores and pet shops, or through Howell Book House Inc., publishers, New York.

BREED BOOKS

AFGHAN HOUND, Complete	Miller & Gilbert
AIREDALE, New Complete	Edwards
AKITA, Complete	Linderman & Funk
ALASKAN MALAMUTE, Complete	Riddle & Seeley
BASSET HOUND, Complete	Braun
BLOODHOUND, Complete	Brey & Reed
BOXER, Complete	Denlinger
BRITTANY SPANIEL, Complete	Riddle
BULLDOG, New Complete	Hanes
BULL TERRIER, New Complete	Eberhard
CAIRN TERRIER, Complete	Marvin
CHESAPEAKE BAY RETRIEVER, Complete	Cherry
CHIHUAHUA, Complete	Noted Authorities
COCKER SPANIEL, New	Kraeuchi
COLLIE, New	Official Publication of the Collie Club of America
DACHSHUND, The New	Meistrell
DALMATIAN, The	Treen
DOBERMAN PINSCHER, New	Walker
ENGLISH SETTER, New Complete	Tuck, Howell & Graef
ENGLISH SPRINGER SPANIEL, New	Goodall & Gasow
FOX TERRIER, New	Nedell
GERMAN SHEPHERD DOG, New Complete	Bennett
GERMAN SHORTHAIRED POINTER, New	Maxwell
GOLDEN RETRIEVER, New Complete	Fischer
GORDON SETTER, Complete	Look
GREAT DANE, New Complete	Noted Authorities
GREAT DANE, The—Dogdom's Apollo	Draper
GREAT PYRENEES, Complete	Strang & Giffin
IRISH SETTER, New Complete	Eldredge & Vanacore
IRISH WOLFHOUND, Complete	Starbuck
JACK RUSSELL TERRIER, Complete	Plummer
KEESHOND, New Complete	Cash
LABRADOR RETRIEVER, Complete	Warwick
LHASA APSO, Complete	Herbel
MASTIFF, History and Management of the	Baxter & Hoffman
MINIATURE SCHNAUZER, Complete	Eskrigge
NEWFOUNDLAND, New Complete	Chern
NORWEGIAN ELKHOUND, New Complete	Wallo
OLD ENGLISH SHEEPDOG, Complete	Mandeville
PEKINGESE, Quigley Book of	Quigley
PEMBROKE WELSH CORGI, Complete	Sargent & Harper
POODLE, New	Irick
POODLE CLIPPING AND GROOMING BOOK, Complete	Kalstone
ROTTWEILER, Complete	Freeman
SAMOYED, New Complete	Ward
SCOTTISH TERRIER, New Complete	Marvin
SHETLAND SHEEPDOG, The New	Riddle
SHIH TZU, Joy of Owning	Seranne
SHIH TZU, The (English)	Dadds
SIBERIAN HUSKY, Complete	Demidoff
TERRIERS, The Book of All	Marvin
WEIMARANER, Guide to the	Burgoin
WEST HIGHLAND WHITE TERRIER, Complete	Marvin
WHIPPET, Complete	Pegram
YORKSHIRE TERRIER, Complete	Gordon & Bennett

BREEDING

ART OF BREEDING BETTER DOGS, New	Onstott
BREEDING YOUR OWN SHOW DOG	Seranne
HOW TO BREED DOGS	Whitney
HOW PUPPIES ARE BORN	Prine
INHERITANCE OF COAT COLOR IN DOGS	Little

CARE AND TRAINING

COUNSELING DOG OWNERS, Evans Guide for	Evans
DOG OBEDIENCE, Complete Book of	Saunders
NOVICE, OPEN AND UTILITY COURSES	Saunders
DOG CARE AND TRAINING FOR BOYS AND GIRLS	Saunders
DOG NUTRITION, Collins Guide to	Collins
DOG TRAINING FOR KIDS	Benjamin
DOG TRAINING, Koehler Method of	Koehler
DOG TRAINING Made Easy	Tucker
GO FIND! Training Your Dog to Track	Davis
GUARD DOG TRAINING, Koehler Method of	Koehler
MOTHER KNOWS BEST—The Natural Way to Train Your Dog	Benjamin
OPEN OBEDIENCE FOR RING, HOME AND FIELD, Koehler Method of	Koehler
STONE GUIDE TO DOG GROOMING FOR ALL BREEDS	Stone
SUCCESSFUL DOG TRAINING, The Pearsall Guide to	Pearsall
TEACHING DOG OBEDIENCE CLASSES—Manual for Instructors	Volhard & Fisher
TOY DOGS, Kalstone Guide to Grooming All	Kalstone
TRAINING THE RETRIEVER	Kersley
TRAINING TRACKING DOGS, Koehler Method of	Koehler
TRAINING YOUR DOG—Step by Step Manual	Volhard & Fisher
TRAINING YOUR DOG TO WIN OBEDIENCE TITLES	Morsell
TRAIN YOUR OWN GUN DOG, How to	Goodall
UTILITY DOG TRAINING, Koehler Method of	Koehler
VETERINARY HANDBOOK, Dog Owner's Home	Carlson & Giffin

GENERAL

AMERICAN KENNEL CLUB 1884-1984—A Source Book	American Kennel Club
CANINE TERMINOLOGY	Spira
COMPLETE DOG BOOK, The	Official Publication of American Kennel Club
DOG IN ACTION, The	Lyon
DOG BEHAVIOR, New Knowledge of	Pfaffenberger
DOG JUDGE'S HANDBOOK	Tietjen
DOG PEOPLE ARE CRAZY	Riddle
DOG PSYCHOLOGY	Whitney
DOGSTEPS, The New	Elliott
DOG TRICKS	Haggerty & Benjamin
EYES THAT LEAD—Story of Guide Dogs for the Blind	Tucker
FRIEND TO FRIEND—Dogs That Help Mankind	Schwartz
FROM RICHES TO BITCHES	Shattuck
HAPPY DOG/HAPPY OWNER	Siegal
IN STITCHES OVER BITCHES	Shattuck
JUNIOR SHOWMANSHIP HANDBOOK	Brown & Mason
OUR PUPPY'S BABY BOOK (blue or pink)	
SUCCESSFUL DOG SHOWING, Forsyth Guide to	Forsyth
TRIM, GROOM & SHOW YOUR DOG, How to	Saunders
WHY DOES YOUR DOG DO THAT?	Bergman
WILD DOGS in Life and Legend	Riddle
WORLD OF SLED DOGS, From Siberia to Sport Racing	Coppinger